Imagination Indulged

Elliott B. Gose, Jr

Imagination Indulged

The irrational in the nineteenth-century novel

McGill-Queen's University Press
Montreal and London 1972

© McGill-Queen's University Press 1972
International Standard Book Number 0-7735-0085-5
Library of Congress Catalog Card Number 70-172486
Designed by Kari Nordby
Printed in Canada by T. H. Best Printing Company Limited

This work has been published with the help of a
grant from the Humanities Research Council of Canada
using funds provided by the Canada Council.

Contents

Preface   vii

Introduction   13

Chapter one: The Gothic Novel   19

Chapter two: *The Monk*   27

Chapter three: The Fairy Tale   41

Chapter four: Romance to Novel   53

Chapter five: *Wuthering Heights*   59

Chapter six: *Bleak House*   73

Chapter seven: *The Return of the Native*   99

Chapter eight: Artist and Magician   127

Chapter nine: *Lord Jim*   141

Chapter ten: The Well of Truth   167

Index   177

Preface

In the Introduction I try to provide a background, framework, and rationale for this book. Here I would like to explain in a more personal way why I wrote the book and why I have taken the approach I do.

Since I use the word "archetype" several times in the pages that follow, my first attempt should be to explain its meaning. In our century the term is inevitably associated with the psychoanalyst, Carl Jung, who borrowed it from classical times:

> The term "archetype" occurs as early as Philo Judaeus, with reference to the *Imago Dei* (God-image) in man. It can also be found in Irenaeus, who says: "The creator of the world did not fashion these things directly from himself but copied them from archetypes outside himself." . . . "Archetype" is an explanatory paraphrase of the Platonic *eidos*. For our purposes this term is apposite and helpful, because it tells us that . . . we are dealing with archaic or—I would say—primordial types, that is, with universal images that have existed since the remotest times.[1]

Psychologically, Jung saw primitive man as more affected by his emotions than we are when looking at external phenomena: "Primitive man is not much interested in objective explanations of the obvious, but he has an imperative need—or rather, his unconscious psyche has an irresistible urge—to assimilate all outer sense experiences to inner, psychic events. . . . The projection [of psychic events on nature] is so

---

1. "Archetypes of the Collective Unconscious," *Collected Works,* Vol. 9, Part I. Quoted here from *The Basic Writings of C. G. Jung,* ed. Violet S. de Laszlo (New York: The Modern Library, 1959), pp. 287–88.

fundamental that it has taken several thousand years of civilization to detach it in some measure from its outer object" (p. 289). But, by becoming conscious and objective, Western man has in the last few centuries managed to detach his feelings from his observation—a triumph according to many scientists, a disaster according to many humanists. Between 1920 and 1960 Jung was one of the most influential of those who doubted the helpfulness of our cultivating impersonality. Because he had broken with Freud and took religion seriously, Jung was at the same time viewed with suspicion or contempt by many liberated thinkers.[2] Since the beginning of the Second World War, however, other schools of thought have developed which make Jung's approach seem less woolly to the religious skeptic than it would have before.

On the one hand many hardheaded thinkers have begun to doubt the human validity of an "objective mind."[3] Some scientists have been repelled by the way colleagues have used their discipline for destructive purposes; some social scientists have become alarmed at the sinister prostitution of their discipline in the name of impersonality. On the other hand, a whole generation has grown up absurd, has adopted the viewpoint of existentialism without necessarily knowing any philosophy. What the thinkers elaborated in words, the postwar generation has lived with since birth: slogans, ideals, and codes may have essence, but man has only existence. Any theory is absurd, meaningless unless felt by someone because it has become part of his experience.

Man, says Sartre, has no nature and can therefore choose what he will be, *has* to choose during each moment he lives, a fact which fills him with such anguish that he usually chooses to hide his freedom from himself and project the choosing function onto his religion, his government, his class, his employer, his family—anywhere but in himself. The present generation has rejected such hypocrisy and has accepted what Robert Lifton calls "the Protean style of self-process."[4] They have

2. On the other hand, the nature of Jung's religious view has been criticized by Martin Buber for, in effect, excessive humanism—that is, locating God in man's soul (the collective unconscious). See *Eclipse of God* (New York: Harper & Row, 1952), Chapters 5 and 9.
3. Cf. Theodore Rozak, *The Making of a Counter Culture: Reflections on the Technocratic Society and its Youthful Opposition* (Garden City: Doubleday & Co., 1969).
4. Robert Jay Lifton, "Protean Man," first published in the *Partisan Review*. Quoted here from *Boundaries* (Toronto: Canadian Broadcasting Co., 1969), p. 30.

accepted that, like Proteus, each of us has many potential shapes, personas, identities into which we can develop; the only process to which we can be true is the one inside us; if we give up following it, to accept some outer form that appeals to one potential of self, we may become caught in that form and develop into a rigid shell, a death mask. These outer forms are vehicles of worldly power and social prestige, but Lifton claims that the younger generation tends not to give itself to them except temporarily or conditionally. Rather this generation keeps searching for what it does not find in Western culture, some process that satisfies the inner need, some symbolic process that will allow the psyche to evolve toward a maturity of wholeness.

This conception brings us back to the relevance of Jung. His explorations were also done in the name of wholeness, and with the essential aid of a symbolic process. In common with this generation, Jung was interested in the Eastern religions and their assumption that behind social forms, intellect, and parental imprintings is a darkness, a seeming nothingness in which lies being. But Western culture has systematically separated man from this self and the means of reaching it.

Shaped by nineteenth-century Swiss Protestantism (his father was a pastor), Jung was in a good position to understand what went on in Victorian England. That is why his formulations of psychic problems are so often useful to someone studying the tradition I have chosen in the Victorian novel. "All ages before us have believed in gods in some form or other. Only an unparalleled impoverishment of symbolism could enable us to rediscover the gods as psychic factors, that is, as archetypes of the unconscious. . . . Since the stars have fallen from heaven and our highest symbols have paled, a secret life holds sway in the unconscious. That is why we have a psychology today, and why we speak of the unconscious" (p. 307). Emily Brontë, Charles Dickens, Thomas Hardy, and Joseph Conrad were all caught in the nineteenth-century "impoverishment." We shall find that they were attracted to the religious view but tended to substitute the psychological view for it. Emily Brontë and Dickens were still overtly committed to Christianity, though I believe the real life of their novels, their spiritual and psychic vitality, is not Christian. Both Hardy and Conrad consciously rejected Christianity; their fiction is thus more overtly psychological. But in fact all four were fighting a battle for the protean self, working against materialism, impersonality, objectivity (mere realism in art); and their novels contain patterns which could lead to the symbolic process of transformation and rebirth.

In analysing these novels I have found that symbols, of the kind Jung called archetypes, are an important key to the process of transformation, whether embodied in characters, in the environment, or in plot patterns. I do not, however, expect the reader to accept the existence of archetypes as an article of faith. I hope the intensity of symbolism in the novels will carry its own conviction. But the reader should certainly emulate protean man and give no more allegiance than is meaningful to him. Jung himself frequently asserted that the archetype cannot be represented to consciousness, that we receive only images of it, mere representations of what he considered the basic matrix of our nature. What that nature is we can know only by inference.[5]

The last chapter of this study is called "The Well of Truth," a title based on a nineteenth-century saying that influenced at least two of the novelists under consideration: "Truth lies at the bottom of a well." The image of the world that lies at the bottom of a well is also important in fairy tales as the place an ordinary person can descend to, go through trials in, and emerge from transformed into the hero. This world may be taken as the land of archetypes and the well itself analysed as an archetypal symbol. To begin with, a well does go down mysteriously to the world below; it allows some of its refreshment to ascend to our everyday world. The water in a well sustains life, not grossly as food does, but purely, coolly. Further, water is the element from which all life came, the amorphous matrix in which we were given our structure, to which we can still return to choose again what form, what identity we will have. Finally the water in a well reflects the outer world, especially the face of whoever looks in. It appears to contain a world, a place that draws us because it contains us.

But we know that picture is a surface image, probably an illusion. Is our desire to descend there not self-indulgent, narcissistic? Undoubtedly more than one person has drowned in the pleasure principle. But Jung's point about the archetypal world is exactly that it is alluring but dangerous, or that to some people it appears dangerous but must be

5. I feel obliged to quote Buber in opposition to Jung's position. "In religious-sounding formulas such as Malebranche's 'we see things in God' it is also philosophical abstraction that speaks. . . . When, on the contrary, the religious man . . . speaks the same sentence, he transforms it. 'Things' mean now to him not archetypes or 'perfect essences,' but the actual exemplars, the beings and objects with which he, this bodily person, spends his life. When he ventures to say that he sees them in God, he does not speak of looking upward but of looking here. He acknowledges that meaning is open and attainable in a lived concreteness of every moment" (*Eclipse of God,* p. 41).

faced in any case. In fact, for the benefit of those who mistrust pretty pictures, I might do well to substitute the image of a dark well for that of the bright reflecting surface. Truth also lies in the frightening descent into darkness.

I offer this latter alternative out of consideration for the kind of existentialist encounterer or Yogic meditator who considers dreams and other fantasy images as "mind games," that is, the effort of the corrupted mind to protect its hegemony over self, a self that lacks confidence enough to take control back from the inculcated principles of authority (the superego). From this point of view, all stories are word-screens, what the mind throws up instead of truth. But also in the purest version of this view, all talk is a word game. One may hear emotion in words or see a reaction in another, but the words themselves must be mistrusted (unless they say the opposite of what the speaker intends). Yet one can be convinced (as I am) of the validity of this relation of one person to another (I-Thou) without completely denying words and story.

From what I know of the life of the novelists whose words are analysed here, my inference is that their novels were called into being in an attempt to cope with acute psychic distress. But the result is, along with some self-deception, documents which show great insight into the sources of stress in their times and their individual lives. Beyond this, their works also embody, consciously and unconsciously, truths about psychic processes important for anyone in any time, if the reader encounters them in the right spirit. Art may thus be said to have something in common with religious experience. In contrasting both to philosophy, the existentialist theologian, Martin Buber wrote, "The religious communication of a content of being takes place in paradox. It is not a demonstrable assertion . . . but a pointing toward the hidden realm of existence . . . . and that which is to be experienced there and there alone. Artistic communication, . . . takes place in the *Gestalt*, from which a communicated content cannot be detached and given independent existence."[6] From this point of view, literary criticism is harmful or superfluous; my own justification of criticism is that it tries to convey a felt sense of the life of a work of literature. Of course, I am supplying my own definition of where the life is to be found. Yet, because fiction deals with characters in thought and action, my emphasis on psychology has at least that much justification.

6. Buber, *Eclipse of God*, p. 43.

On the other hand my approach may alienate those who believe in reading critically but don't want to get involved in depth psychology. I can only say that it seems farfetched to assume that a story will *not* contain something of the psychic life of its author. By using his imagination he is, after all, calling on what he has deeply felt, what animates his nature, what has to come out of him. Such, at any rate, is my premise in this study.

Besides my indebtedness to scholars and publishers as indicated in the footnotes, I must single out two journals which have published articles of mine. The first few pages of the chapter on *Lord Jim* include material that appeared in an article published in *PMLA*. Similarly, the chapter on *Wuthering Heights* includes in revised form material from an article published in *Nineteenth-Century Fiction*.

In concluding this preface, I would like to thank those who have helped me in various ways with the book. First, numerous students who have helped me shape and change my insights into these and other novels. Then three colleagues at the University of British Columbia who read early versions of the first chapters and saved me the embarrassment of trying to foist them on the public: Marc Beach, Bill Hall, Dave Powell. And the University of British Columbia which, through the President's Research Fund and the secretaries of the English Department, has enabled me to get help in typing the manuscript and preparing the book for publication. The fund also made possible my receiving help from Jack Schofield in proofreading and making the index. Finally I must try to express what I owe to my wife Kathleen, for essential financial and moral support, as well as for an editorial and critical acumen which has made the whole book much more readable and sensible than it would otherwise have been.

Introduction

Now that Emily Brontë, Dickens, Hardy, and Conrad have individually received recognition, it seems to me time to try to speak of their place in a common tradition. The connection might be established by suggesting the influence of Emily Brontë on Hardy, or of Dickens on Conrad. But my aim is not to trace the history of an idea. The tradition I am concerned with has several sources which bear unequally on these novelists. The common result, however, is a concern with the possibilities of imaginative perception which transcends differences in sensibility among them.

The nature of the tradition is summed up in the one word "irrational" in the subtitle of this book. Amplified, the subtitle might have read "Fantasy, Romance, Fairy Tale, Dream, and Ritual as Elements in the Nineteenth-Century English Novel." "Fantasy" is a generic term whose Greek meaning of *appearance* hints at both spontaneity and illusion. The most commonly experienced form is a daydream, the mind's sliding away from sensory contact with the outside world into pictures of what might be, deeds of heroism, scenes of success. Besides such gentle compensations for everyday dullness, fantasy can also take the less pleasant form of obsessive living out of possible future conflicts or of past encounters ("What he said, what I said, what I should have said"). The spontaneous nature of these illusory scenes is more obvious if we consider dreams and visions as forms of fantasy too. But we shall be most concerned with less spontaneous forms, those which have passed through a minimal artistic shaping process: fairy tale and romance.

As a formal literary term, the most narrow meaning of "romance" concerns medieval narratives of chivalry, but since the eighteenth century it has broadened to designate a story which moves beyond everyday concerns in search of extravagant adventures. It is in this broader literary sense that I shall use the term. In addition, I shall some-times connect an interest in romance with the Romantic poets, who used it (along with fairy tale and dream) in their poetry, both narrative and lyric. But, as we shall discover in the first chapter, romance had already connected itself with prose fiction before the Romantic poets appeared. I am referring to the gothic novel, which might also be called the gothic romance, since it deals in love and extravagant adventures. Called "gothic" because they are set in medieval times, these romances differ from earlier ones in going beyond the idyllic potential of that remote setting; instead, the gothic novel plays upon the reader's capacity to respond to such emotions as anxiety, remorse, horror, and terror.

The fairy tale has a longer lineage than the romance; in its more scholarly forms, where it is known as folktale or *Märchen*, it dates back, like myth, to the dawn of civilization. These naive tales are now con-signed to the nursery, but we should remember that that urbane and religious Roman, Apuleius, saw fit to devote three chapters of his picaresque tale, *The Golden Ass*, to the well-known fairy tale "Cupid and Psyche." We should also remember that even novelists writing at the height of Victorian materialism felt obliged to use the fairy tale. They adopted its motifs as a reminder to the reader of the reality of emotions which had been forced down by certain aspects of Victorian culture until their only outlet was in "escapist" fantasies. "Escapist" is a pejorative term, and judged by the puritan work ethic, withdrawal from the outside world is morally culpable. But, if we look beyond "once upon a time" and "happily ever after" (the entrance and exit of many such tales), we discover that the sugar coating is very thin in-deed. The violence contained in almost all unbowdlerized tales points to their embodying important psychic conflicts, conflicts which we shall investigate in Chapter Three.

Myth has become one of the favourite tools of a school of modern literary critics. Their interest is an outgrowth of a general recognition that modern man need not scorn as mere ignorant superstition the stories told by primitive peoples: particularly those stories that satisfy a psychic need for pattern and meaning by explaining the origin of the cosmos or of the immediate world and its activities. The advances of archaeological and anthropological investigation, coupled with the de-cline in Christian dogmatism and faith, have given us an interest in what poets have always relished: the way a myth, retold overtly or covertly, with variations or not, can open up vistas of the spirit and the emotions.

As the reader might expect, I am sympathetic to the investigation of mythic patterns in certain works of literature. Because they are so common in literary criticism, I have assumed and mentioned such patterns where relevant in this book. But I have not included them among the analogues to be developed. My main reason for playing them down is that much of what is illuminating in them emerges from an analysis of fairy-tale motifs. As Stith Thompson points out, the line between the two is not clear cut.[1] In ancient times, folktales and myths seem to have drawn on each other. But the folk or fairy tale, being less pretentious, offers fewer temptations to pontificate or allegorize.

Like myth, ritual is a territory much surveyed by scholarly theory, or should I say much hacked at by those with sharply ground axes. Following the Cambridge school, which applied anthropological insights to classical Greek studies, some literary critics championed ritual as the original form from which mythic tales derive. Although this position is demonstrably inaccurate,[2] it gives to its adherents that certainty in a chaotic world which rituals themselves gave to primitive man. Especially where the ritual is based on a seasonal pattern, as in the Mediterranean area, it offers assurance that the cycle of change will repeat itself permanently. Similarly, the literary critic who reduces the ritual pattern to an abstraction—birth, maturity, decay, death, rebirth —can discover "ritual" in most works of literature. I shall discuss ritual in connection with only one of the novels considered in this book, *The Return of the Native*. Hardy made it clear both inside and outside the novel that he took a romantic, antiquarian (not to say anthropological) interest in folk survivals of ritual. In fact we shall discover that he connected the sense of permanence generated by ritual with the sense of doom that overtook many Victorians in the years following Darwin's publication of the theory of natural selection.

The relevance of dreams to everyday life is something the Victorians were beginning to rediscover. As early as 1865, Lewis Carroll had *Alice in Wonderland* begin as a dream and embody the unrealistic transformations of scenes, of characters, and of emotions that charac-

1. "Myth and Folktales," in *Myth: A Symposium,* ed. Thomas Sebeok (Bloomington: Indiana University Press, 1958).
2. See Clyde Kluckhohn, "Myths and Rituals: A General Theory" in *Myth and Literature Contemporary Theory and Practice,* ed. John Vickery (Lincoln: University of Nebraska Press, 1966).

terize dreams. But this was in a romance; no novelist until James Joyce used the dream method in narrative structure. Emily Brontë, Dickens, and Hardy, however, each presented dreams in their work, and in such a way as to indicate the importance of dream images in waking life. In *Wuthering Heights,* for instance, Catherine says, "I've dreamt in my life dreams that have stayed with me ever after, and changed my ideas; they've gone through and through me, like wine through water, and altered the colour of my mind" (Chapter 9). In support of this subjective assertion, we can consider the view of J. A. Hadfield, a psychiatrist, who has suggested that, even without interpreting a dream "cognitively," someone may understand it "intuitively"; thus "quite apart from its interpretation, a dream may have a profound effect upon the dreamer and may be of great therapeutic value."[3]

Elucidating the important practical function of dreams, Hadfield goes farther and claims that although "the dream has a different method of solving [a] problem from that of conscious reasoning," in fact "dreams are a form, probably the most primitive form of ideation" (pp. 71, 70). Conscious thought can deal with a problem "much more explicitly," but dreams are really "more capable of solving our problems by virtue of two characteristics, not shared to the same extent by ordinary ideation, namely the *exaggerated* emotion in the dream and the *dramatization* of dreams, the fact that we actually live in the dream and are actually partakers of it" (p. 72). The two terms italicized by Hadfield are obviously relevant in any consideration of the kind of fiction written by a novelist interested in dreams: Emily Brontë, Dickens, and Hardy are all concerned with dramatization and "exaggerated emotion." The latter quality is clear not only in the emotionalism of their characters but also in the very structure of their plots, which demand an exaggerated emotional response from the reader. In the possibilities that it offers the novelist, the dream may thus be taken as a kind of epitome of the irrational. I would therefore like to use its characteristics as the basis for one side of a contrast, and attempt to distinguish briefly between the novelists I shall be concerned with and other equally prominent ones of the same century. Both Jane Austen and George Eliot, for example, have a sense of drama; both work on their characters' and their readers' emotions, but neither trusts exaggerated emotion, and neither shows much interest in dreams. These two novelists belong to a tradition that can be traced to Aristotle. His

3. *Dreams and Nightmares* (Harmondsworth: Penguin Books, 1954), p. 97.

key conception was that art is mimetic, that it imitates an action in the real world. This conception has given literary criticism some of its basic terms: plot (as action), and character (as actor). These terms are too useful to dispense with, but they take on a different colouring when Aristotle's idea of probability is called in question. In fact, none of the kinds of narrative I have been defining is based on the idea that all actions in a novel must correspond to our sense of how people act or events move in the everyday world. Such latitude may be all very well for romance, but most novel readers demand "probability" before they can take fiction seriously. This is an unfair demand, of course. A writer may satisfy probability of action at every turn of his weary plot and leave us as unenlightened as we are unstimulated. Nor should we think that all violation of probability is mercenary or inartistic, simply because many popular writers sacrifice realism to immediate shock effect. A writer may give very deep thought (in addition to feeling) to a scene which borders on melodrama but satisfies the demands of the plot and the underlying nature of the characters involved. In any case, one important purpose of this study, after its first three chapters, must be to investigate what happens when serious novelists start using motifs from romance, fairy tale, and dream to shift the emphasis in their fiction from verisimilitude of action to validity of feeling.

My approach to literature in this study is on the one hand psychological, concerned with literature as expressive of emotions, and on the other hand formalist, concerned with literature as a self-contained structure. The psychological and the formalist coalesce when one focuses on the workings of the imagination, on the relation of the patterns of a given novel to conscious and unconscious preoccupations and feelings in the mind of the author. As the comments I have made on dreams indicated, this approach necessitates working with the insights of psychoanalysis. Although such insights are essential to this kind of approach to literature, when they are applied without an informed concern or a feeling for literature, they will tend to distort it. My own observation is that strict adherence to the doctrines of either Freud or Jung usually causes such distortion. Consequently, I try to avoid following either of these brilliant theorists rigidly, although I have already indicated my leanings toward Jung. Like any assumption, his theory of archetypes can force a work to mean what we are sure it does not mean. Used discriminately, on the other hand, many of the insights associated with it can lead to the perception of patterns never quite seen before but clearly in touch with the life of a novel and the imagination of its author.[4]

Part of my justification for emphasizing the psychological is that the novelists under consideration demonstrate their own interest in irrational behaviour by the kind of characters they create. I do not mean that the author's concern with the workings of the mind will necessarily result in a character who is a "case study," even if we broaden that term to include any study of a character in the process of change or development. Such a character change, as unfolded in the novels of Jane Austen and George Eliot, for example, belongs to what F. R. Leavis has called the great tradition of the English novel.

Several authors in the tradition of the irrational also pay some attention to representational characterization. But all of them rely more on other means by which to embody in fiction their interest in psychology. Since the Romantic revolt, this interest has often centred, in all areas of European art, on a self-conscious exploration of subjective emotions, or the imagination. Increasingly, therefore, the artist has come to see his problem as how best to embody the tensions, concerns, and insights which he finds in his psychic self. Even before the end of the eighteenth century, English novelists were beginning to discover that image patterns, expressive settings, and melodramatic plots offered more scope for self-expression than did a representational picture of human character and actions. The gothic novel is therefore an appropriate place to begin, and the fairy tale an equally appropriate place to continue, our search for the qualities to be found in a form of fiction shaped less by rational than by irrational forces, by an indulgence of the imagination.

4. A case for the artistic relevance of Jung's theories is well put by Morris Philipson in *Outline of a Jungian Aesthetics* (Evanston, Illinois, Northwestern University Press, 1963). An enlightened version of the Freudian view is presented by Frederick Crews in his introduction to *Psychoanalysis and Literary Process* (Cambridge: Winthrup Publishers, 1970). Crews augments Norman Holland's presentation of an allied approach in *The Dynamics of Literary Response* (New York: Oxford University Press, 1968).

Chapter One

The Gothic Novel

In 1764 Horace Walpole had a dream, a dream in which the gothic novel was born. More than ten years before, Walpole had started remodelling his country house, Strawberry Hill, in the gothic style, and, in his dream, he found himself "in an ancient castle (a very natural dream for a head filled like mine with Gothic story)." On "the uppermost banister of a great staircase I saw a gigantic hand in armour. In the evening I sat down and began to write, without knowing in the least what I intended to say."[1] The result was *The Castle of Otranto*. In this novel, as in Walpole's dream, an ancient castle is the main setting. Included in the large inventory of supernatural items sprinkled through the plot are a huge helmet and sword, a giant form, an animated portrait, blood dropping from a statue, and a speaking skeleton, each of which appears at the theatrically conventional moment to jog the action on its mechanical way. Devoid of literary merit as his work may now appear, Walpole did crystallize the key elements of the gothic novel: its setting (a castle), its mood (mysterious and foreboding), its time (the Middle Ages), and its cast of characters (the tyrant, the persecuted maiden, and the youthful hero).

For the second edition of *The Castle of Otranto*, Walpole wrote an introduction in which he attempted to explain what he had done. Several of the points he made are worth considering both in themselves and as a basis for some definitions which we shall need as we move to

---

1. Editor's "Introduction," *The Castle of Otranto* in *Shorter Novels of the Eighteenth Century*, ed. Philip Henderson (London: J. M. Dent, 1930), p. vi. As with all sources to follow, after the first reference in a footnote, page numbers will be included in the text.

later gothic novels. He had attempted, he claimed, to blend

> two kinds of romance: the ancient and the modern. In the former,
> all was imagination and improbability; in the latter, nature is always
> intended to be, and sometimes has been, copied with success. In-
> vention has not been wanting; but the great resources of fancy have
> been dammed up, by a strict adherence to common life. But if in the
> latter species nature has cramped imagination, she did but take her
> revenge, having been totally excluded from old romances. . . .
>
> The author of the following pages thought it possible to reconcile
> the two kinds. Desirous of leaving the powers of fancy at liberty to
> expatiate through the boundless realms of invention, and thence of
> creating more interesting situations, he wished to conduct the mortal
> agents in his drama according to the rules of probability; in short, to
> make them think, speak, and act, as it might be supposed mere men
> and women would do in extraordinary positions (p. 102).

This theory has much to recommend it.

If we think of the broader context of the eighteenth-century novel as
a whole, we can see Walpole touching on a number of important
developments. Realism is one: Defoe, Fielding and Richardson, each in
his own way, attempted to have his characters "think, speak, and act as
it might be supposed mere men and women" do. By the time Richardson was beginning to write, in the 1740s, the emphasis was shifting to
the first of these verbs, and the thoughts and emotions of a central
character were under scrutiny. From this kind of concern grew what we
have since come to call the novel of sensibility. According to J. M. S.
Tompkins, "sensibility" was to the eighteenth century "a significant, an
almost sacred word, for it enshrined the idea of the progress of the
human race. Sensibility was a modern quality; it was not found among
the ancients, but was the product of modern conditions; the heroic and
tremendous virtues might be dying out with the stormy times that
evoked them, but modern security, leisure and education had evolved a
delicacy of sensation, a refinement of virtue, which the age found even
more beautiful. The human sympathies, which a rougher age had
repressed, expanded widely."[2] This passage provides a clue to an
obvious compensatory reaction which would be among the causes of
the popularity of the gothic novel. "The rougher age," to which the
Augustans contrasted themselves, was also a source of fascination to

---

2. *The Popular Novel in England, 1770–1800* (Lincoln: University of Nebraska
Press, 1961), pp. 92–93. This study was originally published in 1932.

them. The gothic novel paid lip service to the mild emotions of sensibility—pity, sorrow, generous feelings—but mainly as a cushion for its leaps into the ruder chasms of sensation—hatred, fear, and terror. Atmospherically also, the gothic novel moved away from fictional realism. Instead of being content with the contemporary, the natural, and the everyday, these novels cultivated the past, the supernatural, and the mysterious. In doing so they finally moved almost beyond contact with the "formal realism" which Ian Watt sees as the main line of the eighteenth-century novel.[3]

Watt defines formal realism as based on "the premise, or primary convention, that the novel is a full and authentic report of human experience, and is therefore under an obligation to satisfy its reader with such details of the story as the individuality of the actors concerned, the particulars of the times and places of their actions, details which are presented through a more largely referential use of language than is common in other literary forms" (p. 32). This definition fits well the three novelists on whom he concentrates, Defoe, Richardson, and Fielding. It does not fit so well the nineteenth-century novelists with whom we shall be concerned in the chapters ahead. The concept of formal realism is not central to an understanding of Emily Brontë, Dickens, Hardy, and Conrad because of the dramatic shift in literary consciousness and technique which had occurred in the meantime. In fiction that shift began with the gothic novel; for literature generally, it emerged as a significant change of focus in the Romantic movement. The genteel emotions of sensibility were permitted in the middle of the Age of Reason because they were not a real threat to the dominance of good sense. Stronger irrational impulses were, of course, recognized by the establishment, but they were considered the enemy. Thus we have Dr. Johnson's grudging tribute to "that hunger of imagination which preys incessantly upon life, and must be always appeased by some employment."[4] In the gothic novel that hunger usually causes the impulse toward romance to eat away at the common-sense conventions of realism.

Walpole tried to bring together the opposing conceptions of realism and romance in describing what he had done in *The Castle of Otranto*. He wished to combine realism of character with unrealistic events. We

3. *The Rise of the Novel* (London, 1957).
4. This comment is made by Johnson's mouthpiece, Imlac, in *Rasselas*, Chap. 32. See also Chap. 44, "all power of fancy over reason is a degree of insanity."

may appraise the quality of unrealism in the events by looking at the following scene from the end of the novel. Manfred, the tyrannical usurper, is finally forced to recognize the youthful hero Theodore as the rightful heir of Otranto.

> A clap of thunder at that instant shook the castle to its foundations; the earth rocked, and the clank of more than mortal armour was heard behind. . . . The moment Theodore appeared, the walls of the castle behind Manfred were thrown down with a mighty force, and the form of Alfonso, dilated to an immense magnitude, appeared in the centre of the ruins.
>
> "Behold in Theodore the true heir of Alfonso!" said the vision; and having pronounced those words, accompanied by a clap of thunder, it ascended solemnly towards heaven, where the clouds parting asunder, . . . [it was] soon wrapt from mortal eyes in a blaze of glory (p. 190).

In practice Walpole's "romance" includes the improbable, the theatrical, and the supernatural.

His desire to create realism of character in such a setting does not get very far. Here is the reaction to Alfonso's words of Hippolita, Manfred's much abused wife.

> "My lord," said she to the desponding Manfred, "behold the vanity of human greatness! Conrad is gone! Matilda is no more! in Theodore we view the true Prince of Otranto. By what miracle he is so, I know not—suffice it to us, our doom is pronounced! Shall we not—can we but—dedicate the few deplorable hours we have to live, in deprecating the further wrath of Heaven? Heaven ejects us: whither can we fly, but to yon holy cells that yet offer us a retreat?" (p. 190).

This series of rhetorical and attitudinal clichés is typical of the dialogue in the novel and destroys any possibility of the character realism Walpole wished to produce. Yet it was his example not his theory which shaped the tradition. Both supernatural events and melodramatic speeches had become part of the antirealistic heritage of the gothic novel by the 1790s. M. G. Lewis uses them relatively successfully in *The Monk* because he employs fewer and more interesting events and shifts more of the high-flown speeches to demonic or frankly supernatural characters. In *The Mysteries of Udolpho*, on the other hand, Ann Radcliffe explains away the supernatural events while toning down the speeches and making them part of a pattern of character analysis which has considerable psychological subtlety. Consequently, the combination of realism and romance is truly present in *The Mysteries of Udolpho,* as it is not in *The Castle of Otranto.*

The "mysteries" of the title may rightly make us think of sensation rather than sensibility, but in fact, gothic though it is, Mrs. Radcliffe's novel is important for its development in psychological insight, its attempt to humanize the irrational. Although she did not have the insight of Richardson, Mrs. Radcliffe did make a contribution in the area which Ian Watt calls development of personal identity. Watt shows how the growth of this concern in the eighteenth-century novel may be paralleled to an approximately contemporary philosophic concern with the nature of consciousness in relation to time and memory.

As Watt sees it, in characters such as Robinson Crusoe and Moll Flanders, Defoe gave the reader "a sense of personal identity subsisting through duration and yet being changed by the flow of experience" (p. 24). Whereas we shall discover that Lewis' monk, Ambrosio, cannot be understood as this kind of character, Mrs. Radcliffe's heroine, Emily St. Aubert, can. More important, the concern with personal identity was in the forefront of Mrs. Radcliffe's mind; Emily's striving to maintain that identity under duress gives the novel its most interesting continuity.

Most of the duress is provided by the villain of the novel, Montoni. In explaining the difference in sensibility between her heroine and her villain, Mrs. Radcliffe drew an important distinction between two kinds of imagination: "Hers was a silent anguish, weeping, yet enduring; not the wild energy of passion, inflaming imagination, bearing down the barriers of reason and living in a world of its own."[5] Montoni's nature may be taken as an avatar of the Byronic hero. More important for our immediate subject, the Faustian and Satanic overtones of Montoni's character connect him with Richardson's Lovelace as an obvious model for Ambrosio, the title character in *The Monk.* But, where Lewis made Ambrosio the central figure in his novel, Mrs. Radcliffe was more concerned with the personal identity of her heroine. She was, in fact, the last of the novelists for whom sensibility had a central meaning. Where she was willing to place a heroine susceptible to tears and visions of the sublime in situations ranging from the conventional to the terror-filled, Jane Austen would have her heroines find

5. *The Mysteries of Udolpho: A Romance* (London: Oxford University Press, 1966), p. 329.

their identities with a minimum of sensibility, in everyday social situations that demand a response of character. In contrast to both, M. G.
Lewis would show by Watt's standard no realistic conception of personal identity; yet with his unabridged sensationalism he somehow
managed to present us with a compelling anatomy of the irrational.

Before turning to *The Monk*, therefore, we must look a little more
closely into the whole problem of creating characters in fiction. To
begin with we can register Ian Watt's suggestion that the use of a
circumstantial presentation of personality and emotions did not always
result in a truly mimetic novel.

> This combination of romance and formal realism applied both to
> external actions and inward feelings is the formula which explains
> the power of the popular novel: it satisfies the romantic aspirations
> of its readers in a literary guise which gives so full a background and
> so complete an account of the minute-by-minute details of thought
> and sentiment that what is fundamentally an unreal flattery of the
> reader's dreams appears to be the literal truth. For this reason, the
> popular novel is obviously liable to severe moral censure where
> the fairy story or the romance is not: it pretends to be something
> else, and, mainly owing to the new power which accrued to formal
> realism as a result of the subjective direction which Richardson gave
> it, it confuses the differences between reality and dream more insidi-
> ously than any previous fiction (p. 205).

Romance will always be a threat to the rational desire for realism. The
point about the gothic novel is that it altered the balance suggested by
Watt heavily to the side of romance. In *The Mysteries of Udolpho*
realism becomes important at the end when the heroine accepts a
rational explanation of supposed supernatural events. In *The Monk*
romance takes over almost completely.

Following the lead of Hawthorne and others, Richard Chase developed a distinction between the novel and romance in the first chapter
of his study of *The American Novel and Its Tradition* (Garden City:
Doubleday & Co., 1957). His definition of the novel is close to Watt's
idea of formal realism: "The novel renders reality closely and in comprehensive detail. It takes a group of people and sets them going about
the business of life. We come to see these people in their real complexity of temperament and motive. They are in explicable relation to
nature, to each other, to their social class, to their own past" (p. 12).
Against these concerns Chase sets those of the writer of romance:

Following distantly the medieval example, [romance] feels free to render reality in less volume and detail. It tends to prefer action to character, and action will be freer in a romance than in a novel, encountering, as it were, less resistance from reality. . . . The romance can flourish without providing much intricacy of relation. The characters, probably rather two-dimensional types, will not be complexly related to each other or to society or to the past. Human beings will on the whole be shown in ideal relation—that is, they will share emotions only after these have become abstract or symbolic. . . . Character itself becomes, then, somewhat abstract and ideal, so much so in some romances that it seems to be merely a function of plot. The plot we may expect to be highly colored. Astonishing events may occur, and these are likely to have a symbolic or ideological, rather than a realistic, plausibility. Being less committed to the immediate rendition of reality than the novel, the romance will more freely veer toward mythic, allegorical, and symbolistic forms (p. 13).

This analysis is important not only in exempting romance from certain concerns, but also in emphasizing the drive of romance toward consciously heightened methods and altered narrative forms. Since most of what Chase has said will help us to understand *The Monk*, we should clarify the implication of his suggestion that "in some romances" character "seems to be merely a function of plot." The literary form to which this statement most obviously applies is melodrama.

Although we shall be considering *The Monk* as a romance in the next chapter, we should note now that it has many of the characteristics of melodrama. The dialogue often consists of set speeches and fulsome periods in which the characters refer to themselves in the third person, as though they had no personal identity. This tendency is related to the pervasive theatricality of the book. As Lewis Peck puts it, "One frequently gains from these figures as a whole the illusion that they are professional actors in a stock company presenting violent melodrama."[6]

True to that form, its sensations are balanced by a superficial moralism. Virtue is persecuted but finally rewarded, while vice is long successful but finally punished in that crude and mechanical way which so offends the modern sensibility. But, once all these faults are ad-

6. *A Life of Matthew G. Lewis* (Cambridge: Harvard University Press, 1961), p. 40.

mitted, there still remains an attraction in *The Monk*. I do not mean simply the attraction of "camp" literature, in which the very defects are savoured as so naive and transparently schematic that they are delightful. Rather I mean that, once we have adjusted as far as we can to the book's weaknesses, we are in a position to acknowledge the actual power which somehow lies in and behind its sensationalism.

Lewis' plot justifies, if anything can, the excessive rhetoric of his style. Yet the rhetoric does have one obvious virtue by twentieth-century standards. It may not convey a particularized sense of any everyday environment, as Watt would ask it to do, but it does contain images which create vivid scenes and form patterns that emphasize the movement of the plot.

The circumstances of the book's composition provide a clue. It was written by a young man of nineteen to stave off the boredom and restraint of diplomatic life at the Hague. As a *jeu d'esprit* it violates all the cannons of decorum which Lewis would have imbibed at Oxford. But it was this escape into fantasy which opened up the areas of power that the book contains.

By emphasizing the past, the supernatural, dreams, magic, and the antisocial, Lewis liberated his imagination for a flight into the irrational. Formal realism is an irrelevant criterion by which to judge *The Monk* because the novel is based on a psychological premise similar to Coleridge's famous aesthetic: it transfers "from our inward nature a human interest and a semblance of truth sufficient to procure" for Lewis' "shadows of imagination" a "willing suspension of disbelief" (*Biographia Literaria*, Chapter 14). Unlike Coleridge, Lewis was not consciously trying to give his reader a sense of the way the mind operates. Yet he achieved this end, and precisely by creating characters who are not believable in themselves; he achieved it by putting limited characters ("shadows of imagination") in patterned relations to each other and to the dominant imagery of the novel. Lewis' images are the ones common to many romantic works; images of depth, darkness, and cold to convey destruction and unconsciousness; images of height, light, and warmth to convey sublimity and consciousness, growth and love. In *The Monk* these images form a more mechanical and less rich pattern than in the important Victorian novels we shall investigate later. Because its psychological patterns are so overt, *The Monk* makes a good place to begin a detailed study of the part fantasy can play in fiction. In it we shall see in skeletal form how Chase's formulation of romance can work.

Chapter Two

The Monk

According to Freud we must look behind conscious daydreaming, as well as behind unconscious sleep dreaming, for keys to the unsatisfied primitive desires of the self.[1] According to Jung, when investigating such fantasy, we sometimes find ourselves in the presence of a vision that transcends the bounds of the immediate self and its limitations.[2] If we admit the premise of either theory, we are likely to find ourselves approaching fiction as something other than literature. We may if we wish search a novel for keys to the author's psychological problems, or for certain archetypes, universal "superhuman" types, or character relations. But if we do we will have subordinated art to psychological theory. If, on the other hand, we expect a certain kind of novel to reflect distinguishing psychic traits of its author and are not surprised to discover in it mythic patterns, we shall find psychoanalysis a help in approaching fiction, as I shall try to demonstrate in this chapter.

In the last analysis, neither Freud's approach nor Jung's can, in my opinion, provide the grounds for an aesthetic judgement. As Jung admits, a work of great archetypal interest may not have great artistic merit. *The Monk* is by no means devoid of artistic merit, but it is certainly not in a class with *Wuthering Heights* or *Bleak House*. Although it did play a part in establishing the tradition that made them possible, it contains in imperfect form the elements that they brought to artistic greatness.

We shall find in Lewis' novel all the qualities Chase outlined for a

1. Sigmund Freud, "The Relation of the Poet to Daydreaming" (1908), in *Delusion and Dream*, ed. Philip Rieff (Boston: Beacon Press, 1956).
2. Carl Jung, *Symbols of Transformation* (New York: Pantheon Books, Inc., 1956). Jung points out that Freud had earlier opened up this line of thought.

romance: because it is set in the past, its action will not gain much "resistance from reality." Because its characters are "rather two-dimensional types" they will be shown "in ideal relation" and will often act as "a function of plot." The "astonishing events" in which they are caught will contribute not to a realistic effect but to "mythic, allegorical, and symbolic forms."

Fortunately or unfortunately, we lack the evidence to probe very deeply into Lewis' childhood. We can, however, see indications of a psychic split having taken place early in his life. His parents separated in 1781, when he was six, his mother going to live with a music master. Although he stayed with his father and followed his footsteps by attending Westminster School and Oxford, and then entering the Civil Service, his sensibility followed his mother. She enjoyed music and the theatre and wanted to be an author. When young, her son would parade before her mirror "arrayed in a long train, and loaded with all the gauze and feathers that lay within his reach." Once he returned from the theatre and "imitated the actress's shriek with . . . thrilling accuracy." As Lewis' first and very sympathetic biographer commented, "Being the constant companion of his mother—a timid and sensitive woman, whose youthful appearance, when he grew up into boyhood, caused her not unfrequently to be looked upon as his sister—he gradually partook of her own romantic temperament, and somewhat undecided character."[3]

From early childhood, a confusion of sexual roles appears evident in Lewis.[4] In his novel we shall find a study of the disintegration of an "undecided character." Evidence connecting Lewis' nature with that of his hero-villain, Ambrosio, is not hard to find. We know for instance that Lewis suggested a resemblance between himself and Mrs Radcliffe's villain, Montoni.[5] Montoni is also an important source for Am-

---

3. *The Life and Correspondence of M. G. Lewis* (London: H. Colburn, 1839), 2 Vols., I, 12, 44, 28. Peck (p. v) identifies the author as Mrs Cornwall Baron-Wilson.

4. John Berryman takes Lewis' homosexuality for granted in his introduction. Peck (pp. 65–66) is doubtful, arguing that William Kelly, the youth whom Lewis undertook to sponsor in 1802, was only ten at the time. There is more evidence than Peck admits. See André Parreaux, *The Publication of The Monk: A Literary Event 1796–1798* (Paris: M. Didier, 1960), p. 119. Peck is, however, justified in his caveat that homosexuality covers too broad a range to be applied without defining. My case is simply that homoerotic emotions are apparent in Lewis' biography and writing. Whether he ever acted on them need not concern us.

5. See the letter to Lewis' mother in the back of Peck's biography, p. 208.

brosio. In addition we shall see as we analyse *The Monk* how Lewis' naiveté in presenting dreams, daydreams, nightmares, and supernatural scenes affords a relatively clear view of his conflicts. The pattern these elements make is no prettier than the details through which they are rendered, but it is an important pattern, opening up as it does irrational motifs evident in the stuff of Romantic poetry and in a significant number of post-Romantic novels.

The first hint of confused sexual identity comes out in the monk Ambrosio's attraction to Rosario, a young novice whom he loves "with all the affection of a father."[6] Rosario finally reveals himself as a woman, Matilda, who entered the monastery out of love for Ambrosio. After saving his life by sucking the poison out of a deadly bite on his hand, she manages to seduce him. Afterward she confesses that the poison, now in her, cannot be countered by any natural means. But there is some hope. She has been brought up by an enlightened uncle: "Under his instructions my understanding acquired more strength and justness than generally falls to the lot of my sex" (p. 82). In short, she knows something of black magic, and it turns out she will need the aid of the devil if she is to escape death by poisoning. As she leads Ambrosio to the underground burial vaults where she will call up Satan, she assumes "a sort of courage and manliness in her manners and discourse, but ill calculated to please him" (p. 233). Lewis seems at once conscious of the paradoxical relation and confused about it: Ambrosio "regretted Rosario, the fond, the gentle, and submissive; he grieved that Matilda preferred the virtues of his sex to those of her own" (p. 234). The appeal of the effeminate is brought out again later when Ambrosio first sees the devil: "He beheld a figure more beautiful than fancy's pencil ever drew. It was a youth seemingly scarce eighteen, the perfection of whose form and face was unrivalled. He was perfectly naked; a bright star sparkled upon his forehead, two crimson wings extended themselves from his shoulders, and his silken locks were confined by a band of many-coloured fires" (p. 273).

Even when we shift our focus in the novel to male-female relations that are seemingly less ambiguous, we find strange patterns emerging. We may begin with the previous scene in which Ambrosio meets Satan, a scene admired by Coleridge for its demonic "blue trembling flame"

6. Matthew G. Lewis, *The Monk* (New York: Grove Press, 1959), p. 67. Edited by Peck, introduced by John Berryman.

that "emitted no heat."[7] In fact, a "cold shivering" that seizes Ambrosio anticipates the unexpected conclusion of the plot about to be hatched in the vault. To ensure the success of Ambrosio's plan to ravish the heroine, Antonia, Satan gives the monk a myrtle (a flower sacred to Venus) which will send Antonia into "a death-like slumber" (p. 275). But, when the time comes, Ambrosio is successful only to the point of kissing Antonia's lips. At that point her mother, Elvira, rushes in so distraught that Ambrosio finds it necessary to strangle her.

> The blood was chilled in her veins: her heart had forgotten to beat; and her hands were stiff and frozen. Ambrosio beheld before him that once noble and majestic form, now become a corse, cold, senseless, and disgusting.
> This horrible act was no sooner perpetrated, than the friar beheld the enormity of his crime. A cold dew flowed over his limbs. . . . Antonia now appeared to him an object of disgust. A deadly cold had usurped the place of that warmth which glowed in his bosom (pp. 297–98).

But the cold has only temporarily triumphed over the warmth of Ambrosio's passion. He again casts Antonia into a deathlike sleep, this time with a drug. Then he has her placed in the catacombs where Matilda had invoked the devil. When she awakens there, he finally ravishes her in a scene which strengthens the connection between lust and lifelessness. At first he tries to woo her:

> "This sepulchre seems to me Love's bower. . . . Your veins shall glow with the fire which circles in mine."
> . . . Her shroud being her only garment, she wrapped it closely round her.
> "Unhand me, father!" she cried. . . . "Why have you brought me to this place? Its appearance freezes me with horror!" (p. 366).

Afterward he tells her,

> "Wretched girl, you must stay here with me! Here amidst these lonely tombs, these images of death, these rotting, loathsome, corrupted bodies! Here shall you stay, and witness my sufferings; witness what it is to be in the horrors of despondency, and breathe the last groan in blasphemy and curses!—And whom am I to thank for

7. In the *Critical Review* (February 1797). Reprinted by Thomas M. Raysor in *Coleridge's Miscellaneous Criticism* (London: Constable, 1936), p. 373.

this? What seduced me into crimes, whose bare remembrance makes me shudder? Fatal witch! was it not thy beauty? Have you not plunged my soul into infamy?" (p. 369).

Crude as the theatricality of this speech may be, its bald phrase "fatal witch" is a clue to the imaginative patterns which give *The Monk* its unhealthy power.

The real witch in Ambrosio's life is Matilda, who turns out to be in league with Satan. If Matilda and Antonia are enchanting witches, Elvira is that other kind, the old crone, who, like the incubus of conscience, turns cold with fear a man's warmest attempt at wish fulfilment. As I see it, the inevitable replacement of the enchantress by the crone is a central dilemma of Lewis' imagination.

These implications are evident in what Coleridge thought the most compelling part of the novel, the incidents in the section connected with the Bleeding Nun. Visiting in Bavaria, Don Raymond falls in love with a young Spanish woman, Agnes, whose jealous aunt finally denies him entry to her castle. Agnes decides to fly with him to avoid being forced into a nunnery, and she conceives the plan of dressing up as the Bleeding Nun, a ghost who appears once every five years at the castle. On the appropriate night, Don Raymond meets a figure dressed as the nun and swears that he is hers as long as "blood shall roll" in his veins. She turns out to be the actual ghost. He recalls, "I gazed upon the spectre with horror too great to be described. My blood was frozen in my veins. I would have called for aid, but the sound expired ere it could pass my lips. My nerves were bound up in impotence, and I remained in the same attitude inanimate as a statue" (p. 170). Like the Ancient Mariner's Nightmare Life-in-Death, "who thicks men's blood with cold," this witch has Don Raymond in her power and will not let him go until he is reconciled with God. She visits him every night at the same hour for several months, until "the Great Mogul" appears on the scene.

With his help Don Raymond is freed from enchantment in a scene parallel to the one in which Ambrosio is introduced to Satan. But, whereas Don Raymond is guided by a mysterious old man back to a normal life, Ambrosio was guided by a mysterious young woman into a liaison with the devil. And, whereas Ambrosio faced Satan's cold to gain a deceptively easy means of satisfying his hot lust, Don Raymond is liberated from cold by the hot cross on the forehead of the mysterious stranger, who is later identified as the Wandering Jew.

Ambrosio's pursuit of Antonia and Don Raymond's more reward-
ing attempt to unite with Agnes have similar patterns: each desires an
appealing woman but is frustrated by the deadly and chilling interven-
tion of another woman. A similar sequence, wish fulfilment displaced
by terror, is present in a scene near the beginning of the novel. Lorenzo,
the brother of Agnes and one of two youthful heroes in the subplot,
has just met Antonia and fallen in love with her. He goes into "the
gothic obscurity of the church" and abandons "himself to the delusions
of fancy." These melt into a sleeping dream in which Antonia appears
dressed for a wedding. Lorenzo realizes that he is to be the groom.

> But before he had time to receive her, an unknown rushed between
> them: his form was gigantic; his complexion was swarthy, his eyes
> fierce and terrible; his mouth breathed out volumes of fire, and on
> his forehead was written in legible characters—"Pride! Lust! In-
> humanity!"
> Antonia shrieked. The monster clasped her in his arms, and
> springing with her upon the altar, tortured her with his odious
> caresses. She endeavoured in vain to escape from his embrace.
> Lorenzo flew to her succour; but, ere he had time to reach her, a loud
> burst of thunder was heard. Instantly the cathedral seemed crumb-
> ling into pieces; the monks betook themselves to flight, shrieking
> fearfully; the lamps were extinguished, the altar sunk down, and in
> its place appeared an abyss vomiting forth clouds of flame. Uttering
> a loud and terrible cry the monster plunged into the gulph, and in
> his fall attempted to drag Antonia with him. He strove in vain.
> Animated by supernatural powers, she disengaged herself from his
> embrace; but her white robe was left in his possession. Instantly a
> wing of brilliant splendour spread itself from either of Antonia's
> arms. She darted upwards, and while ascending cried to Lorenzo,
> "Friend! we shall meet above!" (pp. 53–54).[8]

We have here one of those allegorical scenes which Chase saw as characteristic of romance. The monster stands for Ambrosio's faults as a man
and a priest; his treatment of Antonia foreshadows Ambrosio's ultimate
rape of her. The allegory also embodies Lewis' conscious anti-Catholicism (the labels on the monster's forehead referring beyond Ambrosio
to the system which produced him), but more important it embodies

8. The parallel with the end of *Clarissa* struck even Lewis, who in the fourth and
fifth editions mentioned it in a footnote. See Peck's list of Variant Readings,
p. 425, *The Monk*. See also Watt's analysis of *Clarissa*.

an unconscious tension in Lewis' psyche and in the novel, a tension between idyllic daydream and destroying nightmare.

The marriage in the church represents the hopeful daydream, while death in the catacombs becomes the dominant (indeed, triumphant) extension of the nightmare ending of the dream. We have already investigated Ambrosio's rape of Antonia in the catacombs. Taking rape as soulless love, we saw it as the yoking of lustful daydream and deathly nightmare. More characteristic, however, is the separation of the two, the hopeful ascent toward light in opposition to the disintegrating descent into darkness. In Lorenzo's dream, the descent caused by the lustful monster is balanced by the ascent of the angelic Antonia. In the death of Ambrosio, we will find an equivalent to the monster's descent. But, although Ambrosio's fall is balanced by the happy marriages of both Lorenzo and Don Raymond, the subplot does not ascend easily toward light.

Forced into a nunnery back in Spain, Agnes is found by Don Raymond, with whom her passion reaches a climax which has an unfortunate, if natural, consequence. The prioress discovers that Agnes is pregnant and locks her deep in the underground burial vaults. There she gives birth to a child that dies immediately. "It soon became a mass of putridity, and to every eye was a loathsome and disgusting object, to every eye but a mother's," says Agnes loyally (p. 393). She also tells us that, when first chained in her prison, her "blood ran cold" as she was struck by "the cold vapours hovering in the air, the walls green with damp" (p. 390). She is found and rescued by her brother Lorenzo, who had believed her dead. As he descends toward her, the cold is again emphasized: "Coldly played the light upon the damp walls, whose dew-stained surface gave back a feeble reflection. A thick and pestilential fog clouded the height of the vaulted dungeon. As Lorenzo advanced, he felt a piercing chillness spread itself through his veins" (p. 355).

In one sense Lorenzo is descending into the abyss about which he had earlier dreamed, and the imagery of light and dark is as pronounced as it was in that dream. The entrance to Agnes' prison is hidden by a statue in the main part of the catacomb. Significantly, that statue is of St Clare, the patron saint of the order to which Agnes belongs. With the statue removed, "A deep abyss now presented itself before them, whose thick obscurity the eye strove in vain to pierce. The rays of the lamp were too feeble to be of much assistance. Nothing was discernible, save a flight of rough unshapen steps, which sank into the yawning gulph, and were soon lost in darkness" (pp. 353–54). The symbolism of St Clare, "Saint Light," hiding a harsh reality of darkness behind her appearance of benevolence and light, is appropriate both to Lewis' conscious anti-Catholicism and to the unconscious ambiguity of his feelings about women.

In Lorenzo's early dream, after the appearance of the monster, "the cathedral seemed crumbling to pieces; . . . the lamps were extinguished, the altar sunk down, and in its place appeared an abyss" (p. 53). Similarly, in the later action, Lorenzo and his followers have descended into the vaults after the convent connected with them has been pulled down and burned by an angry mob. "Lorenzo was shocked at having been the cause, however innocent, of this frightful disturbance," of this "scene of devastation and horror" (p. 345). Like the monster in his dream, he plunges into the gulf below him, but he does so on a kind of redemptive quest.

The overt success of the quest can be measured by the reaction of Agnes when Lorenzo tells her she can at last ascend: "Joy! Joy! I shall once more breathe the fresh air, and view the light of the glorious sunbeams!" (p. 358). Then as they climb, "the rays of the lamp above, as well as the murmur of female voices, guided his steps" (p. 359). For the first time, light appears to triumph over darkness. If, in fact, we consider Lorenzo's experience as an archetypal one, we can see the possibility of a less pathological interpretation of the novel than we have so far been able to find.

Whereas the monster, like Ambrosio, goes down in the pit to be damned, Lorenzo descends into the depths like a hero to offer help. His actions even follow the pattern set by numerous heroes of folktale and myth, as these patterns have been abstracted by mythographers such as Frobenius, Rank, Jung, Lord Raglan, and Joseph Campbell.[9] The journey down into darkness is an important part of this pattern. Jung points out that, although the descent is what Freud would call a regression, it is undertaken with a positive aim. He emphasizes that the hero goes back to the womb in order that he may be reborn, renewed, made strong again.[10]

Since Lorenzo descends through the statue of a woman, Jung's sym-

9. Leo Frobenius, *Das Zeitalter des Sonnengottes* (1904); Otto Rank, *The Myth of the Birth of the Hero* (1914); Carl Jung, *Psychology of the Unconscious* (1916); Lord Raglan, *The Hero* (1936); Joseph Campbell, *The Hero with a Thousand Faces* (1949).
10. *Symbols of Transformation*, pp. 293–94, 308, 330, 335, 408, 419–20.

bolism could be said to hold good for the beginning of his quest. The psychoanalysts would see any movement back to the mother as running into the incest taboo. The overcoming of this taboo is usually represented by the hero's defeating a monster before he can return. The fact that Lorenzo is not forced to face any such monster bodes ill not so much for him as for the story (or its author). As though unconsciously aware of the pattern and its demands, Lewis gives Lorenzo a second chance to face a monster, by having him called back into the catacombs after he rescues Agnes. This time he almost confronts Ambrosio, the monster he should slay to round out the heroic pattern (or, from another point of view, to bring into more effective contact the twin strands of Lewis' plot). But instead Ambrosio escapes and Lorenzo is left with his own love, Antonia, who has just been raped by Ambrosio. She dies in his arms. Clearly something has gone wrong with the archetypal pattern.

In myth the darkness into which the hero descends is always dangerous, but it is also, as Jung shows, a source of life. In *The Monk*, however, it is a place of death only, really a tomb rather than a womb. This fact aligns the novel with an important subpattern that develops when the mythic success pattern is frustrated. As outlined by Joseph Campbell, this subpattern clearly fits *The Monk*. Where an

> Oedipus-Hamlet revulsion remains to beset the soul, there the world, the body, and woman above all, become the symbols no longer of victory but of defeat. A monastic-puritanical, world-negating ethical system then radically and immediately transfigures all the images of myth. No longer can the hero rest in innocence with the goddess of the flesh; for she is become the queen of sin. "So long as a man has any regard for this corpse-like body," writes the Hindu monk Shankaracharya, "he is impure, and suffers from his enemies as well as from birth, disease and death. . . . Throw far away this limitation of a body which is inert and filthy by nature."[11]

The moral that is conscious in the writings of the Hindu monk is largely unconscious in Lewis' work, as the happy ending to Lorenzo's story indicates.

Lorenzo has put his sister in the care of "the beautiful Virginia de Villa-Franca" (p. 348), whom he considers "as a ministering angel descended to the aid of afflicted innocence" (p. 361). Although he goes

11. *The Hero with a Thousand Faces,* (New York: Meridian Books, 1956), p. 123.

into a decline after the death of Antonia, soon Virginia wins him over by her "beautiful person, elegant manners, innumerable talents and sweet disposition" (p. 399). In other words, the happy ending may be seen as an attempt by Lewis to break out of the "world-negating" pattern in which he had immured Lorenzo. But Virginia is a *deus ex machina,* a character functioning more on the level of wish fulfilment than of engaged imagination.

The main impression made upon the reader is of the involvement of love with death in *The Monk*. Matilda risks death to gain Ambrosio (when they make love the first time, a deadly poison is in her veins). Both times that Ambrosio attempts to seduce Antonia, she is first put in a deathlike sleep. The second time, the stage is set appropriately: "By the side of three putrid half-corrupted bodies lay the sleeping beauty" (p. 363). Don Raymond gets the ghost of a corpse the first time he thinks he has Agnes. And Lorenzo, after bringing his sister back from near death in which natural love has placed her, is rewarded by the death of his beloved Antonia. Considering the consistency and force of this pattern, we must attribute success to *The Monk* as an artistic embodiment of certain tensions in Lewis' mind. These tensions reach an effective if morbid resolution in the last chapter of the novel.

While Ambrosio awaits the burning ordained for him by the Inquisition, the devil appears again, not as the beautiful youth of daydream, who had earlier helped seduce the monk to the delights of *contra naturam*, but as a nightmarish reality,

> in all that ugliness which since his fall from heaven had been his portion. His blasted limbs still bore marks of the Almighty's thunder. A swarthy darkness spread itself over his gigantic form: his hands and feet were armed with long talons. . . . Over his huge shoulders waved two enormous sable wings: and his hair was supplied by living snakes, which twined themselves round his brows with frightful hissings. . . . Still the lightning flashed around him, and the thunder with repeated bursts seemed to announce the dissolution of Nature (p. 412).

The last phrase, "the dissolution of Nature," sums up the main direction of the novel, toward descent and disintegration. Life has been drawn irresistibly down into the catacombs to become one with the "rotting, loathsome, corrupted bodies" there. And a similar fate is in store for Ambrosio. Rescued by Satan, he is taken out of the prison to be set upon a precipice in the mountains, where "the disorder of his

imagination was increased by the wildness of the surrounding scenery"
(p. 417). He has found an environment appropriate to his temperament.

Although Ambrosio is unsatisfyingly passive at the end, he has dared
enough to earn Lewis' implied comparisons with Orestes and Tantalus,
if not with Prometheus.

> Darting his talons into the monk's shaven crown, [Satan] sprang
> with him from the rock. The caves and mountains rang with Am-
> brosio's shrieks. The daemon continued to soar aloft, till reaching a
> dreadful height, he released the sufferer. Headlong fell the monk
> through the airy waste; the sharp point of a rock received him; . . . . .
> bruised and mangled, he rested on the river's banks. Life still existed
> in his miserable frame: he attempted to raise himself; his broken
> and dislocated limbs refused to perform their office, nor was he able
> to quit the spot where he had first fallen. The sun now rose above
> the horizon; its scorching beams darted full upon the head of the
> expiring sinner. Myriads of insects were called forth by the warmth;
> they drank the blood which trickled from Ambrosio's wounds; he
> had no power to drive them from him, and they fastened upon his
> sores, darted their stings into his body, covered him with their
> multitudes, and inflicted on him tortures the most exquisite and in-
> supportable. The eagles of the rock tore his flesh piecemeal, and
> dug out his eye-balls with their crooked beaks. A burning thirst
> tormented him; he heard the river's murmur as it rolled beside him,
> but strove in vain to drag himself towards the sound. Blind, maimed,
> helpless, and despairing, venting his rage in blasphemy and curses,
> execrating his existence, yet dreading the arrival of death destined
> to yield him up to greater torments, six miserable days did the villain
> languish. On the seventh a violent storm arose: the winds in fury
> rent up rocks and forests: the sky was now black with clouds, now
> sheeted with fire: the rain fell in torrents; it swelled the stream; the
> waves overflowed their banks; they reached the spot where Ambrosio
> lay, and, when they abated, carried with them into the river the
> corpse of the despairing monk (pp. 419–20).

After plunging from the heights to the abyss, Ambrosio experiences
sunlight not as the "glorious sunbeams" which Agnes looked forward to
earlier, but as the wrath of God. The warmth caused by the sun is no
longer his own hot lust for carnal experience; rather it calls forth insects
which ravish his helpless body. Even the water of life which he desires,

finally brings only death to him. It took six days for God to make the world; on the seventh he rested in peace. It takes six days for Ambrosio to disintegrate completely, physically and spiritually; on the seventh he dies in a storm.

The perversion of nature which Lewis made the moral basis of his conscious didacticism in the novel is also imaged in the development of its thematic patterns. Despite the presence of light and the ascent of some characters toward it, the controlling force in *The Monk*, and the one experienced by its readers, is demonic. All the supernatural visitants have rejected God, and even the one who frees Don Raymond from the Bleeding Nun was damned at Christ's death. Of the ten dreams described or referred to in the novel, six are nightmares, the other four being voluptuous fantasies of the type referred to earlier as leading to a nightmarish retribution. This triumph of the nightmare indicates the plight of Lewis' trapped psyche. In his novel, love leads to lasting union only within the accepted social framework, and then only at the cost of Agnes' natural child or Lorenzo's first love. All the lovers become enmeshed in the machinations of the nunnery and monastery, two institutions which in the novel breed inhumanity while attempting to mask it. Lewis exposes the "truth," rationally by observing that these institutions separate male and female, symbolically by connecting them through the doors that lead from each to the underground burial vaults. But behind the rational distaste lurks a deeper reason for separating the sexes. Lewis could not bring them together convincingly in fulfilled natural love. Behind the loved one as female there stands a jealous aunt, a righteous mother, a damned incubus. Even the loved one as a male turns from a charming lad into a domineering woman or a punishing demon.

Coleridge began his review of *The Monk* with the following sentence: "The horrible and the preternatural have usually seized on the popular taste, at the rise and decline of literature" (*Miscellaneous Criticism,* p. 372). If we think of Coleridge's three great poems, the supernatural comes to mind immediately. The horrible has been less noticeable since he cut from the 1798 version of "The Ancient Mariner" a number of stanzas with a gothic charnel effect. From this point of view, Romantic poetry is the rising form, the gothic novel the declining one. Poetry picks up and transmutes most of the standard gothic accoutrement: horror, terror, the supernatural, the Middle Ages, the sublime, the demonic, incest.[12] Scott, unable to compete in poetry with Byron's dark, soulful hero, turns to the novel, which he reorients towards a more mundane use of the past with more conventional characters and situations. In effect the literary impetus shifts from the novel to poetry. But, with the artistic shift back to the novel after Byron's death in 1824, the techniques and attitudes of romanticism will help bring about a change in the nature of fiction.

The important aesthetic question raised by *The Monk* is one Coleridge tried to solve in the best part of his review. Coleridge's comments, reminiscent of Walpole's much earlier insight, are also a foreshadowing of his famous statement about the suspension of disbelief. In the review he asserted that "The romance-writer possesses an unlimited power over situations; but he must scrupulously make his characters act in congruity with them. . . . We feel no great difficulty in yielding a temporary belief to any, the strangest, situation of *things*. But that situation once conceived, how beings like ourselves would feel and act in it, our own feelings sufficiently instruct us; and we instantly reject the clumsy fiction that does not harmonise with them" (p. 373). In a certain kind of novel we do not ask for a probable environment. We gladly throw away the mirror of exterior nature, partly through joy in the liberation of imagination, but also, Coleridge intimates, because we expect to find out something about our interior nature. It is to this world that Lewis must be true. But, contrary to Coleridge's dictum, and perhaps to common sense, he need not give us deep or consistent characters. That is, any one character may act from shallow or incongruous emotions, but because Lewis embodied in his action powerful emotional and thematic patterns we respond to them intuitively. The sensational sequence of events evokes at least a general sense of unease in the average reader, a response we have seen as based on Lewis' embodying the tensions of his psyche in patterns of sexual conflict, violated taboos, and self-destructive impulses.

Although *The Monk*, with its unresolved tensions, stands as a paradigm of excess, the gothic novel unquestionably did establish the

---

12. Railo treats the evolution of these themes in *The Haunted Castle* (London: G. Routledge & Sons, 1927). See also Peter L. Thorslev, Jr., *The Byronic Hero* (Minneapolis: University of Minnesota Press, 1962). See also Robert Hume, "Gothic versus Romantic: a Revaluation of the Gothic Novel," *PMLA,* 84 (March 1969).

practice of patterned fantasy and psychologically significant settings and action, a practice which influenced many important English novelists in the nineteenth century. A similar case may be made for the fairy tale, another influential form of romance and one we shall consider in the next chapter. One of the triumphs of the novel as a literary form in Victorian times was to transplant the patterns of romance into a nineteenth-century setting.

Chapter Three

The Fairy Tale

The same impulse towards the irrational that manifested itself at the end of the eighteenth century in the novel as gothicism and in poetry as Romanticism also stimulated throughout Europe an interest in the fairy tale. As a result of this concern, folktales became available to nineteenth-century Europeans in a number of written versions; the most notable was the two-volume collection of Märchen by Jacob and Wilhelm Grimm, published in Germany in 1812 and 1815, and translated into English ten years later. Several of the tales collected by the brothers Grimm had indigenous English counterparts, mutilated versions of which had been printed during the eighteenth century, along with abridged romances and translations of Arabian and French fairy tales. Both *The Arabian Nights* and Perrault's *Mother Goose Tales* were also published separately in England in the early eighteenth century. But both collections were composed of tales that had been given literary form rather than transcribed from the oral tradition as the brothers Grimm were to do.[1]

In his guidebook, *The Folktale* (New York: The Dryden Press, 1946), Stith Thompson notes that "the term 'folktale' has always been used loosely to cover the whole range of traditional oral narrative" (p. 21). Within this large category, it is possible to distinguish legends and animal tales from the fairy tale of unrealistic wonders and incredible

---

1. In "A Literary Approach to the Brothers Grimm," *Journal of the Folklore Institute,* Alfred and Mary Elizabeth David point out that Wilhelm Grimm often retouched the tales he and his brother gathered. Partly this activity came from his growing sense of fairy-tale style, partly from the notion both brothers had "of what a folktale should ideally be like. Their ideas on this subject . . . were influenced by their romantic theories of nature and literature" (1: 190, 193).

marvels. Because of its special narrative form, the fairy tale has a psychological import that adds a further dimension to the influence already suggested of the gothic on the novel.

Like the gothic novel, the fairy tale often deals in adventures that are literally impossible in the actual world, and manages quite well with a setting remote from the experience of its readers. Because they share so many of the characteristics attributed to romance by Chase, both the fairy tale and the gothic novel require Coleridge's romantic suspension of disbelief. But fairy tales, in their most typical and effective form, have other literary attributes than does a novel like *The Monk*. Their language is simple, and they are hardly cognizant of passing religious, political, or social manners. To put it another way, the typical fairy tale has a surface simplicity; being short it must rely on straightforward presentation of action to open the reader's perceptions to its vicarious experience. Depending on two-dimensional characters and a highly coloured plot, the action in a fairy tale is not rendered through realistic detail, nor is it typically analysed. The reader is offered a minimum of sense impressions, only enough to catch his imagination. Although the tale embodies psychological processes, it does so impersonally. Most of these characteristics can be correlated with the literary theories and practices of Emily Brontë, Dickens, Hardy, and Conrad.

Of the many differences between these novelists and the anonymous tellers of fairy tales, we can be sure of one: the letters of Dickens and Conrad, and the notebooks of Hardy, indicate their awareness that both fairy tales and their own fiction embody psychological processes. We cannot, of course, know the private intention of the folktellers. Fortunately, however, neither their intentions nor their self-consciousness is relevant. For according to the findings of twentieth-century psychoanalysis, fantasy and dream, romance and fairy tale give representation to the otherwise hidden dynamics of mental life. These forms are able to do so precisely because they turn away from the outside realities of the world. They express an inner reality that is not simply sublimated, unrealistic escape. Interior conflicts and battles are as real and important as any in the outer world.

Stith Thompson organized his *Motif-Index of Folk-Literature* (Bloomington: Indiana University Press, 1955-58, 6 vols.) with the scholarly aim of making the known material most practicably available to workers in the area. But a number of the headings have obvious psychological and anthropological overtones: Tabu, Magic, Marvels,

Tests, Chance and Fate, The Nature of Life. A subheading under "Tests" is "Identity Tests: recognition." Psychoanalysts would suggest that most fairy tales are concerned with an "identity test," the attempt of the self to recognize its shortcomings and conflicts, the impulses toward anarchy or inertia that threaten it, and the possible directions of solution. These problems are personified in the characters, and their dynamics rendered in the plot of the fairy tale.

Under "Magic," Thompson lists four types of "Transformation." I would like to make the psychological implications of this motif the main focus in our consideration of the "identity test" in particular fairy tales. Since the second century A.D., when Apuleius adapted "Cupid and Psyche" from existing folktales, many European fairy tales have dealt with the man who must be freed by a long-suffering lover from a monstrous shape.[2] In two Norwegian tales and one version collected by Grimm, the pattern is quite similar to "Cupid and Psyche."[3] A better-known version, "Beauty and the Beast" is somewhat different, probably because it is farther from an anonymous original.[4] Its appeal to Victorian readers may have rested in its having altered the usual pattern to bring out a latent sentimentality: An ugly but kind beast is finally transformed into a handsome prince only after the beauty he has allowed to leave him realizes he is dying for her and returns to express her love for him. This form of the motif—the transformation of a low beast by a high beauty—appears in the works of the Brontës and Dickens as well as in a number of other Victorian novels.

2. *Amor and Psyche,* with a commentary by Erich Neumann (New York: Pantheon Books, 1956).

3. In the Grimm version, "The Singing, Soaring Lark," he is a lion, while in a very similar Norwegian tale, "White-Bear-King-Valemon," he is a bear, as also in the less similar but better-known Norwegian tale, "East of the Sun and West of the Moon" (both in *East of the Sun and West of the Moon and Other Tales,* translated from the collection of Asbjornsen and Moe, New York: Macmillan, 1963). There is an enchanted bear in Grimm's version of "Snow White and Rose Red," but the story ends with the initial transformation of the bear into a man. In addition, rather than being a true folktale, "Snow White and Rose Red" is according to Thompson "a literary concoction" (*The Folktale,* p. 100). The same is true of the other story of this type that is well known to English readers, "Beauty and the Beast." (See next footnote).

4. *Ibid. "Beauty and the Beast"* is Mme de Beaumont's admirable reworking of a version of the story by Mme de Villeneuve. See *The Borzoi Book of French Folk Tales,* ed. with commentary by Paul Delarue (New York: Alfred A. Knopf, 1956), p. 375. See also Jacques Barchilon, "Beauty and the Beast, from Myth to Fairy Tale," *Psychoanalysis and the Psychoanalytic Review,* 46 (Winter 1959–60): 23–25.

One trouble with "Beauty and the Beast" is that its story is too simple even for a fairy tale; as a contrast, let us take a close look at a more authentic tale, "Iron Hans," from the Grimm collection.[5] Besides offering a different version of the transformation motif, it contains an additional fairy-tale character. A king mysteriously lost all his huntsmen and dogs in a forest full of wild animals near his castle. For many years after, no one went into the forest. Finally a strange huntsman offered to go. Pursuing some game, his dog came to a deep pool, out of which a naked arm reached up, seized the dog, and drew it under. Seeing this, the huntsman brought back three men to empty the pool with pails. Lying on the bottom they found a wild man (Iron Hans) whose body was brown like rusty iron and whose hair hung over his face to his knees. They tied him up and took him to the castle where the king had him locked in an iron cage which no one was allowed to open. The key was kept under the queen's pillow.

The king's son accidently bounced his golden ball into the cage of Iron Hans, who refused to give it back unless the boy freed him. In opening the door for Iron Hans, the boy pinched his fingers. Iron Hans gave the boy his ball and started to leave, but the boy pleaded that he would be punished for freeing the wild man. So Iron Hans put the boy upon his shoulder, and carried him into the depths of the forest where he set him down.

Iron Hans explained that he had gold and treasure, and would treat the prince well if he would be obedient. The next day he asked the boy to guard a well, in the crystal waters of which swam golden fish and snakes. The prince's task was to keep anything from falling in and polluting the well. During the day his finger pained him, so he dipped it in the water, only to draw it out indelibly gilded. Discovering what had happened, Iron Hans let him off that day, and also the next when a hair from the boy's head fell into the well. On the third day, when the prince looked down to admire his reflection in the water, his long hair fell in and turned gold. Though he covered his head with a handkerchief, Iron Hans found him out and banished him. But the wild man said that, since the prince was not really bad, if he ever needed aid he

5. See *The Folktale*, pp. 59–61. A similar tale, closer to Thompson's typical model, is the Norwegian fairy tale of "The Widow's Son" in *East of the Sun*. See also "The Princess on the Glass Mountain" in the same volume. An equally impressive related tale is "The Firebird" in *Russian Fairy Tales*, trans. by Norbert Guterman (New York: Pantheon Books, 1945), p. 304. See also "Prince Ivan and Princess Martha" in the same volume.

should go to the edge of the forest and call out "Iron Hans!"

The boy wandered to a king's court and was put to work in the garden, where one day his hair was seen by the king's daughter. She ordered him to bring her flowers and, when he did, snatched off his cap and gave him some gold pieces. Twice she tried to pull off his cap. Each time he gave her gifts of gold pieces to the gardener's children.

Then the country was invaded, and the king took his followers off to fight, all except the boy who was given a lame horse. He went to the forest, shouted "Iron Hans!" and was supplied with a horse, armour and a troop of iron-clad warriors whose swords flashed in the sun. The boy and his troop saved the king and his followers, and then routed the enemy.

To find the identity of his mysterious saviour, the king held a three-day feast at which his daughter threw out on successive days, three golden apples. Outfitted by Iron Hans, the boy appeared on the first day in red, the second in white, and the third in black. Each day he caught the golden apple, which he afterwards showed to the gardener's children. On the third day he was pursued and wounded in the leg; his helmet fell off, exposing his golden hair which was seen by the king's daughter. When he reappeared as the gardener's helper, she took him to her father, to whom he returned the apples. Asked if he wanted anything, the boy chose the daughter, and the king agreed to their marriage. As it was being celebrated, a stately king appeared. It was Iron Hans, freed from his enchantment by the boy's defeat of the invader king. All the wild man's treasure now belonged to the boy.

The wild man is a variation of the beast who must be accepted and loved.[6] Locked in an iron cage and called Iron Hans because of his rusty colour, he becomes associated with gold from the time the boy's golden ball bounces into his cage. He first offers and later gives the boy treasure; in between he sets him to guard a well with water that gilds whatever it touches, a well of life in opposition to the pool of death in which the wild man's body had presumably been rusted. When the boy proves too self-absorbed to be a worthy guardian of the well, the wild man sends him off to the world of action, where he will later help the boy achieve an heroic destiny.

In giving the boy help, the wild man acts in a role so common in fairy tale and myth that it has been given various names: mentor, donor, wise

6. See *The Wild Man in the Middle Ages* by Richard Bernheimer (Cambridge: Harvard University Press, 1952).

old man.[7] The latter term is the contribution of Carl Jung, whose insights will be helpful in analysing this tale. Jung comments that the wise old man often has both a "positive, favorable, bright side" to his nature and a "negative and unfavorable, partly chthonic" side (p. 82). Or, as we have noted of Iron Hans, the wild man may be a "life-bringer as well as a death-dealer" (p. 82). In this tale, he is first a threat to the boy's father, then a help to the boy; once the boy leaves the forest, Iron Hans both supplies the iron troop which deals death to the invader, and brings treasure to the boy.

From another point of view, we may emphasize the transformation undergone by the boy as a product more of his effort and nature than of those of Iron Hans. We could argue that he has earned the right to dip his finger in the wild man's well: it pains him because it is probably the finger he pinched in freeing the wild man from his iron cage.[8] For the boy's admiring his features in the water there is less excuse. Yet he accepts the (admittedly mild) punishment of banishment as a kind of exchange for the gold hair which attracts the king's daughter. Just as he made no response to Iron Hans's offer of treasure, so he spurns the princess's coins. It is as though he must remain a free agent in order to achieve what he seems to be seeking, the transformation of himself from a gardener's boy to a hero worthy of marrying the king's daughter. His success in battle causes not only his own transformation but also that of Iron Hans, from wild man to king, from iron to gold.

The oppositions associated with "Iron Hans" are worth emphasizing because they are characteristic not only of other fairy-tale characters, but often even of the structure of a tale. Such an opposition is, for instance, embodied in the very conception of the transformation tale. But often the point of the opposition is to enforce a connection, as in Beauty's having to accept the Beast as animal before he turns into a prince. Similarly, the boy's letting Iron Hans out of his prison implies an acceptance of the low, iron captive that leads to the high, gold king. At their most schematized, fairy tales often deal with a low figure (poor

7. "Donor" is the contribution by Vladimir Propp in *Morphology of the Folktale,* trans. by Laurence Scott (Bloomington: University of Indiana Press, 1958), "Wise Old Man" is the contribution of C. G. Jung in "The Phenomenology of the Spirit in Fairy Tales," in Part I of Vol. 9 of Jung's *Collected Works;* all my quotations are from the version of Jung's essay published in *Psyche and Symbol,* ed. Violet S. de Laszlo (Garden City: Doubleday and Co., 1958).
8. This is presumably the same finger that stole the key from under his mother's pillow. Considering the boy's own later trouble with the princess, we may speculate that there is also a Freudian level to this fairy tale.

or small or oppressed) being made high (rich or heroic or successful).
They also often deal with the opposite of this process, the high person
(proud or arrogant) brought low (humbled or killed).

In approaching *Wuthering Heights* and *Bleak House*, we shall discover not only the fact of these two common processes of fiction, but
more important the images and motifs associated with them in the
fairy tale. For example, two images, the well and the treasure, play an
important part in the motif of the boy's transformation to hero. Similarly, in each of the novels by Dickens, Hardy, and Conrad that we
shall look at, the image of the well is related to the problem of individual
transformation.[9] Dickens, Emily Brontë, and Conrad also use the image
of the treasure to deal with the same motif.

The last fairy tale to be considered, "The Glass Coffin," is of more
recent origin than "Iron Hans."[10] While it contains the three fairy-tale
characters we have been discussing, it suggests quite different roles not
only for the wise old man but for the hero and heroine.

A tailor who had lost his way in a forest finally saw a light which
led him to a small hut where he spent the night. Next morning, awakened
by sounds of violence outside, the tailor rushed out in time to see a
battle between a great black bull and a beautiful stag. Eventually the
stag triumphed and killed the bull, whereupon it turned to the tailor
and bore him away on its horns. Finally it set the tailor down unharmed
in front of a wall of rock against which it pushed until a door sprang
open. The tailor entered and discovered two great glass chests and
numerous glass vases filled with coloured liquids and vapours. One
of the chests contained a miniature castle; the other contained a beautiful maiden, who seemed asleep. As the tailor gazed at her, she opened
her eyes and started with joy at seeing a rescuer. When the tailor had
unlocked the lid of the glass coffin, she kissed him and told him her
story.

The daughter of a count, she had been brought up by an older brother
after her parents died. So much affection did each feel for the other

9. The implication of the related fairy-tale motif of the descent into the well
appears in Chapter Nine, and is explored more fully in Chapter Ten, "The Well
of Truth."

10. Joseph Campbell in his "Folkloristic Commentary" to the Pantheon edition
of *Grimm's Fairy Tales* (New York, 1944) places this tale in the seventeenth and
eighteenth century. "Iron Hans", in the form Grimm gives, he dates from the
Middle Ages (p. 856); in both cases he follows Friedrich von der Leyden's
"edition of the *Nursery and Household Tales,* Jena, 1912)."

that they agreed to stay together and not marry. One day a stranger came to the castle and made himself agreeable. That night the sister woke to see the stranger coming through her bolted door; he confessed himself a magician who wished to marry her. She refused. Finally the magician retired angrily, vowing to avenge himself and punish her pride. The next morning the sister went in pursuit of the stranger and her brother, who had gone hunting. She came upon the stranger leading a stag, her brother under a spell. She fired a pistol at the magician, but the shot bounced off him and killed her horse. She fell and was also put under a spell. When she woke in the glass coffin, the magician showed her how he had diminished her castle and transformed her servants into vapour. She still refused to marry him. During the deep sleep into which he again cast her, she had a vision of rescue by a young man and woke to see him there.

Between them, the tailor and the maiden carried the transformed objects outside. There they opened them up, and the castle and its inhabitants were restored to their natural size and shape. Then the brother, who had killed the bull while a stag, appeared from the forest in human form, the spell broken. The tailor and the maiden were married.

Unlike the boy in "Iron Hans," the tailor in this tale neither breaks any commandments nor does any deed of heroism. He is in fact quite passive. Taking the maiden to be the princess he wishes to win, we may note that his only action is unlocking the coffin she is in. But she has to ask this of him, just as earlier a voice had encouraged him to enter the hall and to descend to her chamber. Even more noticeable is the fact that the magician is defeated not by the hero but by the brother as stag. It is also the brother who first directly involves the tailor in the adventure. Both brother and sister are under a spell; it would appear that only an outside male can break it. But the tailor's lack of prominence in the action is a good indication that the theme of the tale does not have much to do with him.

The focus is rather on the maiden. The appearance of a stranger in her life is an intensified form of the natural consequence of her unnatural decision to spend her life with the older brother who has brought her up. In approaching the problem of the unconscious incestuous desire of a child for the parent of the opposite sex, psychoanalysis points out that for a girl, a brother is often an early choice in the process of finding a father substitute. Normally the end of the process is her choice of a male her own age from outside the family. In this case, however, the maiden's brother has acted first *in loco parentis* and then as a sublimated husband for her.

If we see the tale as developing her problem, we can take the stranger as something more than an undesirable suitor: he is the fate that must come if she does not exert her will to free herself from the childhood limitation of loving only a male relative. Even though she has consciously rationalized the incestuous relation, unconsciously she and her brother are still affected by the taboo against incest. As a result both come under a spell; she is emotionally immobilized until she can first dream of an outside hero to rescue her and then agree to marry him.

Jung tended to agree with Freud on the importance of incest (though not on its dynamics or strictly sexual basis); he was also interested in the problem of magic spells and the frequent role of the wise old man as magician. We have seen that the wise old man is usually helpful as an advisor or direction pointer for the hero. As a figure in the experience of the heroine, however, he is usually harmful; of the several explanations possible for this fact, the most logical in "The Glass Coffin" is that the magician represents the male relative who is trying to appropriate what does not belong to him. From this point of view, the relationship of the older man and the younger woman is an important one in many nineteenth-century English novels. It is the use of fairy-tale motifs to explore the problem that distinguishes the particular novelists we shall be concerned with.

Where "Iron Hans" is an active tale of initiation and progressive self-discovery, "The Glass Coffin" is a tale of immobilization, with even the rescue being accomplished by a passive hero. We could say that *The Monk* and "The Glass Coffin" share a heaviness of tone. We may note a source of this oppressiveness by looking at some comparable scenes in the two. The stranger uses magic to approach the maiden in her bed, very much as Ambrosio used the myrtle provided by Satan to approach Antonia. Like Antonia, the maiden is immobilized, though unlike her she is conscious on the magician's first appearance. When she sees the magician the last time, in her glass coffin underground, the situation is somewhat similar to Antonia's waking underground and seeing Father Ambrosio there. One important difference is, of course, that Antonia's "father" rapes her, whereas the magician only pleads again to marry the maiden.

We may take this last difference between a particular gothic novel

and a particular fairy tale as a characteristic difference.[11] Although the
European fairy tale practically never deals directly with sexual encounters, it does often make use of those "gross and violent stimulants"
objected to by Wordsworth in gothic writers ("Preface" to the *Lyrical
Ballads,* para. 8). In Grimm's "Cinderella," the sisters chop off their
toes in the hope of fitting a foot into the glass slipper; subsequently
their eyes are pecked out by birds. These repellent details do not occur
in Perrault's version of the tale, which is the one usually followed in
modern versions of the story. But such details were not so offensive to
the Victorians, who nourished their children on the similarly violent
admonitory tales of *Slovenly Betsy* and *Slovenly Peter,* taken from nineteenth-century German originals. On the other hand, the suppression
of sexual relations in the Victorian novel tends to distinguish it from
the eighteenth-century novel. *The Monk,* in the libidinous scenes of its
first edition, was still a part of its century, while the fairy tale was more
compatible with the Victorian age.

A more general way to make this point is to say that the fairy tale
offered to the Victorian novelist who mistrusted the notion of photo-
graphic realism, a model for saying subliminally what he could not or
did not wish to say openly. The taboo on sex aside, if a writer like Dickens
did not write novels in which he developed complex characters, he was
still able to express his own complex nature, by embodying his emotions
and intuitions in complicated patterns of imagery and character relations. Dickens' work certainly contains patterns of self-discovery or
self-destruction such as we saw in *The Monk,* but more consciously
and characteristically he drew dark patterns of self-binding such as we
have seen in "The Glass Coffin" or light patterns of self-transformation
or integration such as we traced in "Iron Hans."

The connections and influences referred to above come together in
even more concentrated form in Emily Brontë's dark creation, Heathcliff. He is both gothic villain and Byronic hero; he is early the loving
more-than-brother of his foster-sister Catherine, and later the tyrant-
magician of her daughter, Cathy. Adopted in his youth by a wise, older

---

11. It is worth noting, however, that the influence of German folktale is very
strong in *The Monk.* Lewis' main acknowledged source originated in folklore:
the holy man led into evil by the devil. "The Bleeding Nun," Lewis also claimed
as "a tradition still credited in many parts of Germany" (p. 34). Several of the
novel's inserted poems also contain motifs common in folktales. Beside the
particular differences listed in this chapter, the principal general difference
between *The Monk* and folk or fairy tales lies in Lewis' selection from and use
of them for his own grotesque effects.

foster-father who would be his protector, Heathcliff has the misfortune to lose him. Thereafter he can develop not like the youth in "Iron Hans" but only like the Beast in another type of tale, dependent on the pity and love of Beauty. When Catherine fails him by choosing Edgar Linton, Heathcliff remains untransformed. Catherine herself is involved in two equally important fairy-tale patterns. Not only is she the Beauty to Heathcliff's Beast, she wishes to be the Cinderella who is herself recognized and transformed into a princess. In fact, a major conflict develops between the pain of her active stooping to raise another and the passive bliss of her being raised herself.

In the next chapter we shall discover particular evidence in *Wuthering Heights* to indicate Emily Brontë's use of fairy-tale motifs and her emphasis on the problem of transformation. But, before getting fully involved in her novel, we need to face more broadly the question of what kind of novel it is.

Chapter Four

Romance to Novel

The two kinds of prose fiction which we distinguished in Chapter One correspond to two general aesthetic views which came into conflict in the late eighteenth century: these were the dominant notion that art was rightly concerned only with imitating nature, and the emerging idea that art could be self-sufficient. Watt's characterization of the novel as based on formal realism is a sophisticated version of the mimetic theory of art, while Chase's description of romance corresponds to the Romantic theory of the autonomy of a work of art.[1] The case for autonomy was stated as early as 1762, when Bishop Richard Hurd argued in his Tenth Letter on Chivalry, "A poet, they say, must follow *Nature*; and by Nature we are to suppose can only be meant the known and experienced course of affairs in this world. Whereas the poet has a world of his own, where experience has less to do, than consistent imagination."[2] Coleridge gave this literary position its definitive statement in his lectures on Shakespeare: "The romantic poetry . . . appealed to the imagination rather than to the senses. . . . The reason is aloof from time and space; the imagination [has] an arbitrary control over both; and if only the poet have such power of exciting our internal emotions as to make us present to the scene in imagination chiefly, he

1. M. H. Abrams has shown in *The Mirror and the Lamp* (New York: W. W. Norton & Co., 1953) that the doctrine of imitation which had reigned in literary criticism from Aristotle to Johnson was overturned by the doctrine of expressiveness. Poets became interested in mental process. The criterion of success in a work of art became, instead of an objective, consciously imposed form, a suitable organic form which had grown unconsciously.
2. *Hurd's Letters on Chivalry and Romance,* ed. Edith J. Morley (London: H. Froude, 1911), p. 138.

acquires the right and privilege of using time and space as they exist in the imagination, obedient only to the laws which the imagination acts by."[3]

This position is one to which we are willing to give credence when we approach Romantic poetry; its appearance in prose fiction is another matter. Yet the gothic novel is there to testify that the process had begun before Romanticism as such was born; in fact Coleridge's sympathetic review of *The Monk* came two years before the publication of *The Lyrical Ballads*. It may be argued, however, that both the gothic novel and the fairy tale were ephemeral as literary forms, sustainable only in the hothouse atmosphere of Romanticism, and that poetry alone can flourish under the doctrine of autonomy. Perhaps. Certainly it is true that England during the thirties could point to no romance writer of the stature of Poe or Hawthorne in America.[4] Neither did it have any writers of fiction willing to take up the fairy tale as a contemporary form, as Germany did between 1796 and 1822.[5] My claim is that fairy tale and romance were assimilated into the regular stream of English fiction, thereby making a crucial contribution to the strength of the Victorian novel.

In *Wuthering Heights*, for example, we may see Emily Brontë using the transformation motif in a quite sophisticated way. She develops it in contrast to a simple-minded view of the fairy tale which is expressed by the narrator, Lockwood. Hearing that the second Cathy is to marry Hareton, he daydreams aloud about his relation to her: "What a realization of something more romantic than a fairy tale it would have been for Mrs Linton Heathcliff, had she and I struck up an attachment . . . and migrated together, into the stirring atmosphere of the town!"[6] Lockwood's notion of a fairy tale is one still current: Prince Charming comes along, leads Cinderella or Snow White to his castle, they marry and live happily ever after. As I have already commented,

3. *Coleridge's Shakespearean Criticism*, ed. T. M. Raysor (London: Constable, 1911), I, 129–30.
4. See Richard Chase, *The American Novel and its Tradition*. See also Daniel Hoffman, *Form and Fable in American Fiction* (New York: Oxford University Press, 1961).
5. These dates, given for the German writers, span the period of *The Romantic Fairy Tale* (Ann Arbor: University of Michigan Press, 1964), as indicated by the author, Marianne Thalmann in a table on p. 129.
6. Emily Brontë, *Wuthering Heights,* ed. Mark Schorer (New York: Rinehart & Co., 1950), p. 322. Schorer reprints from the original 1847 edition, "except for obvious misprints" (p. xxi).

this idea of the fairy tale as pure escape does not do justice to its special way of facing real problems.

In any case, it is clear that Emily Brontë intends the reader to scorn Lockwood's notion. The "stirring atmosphere" of the town is not what Cathy needs or deserves. Nor would Lockwood have been capable of acting as Prince Charming. The actual happy ending of the novel does involve a kind of transformation, but not of Cinderella from ashes or Snow White from death. Rather, the beauty-and-beast relation is even more obvious between Cathy and Hareton than it had been between her mother and Heathcliff. Coming to the novel with fairy-tale patterns in mind, our eyes are arrested within a few pages of the beginning by Lockwood's description of Hareton: "his thick, brown curls were rough and uncultivated, his whiskers encroached bearishly over his cheeks" (p. 10). Shortly thereafter we hear him growling, and Lockwood refers to him overtly as "that bear." Animal imagery is common in the novel, of course, and like other images this one falls into a larger pattern.

Cathy decides to work on Hareton, if not to give him love growing out of pity, as Beauty does her Beast, certainly to raise him into a civilized creature if she can rouse him: "He's just like a dog, . . . or a cart-horse. He does his work, eats his food, and sleeps, eternally! What a blank, dreary mind he must have! Do you ever dream, Hareton?" (p. 329). But she employs subtlety as well as raillery in her efforts. As Nelly Dean testifies, Cathy would often "bring some pleasant volume, and read it aloud to me. When Hareton was there, she generally paused in an interesting part, and left the book lying about—that she did repeatedly; but he was as obstinate as a mule, and, instead of snatching at her bait, in wet weather he took to smoking with Joseph, and they sat like automatons, one on each side of the fire" (p. 330). Finally, however, his brute existence rebounds on him. He usually spends Sunday, when he might be reading or sharing Cathy's company, shooting on the moors. But one day his gun bursts and wounds him. As a result "he was condemned to the fire-side and tranquility, till he made it up again" (p. 330). Cathy exerts her charm, calling forth a defensive assertion which indicates that he is capable of dreaming. "Nay, if it made me a *king,* I'd not be scorned for seeking her good will any more" (p. 332, my italics). Nelly has told us that Cathy had always been called "queen" and "angel" in her own home at the Grange (p. 210). It demands all the magnanimity she possesses to break through Hareton's brute reserve and try to lift him to the level of king.

Cathy's motives for helping Hareton are not merely altruistic, of course. Not only does she feel affection for him (before it grows into love), she realizes that at Wuthering Heights she can regain her lost queenship not by acting as the ruler who must be obeyed but only by giving herself to another. As she "frankly extended her hand" to Hareton in a direct plea, however, "he blackened, and scowled like a thunder-cloud, and kept his fists resolutely clenched, and his gaze fixed on the ground. Catherine, by instinct, must have divined it was obdurate perversity, and not dislike, that prompted this dogged conduct; for after remaining an instant, undecided, she stooped, and impressed on his cheek a gentle kiss" (p. 332). This begins the thawing. Looking at them, shortly after, Nelly perceives two "radiant countenances," and we realize there has been a successful transformation from dark to light, from beast to man, from brutishness to royalty. Nelly tells us that "his brightening mind brightened his features, and added spirit and nobility to their aspect" (p. 341). She also attributes the elevation of both to their lack of "disenchanted maturity" (p. 342). If they are enchanted, even prosaic Nelly considers it hopeful.

Before this enchantment, Cathy was doomed to slavery at the Heights and Hareton to a subhuman state. The source of that malign spell was Heathcliff, who had announced to Nelly two years earlier that Hareton would "never be able to emerge from his bathos of coarseness, and ignorance. I've got him faster than his scoundrel of a father secured me, and lower; for he takes a pride in his brutishness. I've taught him to scorn everything extra-animal as silly and weak" (pp. 231–32). This quotation heightens the contrast with Hareton's enlightenment at the end, but the mention of Heathcliff should remind us that the happy ending we have traced is only a small portion of a story filled with hate and violence. Before we enter seriously into an analysis of *Wuthering Heights*, we shall therefore have to discuss the basis of its complexity and see how it transcends simple romance.

We must, in fact, begin with the admission that it is a realistic novel. It is filled with detail, not the mechanical lists of *Robinson Crusoe* or the nonsensuous "things" that Dorothy Van Ghent complains of in *Moll Flanders*. Rather it has the concreteness, the objectivity, and impersonality of a case history, what Ian Watt calls the "circumstantial view of life." The case for putting *Wuthering Heights* in this tradition has been so eloquently made by Arnold Kettle that I must refer the reader to his penetrating analysis: "The story of *Wuthering Heights* is concerned not with love in the abstract but with the passions of living people, with property-ownership, the attraction of social comforts, the arrangement of marriages, the importance of education, the validity of religion, the relations of rich and poor."[7] On the other hand, Kettle insists, "the power and wonder of Emily Brontë's novel does not lie in naturalistic description, nor in a detailed analysis of the hour-by-hour issues of social living" (p. 140). As he goes on to show, the novel does probe social issues, but with the radical penetration and intensity of Blake (pp. 146–47). In other words, there is in *Wuthering Heights* a kind of testing and questioning of human relations that goes behind our waking adherence to the temporal standards of conduct we like to think we share. This radical questioning is based on an irrational, imaginative view of reality. As Kettle puts it, "Emily Brontë works not in ideas but in symbols, that is to say concepts which have a significance and validity on a different level from that of logical thought" (p. 140). It could, of course, be argued that symbolic writing is not natural fiction, because prose normally does not insist on the slow reading, the focusing on and savouring of detail that lyric poetry does. But, if we let ourselves accept Kettle's point, we shall discover how romance could be assimilated to the novel.

Several modern literary critics believe that the Romantics got tangled in the philosophic problems they often used as a theme in their work.[8] According to this view, neither Wordsworth, nor Coleridge, nor Keats, nor Shelley, nor Byron was able to resolve the conflict between objectivity and subjectivity, between inner and outer, between self and nature, between feeling and perception. The reader need not accept the absolute validity of this characterization to appreciate the possibilities offered to some Victorian novelists by the problem. As Victorians they were greatly concerned with the environment, both social and natural; as artists they were influenced by the Romantic preoccupation with the inner self. In several cases, they believed they had a duty to reconcile the two; in the novel they discovered the vehicle for a convincing solution of the problem; and in the symbol they found a microcosm of the means of bridging the gap.

7. Arnold Kettle, *An Introduction to the English Novel* (London: Hutchinson University Library, 1951), I, 139.
8. Cf. Edward Bostetter, *The Romantic Ventriloquists* (Seattle: University of Washington Press, 1963) and Masao Miyoshi, *The Divided Self* (New York: New York University Press, 1969).

The point about a symbol, of course, is that it is at once an image, appealing mimetically to the senses, and a conveyor of meaning, appealing figuratively to our emotions, our imagination. If introduced unobtrusively or "naturally," symbols provide details to give the realistic texture Ian Watt demands. They also function as part of the "referential language" which he suggests as a characteristic of formal realism. But this function does not stop the symbol from referring to more than a designated object, nor does it keep the symbol from being part of a system of figurative language by which a novelist may express the heights and depths of the spirit. Although we shall find in the next chapter that *Wuthering Heights* is very much a novel dealing with archetypal adventures of the spirit, we shall also discover that Emily Brontë was aware of the binding qualities of the social and physical environment and of a determining basis for human morality in psychic patterns of action and reaction, of dominance and submission.

Chapter Five

Wuthering Heights

It would be an error to claim that the fairy-tale patterns are the only figurative patterns in *Wuthering Heights*. But they are very important because of the levels of meaning they open up, and they do provide an obvious area for further investigation of the relation between romance and the novel. The brevity of most fairy tales and the lack of complexity in their structure, description, and characterization make the task of recognizing and interpreting their symbols if not easy at least simpler and more straightforward than it is with a novel like *Wuthering Heights* where the symbols appear as part of the realistic fabric. I shall therefore enter into a more detailed consideration of the novel with a passage that has two immediate virtues: it reads like the beginning of a fairy tale; it names several things that clearly carry some symbolic weight.

Nelly Dean starts her story for Lockwood not only in the style of a fairy tale but with the incident that begins the Beauty-and-Beast type of tale—the father about to go on a trip. Like that father, Mr Earnshaw promises each of the three children a present on his return. He addresses first Hindley, his oldest:

> "Now, my bonny man, I'm going to Liverpool today . . . What shall I bring you? You may choose what you like; only let it be little, for I shall walk there and back; sixty miles each way, that is a long spell!"
>
> Hindley named a fiddle, and then he asked Miss Cathy; she was hardly six years old, but she could ride any horse in the stable, and she chose a whip.
>
> He did not forget me [says Nelly]; for he had a kind heart, though he was rather severe, sometimes. He promised to bring me a pocket-

ful of apples and pears, and then he kissed his children good-bye, and set off.

It seemed a long while to us all—the three days of his absence—and often did little Cathy ask when he would be home. . . . Just about eleven o'clock, the door-latch was raised quietly and in stept the master. He threw himself into a chair, laughing and groaning, and bid them all stand off, for he was nearly killed—he would not have such another walk for the three kingdoms.

"And at the end of it, to be flighted to death!" he said, opening his great coat, which he held bundled up in his arms. "See here, wife! I was never so beaten with anything in my life; but you must e'en take it as a gift of God, though it's as dark almost as if it came from the devil" (pp 36–37, second ellipsis mine).

Again like the father in "Beauty and the Beast," Mr Earnshaw brings home trouble instead of presents for his children. Unlike that father, however, the trouble he brings is the beast itself; all three children are confronted with the creature responsible for their not receiving presents. Although Mr Earnshaw offered to bring whatever they wanted that he could carry, what he actually carries home is a gift that none of them would have chosen, not even the father. Heathcliff's initial appearance is symbolic: the pronoun *it* applied to him indicates an alien, subhuman nature, an object of fate. Since he is "as dark almost" as if he comes "from the devil" we can adopt Dorothy Van Ghent's view of him as a "daemonic archetype." But we must qualify this view with that of Kettle, who connects Heathcliff's energy with "moral emotion" (p. 147).[1] We shall delve further into his symbolic name and nature presently, but for now we must at least see this gift from the father as a means for a testing by fortune of Hindley and Catherine.

This brings us to the three simpler symbols in the passage above, the objects the children originally asked for. Hindley had wanted a fiddle, Catherine a whip. Similarly, he cries upon seeing the fiddle, smashed, she threatens upon hearing the whip was lost while her father tended "the stranger." Although we might expect the desires and re-actions of the two to be reversed, we should remember that, when

1. Dorothy Van Ghent, *The English Novel: Form and Function* (New York: Rinehart & Co., 1953), p. 164. She argues that, unlike the other examples of this archetype with which she deals, Heathcliff cannot be connected with "ethical thought." Kettle's best analysis is of the Blakean morality of Heathcliff's statement, "The more the worms writhe, the more I yearn to crush out their entrails! It is a moral teething" (pp. 161–62).

Symbolism + Irony

children speak from their heart's desire, they often ask for what they really want, which may very well be the opposite of what they are conventionally supposed to want. Taking the gifts symbolically, we may say that Hindley wants to develop the finer, more cultural, less active side of his nature. His gift is crushed. Catherine wants to develop the rougher, more physical and active side of hers, and indeed has already begun to do so. She is consequently soon able to accept Heathcliff. Hindley, on the other hand, sees his hopes for refinement being thwarted by his father's subsequent favouring treatment of this alien. Ironically, in rejecting what Heathcliff stands for, he rejects self-knowledge. His dark side emerges negatively, in destructiveness, including self-destruction.

Nelly Dean, who is Hindley's age (p. 196) and calls herself "his foster sister" (p. 68), had not asked for anything but was promised "a pocketful of apples and pears." She is presumably also disappointed, but, whereas we never after see Hindley with a fiddle or Catherine with a whip, we do see Nelly with fruit and can judge from later scenes its symbolic overtones. Her use of it in a scene where she is trying to entice Hareton shows the meaning clearly. He swears at her, not recognizing his old nurse after a separation of ten months. "This grieved, more than angered me," reports Nelly. "Fit to cry, I took an orange from my pocket, and offered it to propitiate him" (p. 115). This act shows the same kind of encouragement of deprived humanity which she had earlier demonstrated with Heathcliff. The first time the Linton children come to visit the Heights, Nelly tries to make Heathcliff presentable enough to take part in the Christmas dinner. Unfortunately Hindley intervenes, ordering Heathcliff "into the garret till dinner is over. He'll be cramming his fingers in the tarts, and stealing the fruit, if left alone with them a minute" (p. 60). Like other self-fulfilling prophecies, this one comes true when Heathcliff dashes "a tureen full of hot apple sauce" against Edgar Linton. But this aggressive use of fruit should not obscure the nourishing use intended by Nelly.

Her life-giving warmth is quite apparent in the description she gives of the kitchen the night before these events.

> Putting my cakes in the oven, and making the house and kitchen cheerful with great fires befitting Christmas eve, I prepared to sit down and amuse myself by singing carols. . . . I smelt the rich scent of the heating spices; and admired the shining kitchen utensils, the polished clock, decked in holly, the silver mugs ranged on a tray

ready to be filled with mulled ale for supper; and, above all, the speckless purity of my particular care—the scoured and well-swept floor.

I gave due inward applause to every object, and, then, I remembered how old Earnshaw used to come in . . . from that I went on to think of his fondness for Heathcliff, and his dread lest he should suffer neglect after death had removed him; . . . It struck me soon, however, there would be more sense in endeavouring to repair some of his wrongs than shedding tears over them—I got up and walked into the court to seek [Heathcliff] (pp. 56–57).

The emotional gamut here is from applause for the physical, to memory of affection, to sadness, to determination.

This thought sequence would not be worth remarking if it did not lead to the interesting advice that Nelly gives Heathcliff when she finds him.

You're fit for a prince in disguise. Who knows, but your father was Emperor of China, and your mother an Indian queen, each of them able to buy up, with one week's income, Wuthering Heights and Thrushcross Grange together? And you were kidnapped by wicked sailors, and brought to England. Were I in your place, I would frame high notions of my birth (p. 59).

Because of his dark skin, Heathcliff is connected with the devil by his foster father, is called a gipsy by the Lintons, and is here offered a third possibility, a royal eastern parentage by Nelly Dean. As Dorothy Van Ghent phrases this possibility: "If Heathcliff is really of daemonic origin, he is, in a sense, indeed of 'high birth,' a 'prince in disguise,' and might be expected, like the princes of fairy tale, to drop his 'disguise' at the crisis of the tale and be revealed in original splendor" (p. 168). Unlike Hareton, however, who later does shine forth, Heathcliff remains untransformed because rejected by Catherine. He does disappear at one point, to return after Catherine's marriage to a different person, but he is changed by loneliness and hate rather than transformed by love. On the other hand, we have Nelly's reaction to his return: "I was amazed more than ever, to behold the *transformation* of Heathcliff." His face "looked intelligent, and retained no marks of former degradation. A half-civilized ferocity lurked yet in the depressed brows, and eyes full of black fire, but it was subdued" (pp. 100–101, my italics). Although subdued, this "black fire" is characteristic of the violent

Imagery Symbolism

Heathcliff we come to know. In our fairy-tale sense he is untransformed and never turns into a bright prince of light or gold.[2]

An extension of the symbolism of darkness associated with Heathcliff is indicated by Catherine's earlier characterization of him as "bleak, hilly, coal country" (p. 73). This image suggests not only his exterior appearance but his interior being, compressed to rich dark fuel. Similar associations attach to his name. The *heath* is bleak, while *cliff* connects with Catherine's description of her love for Heathcliff, which "resembles the eternal rocks beneath—a source of little visible delight, but necessary" (p. 86). Cliff and rocks together connect with Peniston Crag, the landmark whose cave is associated with fairy power (p. 210).

Like the magician in "The Glass Coffin," Heathcliff because he is rebuffed has chosen to strive for revenge, to bring down pride. Just as the magician transformed the brother of the woman he loved into a stag, Heathcliff played a key role in the dehumanization of both Hindley and Hareton. Just as the magician became a vicious black bull after casting his spells, Heathcliff becomes a vicious person until he is finally opposed. One important difference between the novel and any of the fairy-tale analogues we have noted is, of course, the complexity of *Wuthering Heights*. Heathcliff perverts Hareton's nature, yet wins Hareton's love. Heathcliff stops his revenge because he sees the spirit of Catherine in the face of Cathy (pp. 340, 342) and of Hareton (p. 343). He wins not mere death but presumably union with the spirit of Catherine.

Irony — Heathcliff

In his single-minded effort to create revenge, Heathcliff works with the negative force of destruction. In doing so he acts counter to Nelly Dean. Through most of the novel she is a frustrated mother, as we have seen in her unsuccessful attempts to help Heathcliff and Hareton. But by the end she is fulfilled in the coming marriage of Hareton and Cathy, whom she calls "in a measure, my children" (p. 341), having nursed them when their mothers died soon after each was born.

In the fairy-tale pattern, Nelly takes the role of helpful provider, the good fairy who offers the young man a token and advice for achieving his destiny, or for finding his true identity. If she is motherly in addition this only confirms the findings of psychoanalysis that the good fairy represents one side of the mother, just as the bad fairy represents another. Sometimes, indeed, the fairy who appears good at first (offer-

Nelly — good fairy

2. Edgar says of Heathcliff just before this description, "He never struck me as such a marvellous treasure."

ing sweets to eat, as in "Hänsel and Gretel") may turn out to be a witch who really means harm. It has, in fact, been argued that Nelly is the villain of the novel.[3] Certainly it is true that Catherine at one point views Nelly as a potential witch. "'I see in you, Nelly,' she continued, dreamily, 'an aged woman—you have grey hair, and bent shoulders. This bed is the fairy cave under Peniston Crag, and you are gathering elf-bolts to hurt our heifers; pretending, while I am near, that they are only locks of wool. That's what you'll come to fifty years hence: I know you are not so now'" (p. 130).[4] Then finding that Nelly has not told her husband what she wished. Catherine bursts out, "Nelly is my hidden enemy—you witch! So you do seek elf-bolts to hurt us!" (p. 136). As Heathcliff points out to Catherine in their last interview, however, she is her own "hidden enemy." Nelly does meddle, has human failings, but she always acts from good motives, by her standard. That standard is based on a natural sympathy with the comfortable, orderly world of Thrushcross Grange. She is at home in its cultivated comfort and its orchard of fruit trees. But she has known Catherine and Heathcliff as children at the Heights, and she is willing to compromise and allow room for their values. In their generation, however, the world of the Heights cannot be reconciled with that of the Grange. Nelly is successful only with the next generation, Hareton and Cathy.

Having cleared Nelly of being a witch, we seem to be well on our way to demonstrating that the characteristic atmosphere of *Wuthering Heights* is sweetness and light. Any reader's experience is quite different, of course: we all know that *wuthering* really is descriptive of "atmospheric tumult" (in Lockwood's decorous phrase). We also know that the first half of the novel is the best place to look for the violence which we have already admitted to be in the novel. In turning our attention there, I propose, however, to begin with another fairy-tale scene, also apparently filled with sweetness and light. Here is Heathcliff's description of the living room at Thrushcross Grange as seen by him and Catherine. "It was beautiful—a splendid place carpeted with crimson, and crimson-covered chairs and tables, and a pure white ceiling bordered by gold, a shower of glass-drops hanging in silver chains from the centre, and shimmering with little soft tapers" (p. 49). This is the palace where lives the prince whom Catherine will marry. Taken inside,

---

3. James Hafley, "The Villain in *Wuthering Heights*," *Nineteenth-Century Fiction,* 13, (December 1958).
4. "Elf-bolts, the ancient British flint arrow-points." Mrs. Gutch, *North Riding of Yorkshire . . . County Folklore* (London: D. Nutt, 1901), p. 181.

she finds there a fulfilment of her wish to be queen. "Then the woman servant brought a basin of warm water, and washed her feet; and Mr. Linton mixed a tumbler of negus, and Isabella emptied a plateful of cakes into her lap, and Edgar stood gaping at a distance. Afterwards, they dried and combed her beautiful hair, and gave her a pair of enormous slippers, and wheeled her to the fire" (p. 52). All we need is the marriage itself and we shall know that Catherine and Edgar will live happily ever after. The marriage takes place, and a certain kind of happiness does follow; but it is not the kind forecast by the two scenes above, nor does it last very long. Why not?

The problem is that Catherine cannot decide which kind of fairy tale she is participating in. Or, to put it from her point of view, she cannot decide which kind of identity to choose, the easy one of material comfort, or the difficult one of sympathy with an outcast. The second corresponds to "Beauty and the Beast" or perhaps to "The Frog Prince." There the father makes the princess go through with her bargain, after which the frog, like the Beast, is transformed into a handsome prince. But Catherine has lost her father by the time marriage becomes a possibility. Her brother, as the new authority, separates her from Heathcliff and pushes her toward Edgar Linton. But, if she cannot function as the princess who helps the beast to become human, why should she not choose another role, and become the poor little girl who is taken into the king's palace and herself transformed into a queen? She could make this shift, on one condition: that she had never committed herself to the first role, never made a promise to the beast (or frog). But she has committed herself, has already so bound up her identity with Heathcliff's that she can choose a destiny demanding another identity only at the cost of splitting her nature.

That split is evident in her delirium following Heathcliff's return after her marriage to Edgar Linton. Nelly tries to restrain her from looking in the mirror, where Catherine sees a face which she does not recognize as her own. When Nelly finally convinces her, Catherine makes a strange comment.

"There's nobody here!" I insisted. "It was *yourself*, Mrs. Linton; you knew it a while since."

"Myself!" she gasped, "and the clock is striking twelve! It's true, then, that's dreadful!" (p. 131).

As Nelly confirms further on (p. 132), the clock really has struck twelve midnight. In her delirium, however, Catherine puts a different

kind of weight on the fact than Nelly. We discover that she dreamed she
was back at Wuthering Heights, "the whole last seven years of my life
[grown] a blank" (132). The face in the mirror appears alien because
she expected to see her earlier self. What is true and dreadful is that she
is actually at the Grange. Heathcliff's reappearance has made her aware
of the split, of her mistake in marrying Edgar. The clock striking twelve
brings it home because midnight, the traditional time of change, indicates the end of the spell, the enchantment which made the girl who
belonged in the cinders appear as a princess. She cannot fool herself
any longer.

We have made Catherine sound perhaps too culpable in our analysis
(though we have not been as hard on her as Heathcliff is just before
her death). One detail from her dream may give us a clue to balancing
our judgement. "I was a child; my father was just buried, and my
misery arose from the separation that Hindley had ordered between
me and Heathcliff—I was laid alone, for the first time" (p. 132). This
makes clear that the original split occurred, not when Catherine de-
serted Heathcliff for the Lintons, but when she was separated from him
by authority. Her fairy-tale task is to work and suffer to heal the split,
as she is well aware. Her rationalization to Nelly for marrying Edgar
is that it will help Heathcliff. But this move is a mistake, as Nelly tries
to tell her; she is actually choosing physical comfort when only suffering
will resolve the problem.

But once again we are being too hard on Catherine. Circumstances
separated her from Heathcliff before she ever agreed to marry Edgar,
and they held her at the Grange before she ever agreed to enter and
allow herself to be charmed. I am thinking of a scene the very opposite
of Catherine on a sofa being waited on, of the incident which in fact
causes that scene to take place. Earlier outside, Heathcliff and Catherine
had started to run, and she had fallen. " 'Run, Heathcliff, run!' she
whispered. 'They have let the bull-dog loose, and he holds me!' "
(p. 50). Heathcliff continues,

> The devil had seized her ankle, Nelly; I heard his abominable snort-
> ing. . . . I got a stone and thrust it between his jaws, and tried with
> all my might to cram it down his throat. A beast of a servant came
> up with a lantern, at last, shouting—
> "Keep fast, Skulker, keep fast!" . . .
> The man took Cathy up; she was sick—not from fear, I'm certain,
> but from pain. . . .

"How her foot bleeds!" . . .
"She may be lamed for life!" (pp. 50–52).

She is not lamed for life physically, but she does not recover her psychic freedom until death liberates her spirit.

The connection between physical and psychical impressions and reactions was covertly present in an earlier scene between Lockwood and the Heights' dogs. When they attacked him, he defended himself with a poker and afterward answered Heathcliff's query whether he was bitten, "If I had been, I would have set my signet on the biter" (p. 6). But in fact they were about to set their sign on him. Wanting to leave, he picked up a lantern outside, at which Joseph sicked Gnasher and Wolf on him. Again he was not bitten, just knocked down, "but they would suffer no resurrection, and I was forced to lie till their malignant masters pleased to deliver me." Once on his feet, he trembled and threatened, and "the vehemence of my agitation brought on a copious bleeding at the nose" (p. 16). He finally stayed at the Heights to dream first of being attacked by men with staves in a chapel near a graveyard, and then of his own aggression, sawing a girl's wrist on a broken window while "the blood ran down and soaked the bedclothes" (p. 25). Lockwood had been initiated by the forces of power and violence, into the inner world of darkness.

Like Catherine after her indoctrination, he had to stay in bed at Thrushcross Grange for a few weeks, but, whereas he recuperated in a house that suited his social nature, she became acclimated to an unfamiliar environment. Also like hers his blood flowed after contact with ferocious dogs. In her case, however, there was a physical wound, and a psychic scar. Her contact with the beast led to the more genteel initiation inside the house, and the two together form the upper and lower half of the force that tests the strength of her spirit. That is, we can contrast the "lower" dog bite in the dark on Catherine's leg with the "upper" combing of her beautiful hair in the light.

Similarly, we have noted a fairy-tale pattern of reconciliation between the low beast and the high beauty. But Skulker is no transformable beast; he is a watchdog, the brute force by which those who own protect what they have from those who own not. But he is also the necessary prelude to a test. Fairy tales are full of palaces and castles guarded by beasts and monsters. To fail in dealing with them is to come under an alien power. The nature of the new identity "forced" on Catherine is revealed when she returns to the Heights. Nelly reports,

"I removed the habit, and there shone forth, beneath a grand plaid silk frock, white trousers and burnished shoes; and, while her eyes sparkled joyfully when the dogs came bounding up to welcome her, she dare hardly touch them lest they should fawn upon her splendid garments" (p. 54). Catherine is now too clean and bright to be touched by dirty dogs, too high to live intimately with such beasts as Heathcliff. "If the wicked man [her brother, Hindley] in there had not brought Heathcliff so low," she would not have considered marrying Edgar. But "it would degrade me to marry Heathcliff, now" (pp. 84–85). In fairy tales the pride of the person who is unwilling to stoop is invariably punished severely.

The polarized thinking responsible for Catherine's predicament is made a paramount psychological and moral theme in the novel. Even at the very beginning, it is tellingly embodied in Lockwood's responses, again in fairy-tale terms. Leaving aside such obvious blunders as his mistaking dead rabbits for live cats, we may look at the mistake he makes about the younger Catherine's position in the household. Finding his error in assuming her to be Heathcliff's wife, he again puts his foot in it by suggesting to Hareton that "you are the favoured possessor of the beneficent fairy" (p. 12). Not only is this superficial compliment, "favoured possessor," denied by "a brutal curse" from Hareton; its twin, "the beneficent fairy," is shown to be equally wrong as a characterization of Cathy. She quickly gets into an argument with Joseph in which she threatens to ask his "abduction as a special favour" (p. 13). She then takes "a long, dark book" from the shelf, mentions "the Black Art" and again threatens Joseph, "I'll have you modelled in wax and clay" (p. 14). Lockwood for once is able to interpret correctly: "The little witch put a mock malignity into her beautiful eyes, and Joseph, trembling with sincere horror, hurried out" (p. 14). She is only playing the witch, then, but she is playing it for real, as a means of holding her own with Joseph. It is this vitality that Lockwood instinctively shrinks from.

Lockwood's incapacity with a marriageable woman is, however, indicated even before his blunders with Cathy. He tells the reader a revealing anecdote about himself. "While enjoying a month of fine weather at the sea-coast, I was thrown into the company of a most fascinating creature, a real goddess in my eyes, as long as she took no notice of me. I 'never told my love' vocally; still, if looks have language, the merest idiot might have guessed I was over head and ears; she understood me, at last, and looked a return—the sweetest of all imaginable looks—and what did I do? I confess it with shame—shrunk icily into myself, like a snail" (p. 4).[5] Lockwood understands that "looks have language," and yet he immediately turns around and acts as though they do not. Left alone with the dogs, as mentioned before, and "imagining they would scarcely understand tacit insults, I unfortunately indulged in winking and making faces at the trio" until he "so irritated madam, that she suddenly broke into a fury, and leapt on my knees" (p. 5). In case any reader is in doubt as to the parallel between these two contiguous scenes, the name of "madam" is presently revealed as "Juno"—a real goddess who, we might say, pays Lockwood back for his earlier refusal of engagement with her sex. More to our purpose is the point that his insistence on consciously idealizing women seems to be balanced by an unconscious hostility to them. His calling a woman a goddess or a good fairy seems to call up the bitch and the witch to remind him that human nature has connections with the physicality of animals and the twisted spirituality of aggression. Essentially these themes are also present in his two dreams.[6]

Although Lockwood is too defensively bound up in himself to learn from his experiences, Cathy can modify her nature, as a brief comparison with her mother will indicate. Catherine, learning intransigence in the face of Hindley's unfair authority, was indoctrinated into a life of civility and ease during her enforced stay at the Grange. Her daughter, being spoiled by comfort and indulgence at the Grange, is indoctrinated into a life of hardship and neglect at the Heights. The mother could only retreat to the Heights in fantasy or to the grave in reality as an escape from the split embodied in husband and first love. The daughter is able to learn through suffering the patience and humility needed to love another and transform him. More than this, though, as we have seen, she transforms her dependent egoism into a rebellious self-reliance which is equally necessary to survival. The girl who was used to being called "angel" learns to depend on her potential as witch; the lady who has been treated as a queen is finally condemned by Joseph as a "quean" (that is a "jade, wench, slut") for encouraging Hareton to pull up Joseph's thorny bushes and plant flowers at the

5. Cathy later gives a smile "as sweet as honey" (p. 333) to Hareton; obviously, Lockwood could never have responded to such a stimulus.
6. For consideration of the dreams, see Dorothy Van Ghent. See also Edgar F. Shannon, Jr., "Lockwood's Dreams and the Exegesis of *Wuthering Heights*," *Nineteenth-Century Fiction*, 14 (September 1959).

Heights. As this act shows, she is trying to reconcile the creative with the destructive.

Hardly an unsophisticated fairy tale, *Wuthering Heights* incorporates its oppositions in the same subtle way a fairy tale does. We do not consciously register the fairy-witch, goddess-bitch, queen-quean pairs or their final reconciliation except in the sense of a generalized tempering of Cathy's nature by the end. But, as often in a fairy tale, a structure that feels powerful on reading turns out on examination to have such oppositions and resolutions within it.

Despite the presence of fairy-tale motifs in *Wuthering Heights*, it is not simply a fairy tale. Emily Brontë wrote a novel; the fairy tale is by our definition a form of romance. The transformation of the brother into a stag in "The Glass Coffin" is, for instance, an impossibility which the reader allows without thinking to employ realistic standards. Like other works of the romance type, the fairy tale demands an indulgence which frees it from the bonds of particularized verisimilitude. It may then give full rein to the tendency to make believe, though it may at the same time redeem its licence by treating seriously some problem of human nature. It may even call in question the reality of the everyday world it has left behind, usually by means of the make believe which inspired the original departure from the everyday (see *Through the Looking Glass*). Such questioning will consequently strike most readers as the game it often is.

Wuthering Heights works differently. It tries to keep in contact with the everyday, but insists at the same time in pushing beyond simple realism. Thus, for contemporaries of Emily Brontë, the oddity of the novel, as of Blake's poetry earlier, lay in its inability to be superficial or sentimental. She did not indulge in crude realism or spiritual perversity to shock the philistines as the late Victorians often did; rather she carried on the search started by the Romantic movement to discover the place of the individual in the universe.

Such a search obviously included due respect for the ravages of the flesh, just as it also accepted the possibility of the separate existence of the spirit.[7] Lockwood has an intimation of this possibility in his dream of the waif Catherine outside his window: Catherine and Heath-

7. For a comprehensive analysis of the relation of physical destructiveness to spiritual union in *Wuthering Heights,* see J. Hillis Miller, *The Disappearance of God* (Cambridge: Harvard University Press, 1963), Chapter 4. Miller also analyses the relation between the Catherine-Heathcliff and the Cathy-Hareton love stories.

cliff, before their respective deaths, also affirm it. And I think the reader of the novel is intended to register it as a latent permissible reality. Just before the end of *Wuthering Heights,* Nelly tells of meeting "a little boy with a sheep and two lambs." He is frightened and tells of having encountered the ghosts of Catherine and Heathcliff on the moor. Nelly's conclusion is interesting: "I saw nothing; but neither the sheep nor he would go on" (p. 357). Lockwood can see nothing either. Visiting the graves under a "benign sky," he wonders "how anyone could ever imagine unquiet slumbers, for the sleepers in that quiet earth" (p. 358). Since these words end the novel, they are often taken as expressing their author's final position. It seems to me evident that they are a last ironic revelation of Lockwood's character. First of all, he has forgotten his dream, with its accurate cry from Catherine, "I've been a waif for twenty years" (p. 25). Second, his logic has a flaw. Suppose the sky were not benign? Suppose it were "wuthering," what would one be able to imagine for those two passionate sleepers then? Like Nelly, Lockwood by choice belongs to the calm and regulated life of the Grange. But I believe the reader who has experienced the tumult of the novel is invited to imagine that spirits do roam, not visible to the rational eye, but as a sufficient testimony to the durability of psychic energy.

This notion may be romantic, but is it novelistic? Balanced as it is against the brute force of temporal circumstance, I believe it is, for this spiritual state is given a physical correlative in the elemental world of the moors, the place where young Catherine and Heathcliff were free from the tyranny of Hindley. The elements of wind and rain as non-human thus become a lyric part of the circumstances of the novel.[8] The final freedom of Heathcliff and Catherine there may stretch the form of the novel, but without breaking it.

8. On the elements, see again Dorothy Van Ghent. See also Elliott B. Gose, Jr., *"Wuthering Heights*: the Heath and the Hearth," *Nineteenth-Century Fiction,* 21 (June 1966).

Chapter Six

Bleak House

The separation of the world of *Wuthering Heights* from that of *Bleak House* seems far wider than the five years that elapsed before Dickens' novel appeared in 1852. While Emily Brontë was working out the problem of Romantic duality, man's relation to nature and to his own spirit, Dickens was involved in a version of the typical Victorian problem, how to maintain humanity among the rigid forms of tradition and of urban materialism. We might expect, then, that in moving from the moors to the streets of London we shall have to leave behind much of what we have learned about the imagination. The actual case is less clear cut.

Whereas the moor was "romantic" in the popular sense of being far enough removed from most readers' experience to make possible the suspending of disbelief about irrational happenings, Dickens faced a much more difficult task when he tried to construct an environment which purported to be drawn from the immediate experience of most readers. Dickens was aware of this problem and addressed himself to it in his prefaces and the magazines he edited. In a well-known passage from the preface to *Martin Chuzzlewit,* he commented, "I sometimes ask myself whether it is *always* the writer who colours highly, or whether it is now and then the reader whose eye for colour is a little dull." This is actually a rather mild complaint for someone who had taken on the task of bringing alive an urban environment by which many of his readers were either anesthetized or overwhelmed.

In his efforts to vivify the city, Dickens fell into a mode similar to that of other nineteenth-century novelists who dealt with the urban scene. As Donald Fanger suggests, these writers tended to develop a black and white vision, "a Manichean world view, in which human beings and human societies become a battleground." This view presents

each man's struggle, however obscure, in the light of the ultimate contest between good and evil; and it dramatizes this framework by incarnating the opposed principles through the introduction of purely good characters (most often women and children) and, more important, of characters clearly identified as diabolic surrogates. The former tend often to be sentimentalized portraits; they tend almost always to be victims, beatified by Christian passivity and resignation. The latter are active, aggressive, predatory; and they tend to appear suprahuman, surrounded with a demonic aura and seemingly possessed of at least quasi-demonic powers.[1]

Such a view is of course very close to the fairy tale, and it was to the fairy tale that Dickens himself actually turned for his vision. In a series of articles on Dickens' Christmas books and on the novel (*Dombey and Son*) which immediately followed them, Harry Stone has demonstrated convincingly how important the fairy tale was as a background form to Dickens' narrative imagination.[2] A slightly different but equally strong case can be made for *Bleak House*.

As Dickens said in his preface to it, "I have purposely dwelt upon the romantic side of familiar things." In this approach, he was influenced as much by social and humane considerations as by aesthetic ones, as is apparent in the foreword he wrote for the first issue of *Household Words* in 1850, the year before he began *Bleak House*. He wanted the magazine he was starting "to show all, that in the familiar things, even in those which are repellent on the surface, there is Romance enough, if we will but find it out—to teach the hardest workers at this whirling wheel of toil that their lot is not necessarily a moody, brutal fact excluded from the sympathies and graces of imagination." This attitude was again evident three years later in an article Dickens wrote for the magazine. "In an utilitarian age, of all other times, it is a matter of grave importance that Fairy tales should be respected. . . . Every one who has considered the subject knows full well that a nation with-

1. *Dostoevsky and Romantic Realism* (Cambridge: Harvard University Press, 1965), p. 18.

2. "Dickens' Artistry and *The Haunted Man*," *South Atlantic Quarterly*, 61 (1962); "Dark Corners of the Mind: Dickens' Childhood Reading," *Horn Book Magazine*, 39 (1963); "The Novel as Fairy Tale: Dickens' *Dombey and Son*," *English Studies*, 67 (1966).

out fancy, without some romance, never did, never can, never will, hold a great place under the sun" (Oct. 1, 1853).[3] The emphasis on romance which connects Dickens' view of his own novels with fairy tales, does not necessarily mean that he intended them to *be* modern fairy tales.

It is certainly true that Dickens was not the type of Romanticist who worshipped the past. The made-up titles of his false bookcase and the articles he wrote or solicited for *Household Words* make clear his scorn of earlier superstitions.[4] Yet precisely because he could distinguish between the figurative imagination of art and the literal horrors of history, he was able in *Household Words* both to praise fairy tales and to debunk goblins, witches, giants, and vampires. This debunking did not, however, prevent him from using these specific types figuratively in *Bleak House* and other novels. More important, one of Dickens' favourite devices of character linkage—in which one character serves as a "double, *alter ego*, or shadow"[5] of another—has a fairy tale origin. This device is of great psychological importance in *Bleak House*: not only does it add depth to the novel, it also has connections with Dickens' own experience and his conception of himself as an artist.

Dickens began the *Household Words* article already cited with a personal statement (slightly diluted by the editorial pronoun): "We may assume that we are not singular in entertaining a very great tenderness for the fairy literature of our childhood. What enchanted us then . . . has . . . enchanted vast hosts of men and women." That this was no conventional tribute can be verified by the frequency with which references to various fairy tales appear in his fiction, sometimes with the same emphasis on the good they do children. Thus David Copperfield claims that reading fairy tales and eighteenth-century novels "kept

3. Page 97. See the use made of this article by Shirley Grob, "Dickens and Some Motifs of the Fairy Tale," *Texas Studies in Literature and Language,* 5 (Winter 1964).

4. These mock titles are given in part by Edgar Johnston in his important biography, *Charles Dickens His Tragedy and Triumph* (New York: Simon and Schuster, 1952), pp. 749–50.

5. These terms are used by Julian Moynihan to characterize the relations between Pip and Orlick in "The Hero's Guilt: the Case of *Great Expectations*," *Essays in Criticism,* 10 (Jan 1960): 67. The notion of the alter ego character had earlier been developed by several other critics, including Dorothy Van Ghent and M. D. Zabel.

alive my fancy . . . and did me no harm" (Chapter 4).[6] Contrariwise, Dickens believed that lack of fairy tales could damage the development of humanity in a child. Introducing the Smallweed family in *Bleak House,* he put heavy emphasis on their unnaturalness. "The house of Smallweed, always early to go out and late to marry, has strengthened itself in its practical character, has discarded all amusement, discountenanced all story-books, fairy tales, fictions, and fables, and banished all levities whatsoever. Hence the gratifying fact, that it has no child born to it, and that the complete little men and women whom it has produced, have been observed to bear a likeness to old monkeys with something depressing on their minds."[7] Thus Judy Smallweed "never owned a doll, never heard of Cinderella" (p. 220).

Another deprived character in the novel does at least own a doll, and in telling of her childhood, Esther Summerson refers to herself as "like some of the princesses in the fairy stories, only I was not charming" (p. 11). She remembers crying herself to sleep with a doll, realizing "that I was to no one on earth what Dolly was to me" (p. 13). One obvious parallel between Esther and Cinderella is the way she is treated. The woman who takes care of her acts like a cruel stepmother while calling herself Esther's godmother; she fulfils this latter role in the narrow Christian sense that Dickens disliked, rather than in the benevolent fairy-tale sense of which he approved. She will not, for instance, allow Esther to celebrate her birthday because it is a reminder of her bastard condition: "Submission, self-denial, diligent work, are the preparations for a life begun with such a shadow on it. You are different from other children, Esther, because you were not born, like them, in common sinfulness and wrath. You are set apart" (p. 13). Like a fairy-tale heroine, also, Esther at first accepts her fate and then triumphs over it, transforms it into an exalted state of being "set apart" from common mankind by her goodness.

All Dickens' sympathetic characters suffer; some like Jo must die to find happiness, while others like Esther finally earn their heart's desire. Her greatest trial is to catch the smallpox, but loss of beauty

6. In addition to the formal influence on Dickens' fiction of the eighteenth-century novelists, other influences have been found in minor traditions such as the Newgate novel. See Earle Davis, *The Flint and the Flame* (1963); Jack Lindsay, *Charles Dickens: A Biographical and Critical Study* (1950); and Walter C. Phillips, *Dickens, Reade, and Collins: Sensation Novelists* (1919).

7. *Bleak House,* ed. with an Introduction by M. D. Zabel (Boston: Houghton Mifflin Co., 1956), p. 219. All ellipses in quotations indicate my omissions.

opens the door to the magic transformation of the fairy tale. Of the time she spends recuperating at Boythorn's, Esther says, "If a good fairy had built the house for me with a wave of her wand, and I had been a princess and her favoured godchild, I could not have been more considered in it" (p. 381). The transformation is quickly brought to a climax by Lady Dedlock's revealing herself to Esther as her mother. Afterward Esther remembers her old-testament upbringing and rises above it. "For, I saw very well that I could not have been intended to die, or I should never have lived . . . and that if the sins of the fathers were sometimes visited upon the children, the phrase did not mean what I had in the morning feared it meant. I knew I was as innocent of my birth as a queen of hers; and that before my Heavenly Father I should not be punished for birth, nor a queen rewarded for it" (p. 391). Later, during the gruelling ride in search of her mother, Bucket says to Esther, "My dear, . . . when a young lady is as mild as she's game, and as game as she's mild, that's all I ask, and more than I expect. She then becomes a Queen, and that's about what you are yourself" (p. 606).[8] Among other things, this statement indicates that Esther is worthy to marry her Prince Charming, Allan Woodcourt; the images in the two words that make up his name indicate his natural royalty. Although the family is poor, Woodcourt's mother insists on the family tree; she more than once throws her son's "royal lineage" in Esther's face (pp. 182, 313).

Besides the central role Esther plays in her own drama of personal identity,[9] she also has a part in another drama, connected with several fairy-tale motifs which Dickens uses to voice his concern with the state of English society. Ada Clare and Richard Carstone, important characters in this part of the story, are fairy-tale victims, as comes out in an early scene combining motifs from both "Hänsel and Gretel" and "The Children in the Wood."[10]

8. Dickens' unbending insistence on his dignity when he later had contact with Queen Victoria can be connected with this attitude, which is repeated in letters of the period: See Vol. II of the three volumes of collected letters in *The Nonesuch Dickens* (London, 1938), pp. 203 and 269. See also his essay, "Lying Awake."

9. This question is dealt with in an article on "The Identity of Esther Summerson," by James Broderick and John Grant in *Modern Philology*, 55 (May 1958).

10. "Hänsel and Gretel" is from Grimm, the other being an English folktale about a boy and a girl left to starve in the woods by a grasping uncle. See Percy's *Reliques*. One chapbook version has only one child: John Ashton, ed., *Chapbooks of the Eighteenth Century* (London: Chatto and Windus, 1882), p. 447.

"Well!" said Richard Carstone, "*that's* over! And where do we go next, Miss Summerson?"

"Don't you know?" I said.

"Not in the least," said he.

"And don't *you* know, my love?" I asked Ada.

"No!" said she. "Don't you?"

"Not at all!" said I.

We looked at one another, half laughing at our being like the children in the wood, when a curious little old woman in a squeezed bonnet, and carrying a reticule, came curtseying and smiling up to us, with an air of great ceremony.

"O!" said she. "The wards in Jarndyce! Ve-ry happy, I am sure, to have the honour! It is a good omen for youth, and hope, and beauty, when they find themselves in this place, and don't know what's to come of it" (p. 25).

The nature of this unfortunate woman is indicated by her name, Miss Flite. The fact that she is pathetically mad (her wits having flown) should not keep us from noting the other association of flight; she is plainly a witch, though without broomstick or a conscious malevolence. Her blessing on the three babes in the woods of Chancery is in reality a prefigurement of evil (they "don't know what's to come of?" being in Chancery, but we can guess). The attributes of youth, hope, and beauty she later bestows one to each of the wards (p. 43). Since Ada is the youngest, and Richard is hope, Esther must be beauty (though she would never let the reader know it). Ada will lose her youth through too early marriage and sorrow; Esther will lose her beauty when she catches smallpox; and Richard's hope will ruin him, giving an ironic reversal to the comparison he early makes of himself to Dick Whittington (p. 46). He returns to London, like his namesake, but he is drawn there by the false hope of great expectations, the pursuit of which brings him early death instead of fame and happiness.

Like the witch in "Hänsel and Gretel," or "Jorinda and Joringel" Miss Flite keeps wretches caged in her abode. Hers are birds whom she protects from the cat belonging to her landlord, Krook. Although she will not reveal their names, Krook does: "Hope, Joy, Youth, Peace, Rest, Life, Dust, Ashes, Waste, Want, Ruin, Despair, Madness, Death, Cunning, Folly, Words, Wigs, Rags, Sheepskin, Plunder, Precedent, Jargon, Gammon, and Spinach. That's the whole collection . . . all cooped up together, by my noble and learned brother [the Lord Chancellor]" (p. 152). After Richard marries Ada and becomes a frequenter of the Court of Chancery, Miss Flite tells Esther that she has added two birds called "the Wards in Jarndyce" (p. 620). Seeing that Miss Flite does not intend ill (even Krook says that it is the Lord Chancellor who keeps the birds caged), we realize that she is an unknowing witch. The explanation of this paradoxical circumstance is that she is herself under a spell. She hopes for "*the* judgment that will dissolve the spell upon me of the Mace and Seal" (p. 379). Those two "cold and glittering devils" on the table in Chancery constitute part of the "dreadful attraction in the place." They "draw people on. . . . Draw peace out of them. Sense out of them. Good looks out of them. Good qualities out of them. I have felt them even drawing my rest away in the night" (p. 378). The hidden image implicit in Miss Flite's description comes out as she recounts how she originally came under the spell she is in. "Then I was ill, and in misery; and heard, as I had often heard before, that this was all the work of Chancery. When I got better, I went to look at the Monster. And then I found out how it was, and I was drawn to stay there" (p. 378).

Inevitably we are led to Chancery as the villain of the novel. And the monster image used to characterize it had already been introduced in the first paragraph of Dickens' brilliant opening chapter, where we were told that, considering the weather, "it would not be wonderful to meet a Megalosaurus, forty feet long or so, waddling like an elephantine lizard up Holborn Hill." That such a creature is in fact abroad, we can infer first from the description of Temple Bar as a "leaden-headed old obstruction" and then from a reference to "the groping and floundering condition which this High Court of Chancery, most pestilent of hoary sinners, holds, this day, in the sight of heaven and earth" (p. 1). The pestilence of Chancery has its literal form in the disease which began spreading from Tom-all-Alone's after the tenement was allowed to decay because its master became entangled in the case of Jarndyce and Jarndyce.

In a real fairy tale, the monster is slain by the resourceful prince, but Dickens stopped short of such revolution against even a corrupt order and contented himself with the somewhat mystic pronouncement on Krook's death: it is "the death of all Lord Chancellors in all Courts, and of all authorities in all places under all names soever, where false pretences are made, and where injustice is done. . . . it is the same death eternally—inborn, inbred, engendered in the corrupted humours of the vicious body itself" (p. 346). In generalizing against "all authorities" who perpetuate injustice, Dickens was probably including Parliament,[11] and was certainly thinking of the aristocracy, which he satirized directly in his portrait of the Dedlocks. An imagistic connection of Chancery and the aristocracy is initiated on the first visit of the wards to the court. While they wait, "the fire, which had left off roaring, winked its red eyes at us—as Richard said—like a drowsy old Chancery lion" (p. 23). Not until the image is applied to Chesney Wold much later does Dickens' implication become clear: "old stone lions and grotesque monsters bristled outside dens of shadow, and snarled at the evening gloom over the escutcheons they held in their grip" (p. 390). Like the prehistoric monsters of the first chapter, these savage beasts belong to an earlier age. But, somehow, like anachronisms in nature, outmoded laws and titles get passed on from one generation to the next.

In other words, Dickens took seriously the implicit theme of many fairy tales, that older authority needs to make room for the vitality of youth, though if it has become rigid it may not allow youth to grow, if grasping it may try to appropriate young life to itself. Dickens' literal application of this notion comes out clearly as Miss Flite reacts to Esther's explaining why Woodcourt will not receive official recognition for lifesaving heroism. "How can you say that? Surely you know, my dear, that all the greatest ornaments of England in knowledge, imagination, active humanity, and improvement of every sort, are added to its nobility! Look round you, my dear, and consider. *You* must be rambling a little now, I think, if you don't know that this is the great reason why titles will always last in the land!" (p. 380). Dickens' irony needs no comment.

Having seen Dickens' use of the simple fairy-tale motif and his connection of it with his social theme, we must now turn to the more complicated psychological concept of the *alter ego* character. In 1843 Dickens had drawn an allegorical picture of "Ignorance" and "Want" in Stave Three of *A Christmas Carol*. "They were a boy and girl.

11. In 1826 the method of keeping parliamentary accounts on notched sticks was abandoned; when the sticks were finally burned in the House of Lords in 1834, a fire started which consumed both Houses of Parliament. Two years after publishing *Bleak House*, Dickens used the incident as an example of how "all obstinate adherence to rubbish which the time has long outmoded is certain to have at the soul of it more or less what is pernicious and destructive, and will one day set fire to something or other" (Johnson, p. 97). Dickens wished that all the injustice and misery caused by Chancery "could only be locked up with it, and the whole burnt away in a great funeral pyre" (p. 5).

Yellow, meagre, ragged, scowling, wolfish; but prostrate, too, in their humility. . . . Where angels might have sat enthroned, devils lurked, and glared out menacing. No change, no degradation, no perversion of humanity in any grade, through all the mysteries of wonderful creation, has monsters half so horrible and dread."[12] The Spirit warns Scrooge, "beware this boy, for on his brow I see that written which is Doom, unless the writing be erased." This statement should sound familiar, since we all know that Tiny Tim also has a doom awaiting him. As the same Spirit tells Scrooge earlier, "if these shadows remain unaltered by the Future, the child [Tim] will die." It seems clear to me that Tiny Tim, the angelic good boy, has the devilish wolf boy as an *alter ego*. The Spirit tries to arouse Scrooge to action through pity for Tim and then fear of his counterpart.

Although the two boys are not overtly connected, Dickens provided a hint for the pattern that would connect them. In Stave Two, the Spirit of Christmas Past shows Scrooge himself as a small boy, reading alone at school. Outside the window appear characters from the story the boy is reading. Scrooge becomes excited at recapturing this childhood experience; it is through his description that the reader sees it. Knowing Dickens' theory of the humanizing effect of such stories, we can see the scene as a psychologically justified preparation for Scrooge's conversion at the end of the story. One of the tales referred to contains characters, Valentine "and his wild brother, Orson," who can be paralleled to Tim and his wolfish *alter ego*. Dickens read about these two brothers in his youth, presumably in a chapbook, where many fairy tales were published; the story has a courtly milieu with clear indications of a folk background.[13] Valentine, a Knight, goes off to fight a Wild Man in the woods. When both are wounded, Valentine takes the bear-man, Orson, back to court, after which they have various adventures together. In the first of these, Orson in Valentine's armour defeats another knight. Later

12. Compare this description with the advice Nelly gives Heathcliff in *Wuthering Heights*: "Do you mark . . . that couple of black fiends, so deeply buried who never open their windows boldly, but lurk glinting like devil's spies? Wish and learn . . . to raise your lids frankly, and change the fiends to confident innocent angels. . . . Don't get the expression of a vicious cur" (p. 59). See also Dickens' *Haunted Man* (1848).

13. The story was also recorded in Percy's *Reliques* in a simplified and polished version, "Valentine and Ursine." Dickens could also have come to know this story through a pantomime version. Grimaldi, whose biography Dickens later edited, had acted the part of Orson during the years of Dickens' youth. See A. E. Wilson, *Christmas Pantomime* (London: G. Allen & Unwin, 1934), p. 69.

Orson gets the gift of speech and is revealed as Valentine's brother who had been taken off by a bear after both were born in a forest. Orson and Valentine each marry and cap their adventures by ruling in turn over a large empire in the Middle East.

This story brings together, as Dickens did in his fiction, high and low, noble and base, man and beast. Such couplings are the stuff of the fairy tale, as we have seen. It is also a frequent conjunction in Dickens' mind, one that he characteristically expressed in a fairy-tale form.[14] In his letters, for instance, he could allude playfully to a story we have considered: "Am I a Beast whom Begging-Letter Writers have made out of a Beautiful Prince?" Or, more pointedly, "The nation is a miserable Sindbad and its boasted press, the loathsome old man upon his back" (*Letters,* II, 334; I, 557).

But they also show that his personality, being the expressive sort, made him aware of and very sensitive to social and psychological repression. As he told Forster in 1857, "You are not so tolerant as perhaps you might be of the wayward and unsettled feeling which is part (I suppose) of the tenure on which one holds an imaginative life, and which I have, as you ought to know well, often only kept down by riding over it like a dragoon." (*Letters,* II, 877). He was not only more responsive but more aware than most people of what goes on in the depths of the psyche. Praising Bulwer-Lytton's fanciful *Strange Story,* Dickens assured his friend that it would have some appeal even to "readers who have never given their minds . . . to those strange psychological mysteries in ourselves, of which we are all more or less conscious." He continued, "If you were the Magician's servant instead of the Magician, these potent spirits would get the better of you; but you *are* the Magician, and they don't, and you make them serve your purpose" (*Letters,* III, 218). If this analysis sounds extravagant, let us also admit that it gives a good sense of inner mysteries and powers hardly plumbed and rarely tapped in any systematic way by most men, forces which can overpower the user who is not an adept. The relevance of magic in such an experience is indicated by Dickens' own inability

14. As Harry Stone puts it, "For Dickens, then, the Doppelganger technique, although he invariably interfused it with realistic and autobiographical materials, is part of a fairy-tale Gestalt." "Fire, Hand, and Gate: Dickens' *Great Expectations,*" *Kenyon Review,* 24 (Autumn 1962): 667. For a brief but effective placing of the Doppelganger in romantic literature, see Ralph Tymms, *Doubles in Literary Psychology* (Cambridge, England: Cambridge University Press, 1949).

to write unless he had on his desk the bronze desk ornaments which were his fetishes (Johnson, p. 593).[15]

As we continue our investigation of the *alter ego* character, we shall discover that Lady Dedlock also possesses an object filled with magical potency for her and for Dickens. Of the numerous *alter ego* characters in the life of Lady Dedlock, the most emphasized is the lowest, Jenny, a brick-maker's wife. At first neither woman knows love except through a child each loses. Dickens establishes the connection between Jenny and Lady Dedlock by more than mere parallels, however. Discovering that Jenny has one of Esther's handkerchiefs, Lady Dedlock obtains it from her and keeps it as a kind of talisman. In the recognition scene between mother and daughter, Esther says, "I cannot tell in any words what the state of my mind was, when I saw in her hand my handkerchief" (p. 386). This handkerchief later becomes an important clue for Inspector Bucket, who finds it in Lady Dedlock's room after she flees. At the end of the chapter in which the search for her begins, the objective narrator asks "Where is she? Living or dead, where is she? If, as he folds the handkerchief and carefully puts it up, it were able, with an enchanted power, to bring before him the place where she found it, and the night landscape near the cottage where it covered the little child, would he descry her there?" (p. 581). The answer is *yes*, for, as if by enchantment and certainly for no logical reason, Lady Dedlock has gone to St Albans where she finds Jenny. She and Jenny trade clothes; Jenny as Lady Dedlock continues the journey and disappears; Lady Dedlock as Jenny goes back to London and dies of the cold outside the yard where Esther's father is buried. The change of identity is so complete that it allows Esther, approaching the corpse, to describe it as Jenny in terms which are equally applicable to Lady Dedlock (p. 615).[16]

15. Taylor Stoehr speaks of the importance of magic to bind or control the compelling figures and scenes thrown up by Dickens' imagination. See *Dickens: the Dreamer's Stance* (Ithaca: Cornell University Press, 1965), pp. 85–88 and 284.

16. Disguises are important in indicating other *alter ego* characters in Lady Dedlock's life. She had earlier dressed as a servant to enquire about her dead husband (p. 170). Then her maid Hortense appears in her mistress's clothes before Jo, who takes her for Lady Dedlock (p. 240). Later, when Jo is sick, he mistakes a veiled Esther for her mother (pp. 327, 329). Finally on the night of Tulkinghorn's murder, George Rouncewell sees a figure that looks like Esther in the lawyer's house. Whether it is Hortense or Lady Dedlock is left open even in Inspector Bucket's reconstruction (p. 561). For a discussion of the relation of Hortense and her mistress see Stoehr, pp. 165–67.

We may see Dickens then as a kind of secular magician, one who insists that true white magic is human love and that black magic comes either from hate or denial of emotions. Admitting the emotions means removing the lid of unfeeling sophistication which can keep real human nature repressed. Looking beneath that lid, Dickens sometimes hinted at the finding of the hidden gold of the fairy tale, but he was best at examining the pathology caused by repression. His imagination excelled in the creation of wolfish boys, bear-like men, and dark magicians.

Much of Dickens' insight into pathology comes out in his use of imagery. The reaction of his characters to light and dark will often let us know how to judge them. When, late in *Bleak House,* we are told that Richard asks for the lamp to be "removed into the next room, as he complained of its hurting his eyes" (p. 623), we know that he has been lured as irretrievably into the dragon's den as Miss Flite was. But even incorruptible characters must be tested by contact with the dark, as Ada was in marrying Richard, and Esther was in her childhood, her sickness, and the final search for her mother. Even Jarndyce, who has successfully kept clear of the den of Chancery, gets involved with darkness, though he tries to insulate himself through the use of intermediaries.

High and disinterested though he appears, Jarndyce is as much a character with a fairy-tale part to play as any of the three young people he tries to help. He first appears in the story as an anonymous and suggestive figure. He has determined to be Esther's fairy godfather, providing her with a carriage ride to a new life. Sitting across from her as a stranger and the only other passenger, he inquires why she is crying. On finding that it is partly because of the housekeeper's not being sorry to part with her, he says, "Con-found Mrs. Rachael! . . . Let her fly away in a high wind on a broomstick!" Then he attempts to comfort Esther in a very odd and significant way. He offers her "a piece of the best plum-cake that can be got for money—sugar on the outside an inch thick, like fat on mutton chops. Here's a little pie (a gem this is, both for size and quality), made in France. And what do you suppose it's made of? Livers of fat geese. There's a pie! Now let's see you eat 'em." But Esther declines politely, saying they are "too rich" for her (p. 18). Jarndyce is trying to bring Esther out of the shadow of her early life into the light by changing her environment, but in this scene he discovers that the change cannot be effected so simply. Esther instinctively realizes that royal food is not for the likes of such as she;

that is, she can never consent to act like a literal queen or member of the aristocracy.

Other details connected with this first appearance of Jarndyce suggest a fairy-tale character more strongly. Esther describes him and his actions:

> He came quite opposite to me from the other corner of the coach, brushed one of his large furry cuffs across my eyes(but without hurting me), and showed me that it was wet. . . . He was wrapped up to the chin, and his face was almost hidden in a fur cap, with broad fur straps at the side of his head, fastened under his chin; but I was composed again, and not afraid of him. . . . After a little while, he opened his outer wrapper, which appeared to me large enough to wrap up the whole coach, and put his arm down into a deep pocket in the side. . . . I must say, I was relieved by his departure. We left him at a milestone. I often walked past it afterwards, and never for a long time, without thinking of him and half expecting to meet him (p. 18).

As these quotations indicate, Dickens was at some pains to give magical overtones to the interview, and to emphasize the forbidding appearance and startling actions of the benign Jarndyce.

When we connect "his large furry cuffs" and "broad fur straps at the side of his head" with the "growlery" which is so important a part of Jarndyce's house, we may begin to feel both enlightened and confused. Since he is so good, why is Jarndyce characterized as a beast of whom Esther is at first somewhat afraid? The answer is that these characteristics, combined with his fatherly helpfulness, put Jarndyce in that special category of fairy-tale characters, the magician or "wise old man." This character according to Jung "represents knowledge, reflection, insight, wisdom . . . on the one hand, and on the other, moral qualities such as good will and readiness to help, which make his spiritual character sufficiently plain."[17] More particularly, Jung noted that "in certain primitive fairy tales" his "illuminating quality . . . is expressed by the fact that the old man is identified with the sun" (p. 80). Jarndyce, when he gives Esther to Woodcourt, speaks "radiantly and beneficently, like the sunshine" (p. 649). Jung also pointed out that this same figure is often either associated with an animal or able to turn into one, but that this association does not "imply any

17. "The Phenomenology of the Spirit in Fairy Tales," p. 77.

devaluation" (p. 86). In fact, as Jung saw it, high and low, or noble and bestial forms are necessary complements to one another. Since we have discovered this view to be a preoccupation with Dickens, we should not be surprised if one area of the novel responds to a Jungian analysis.

Where there are two old men in a fairy tale, one good, one evil, details in imagery or plot often indicate, in Jung's words, "that the old man is his own opposite, a life-bringer as well as a death-dealer" (p. 82). Before looking any further at Jarndyce as wise old man, therefore, we need to bring back a less savoury character, Krook, who will allow us to investigate further the dark side of this fairy-tale figure. Jung asserts that part of his dark nature may indicate a "chthonic" quality in the wise old man. For instance, if he appears as a dwarf, it may imply a less than animal nature, what Jung characterizes as "a naturalistic vegetation numen sprung from the underworld. In one Balkan tale the old man is handicapped by the loss of an eye." He "has therefore lost part of his eyesight—that is, his insight and enlightenment —to the daemonic world of darkness" (p. 82). We find a quite unexpected representation of such a figure in Dickens' initial characterization of Krook. Esther tells us that his "shop was blinded . . . by the wall of Lincoln's Inn, intercepting the light." As for Krook, "his throat, chin, and eyebrows were so frosted with white hairs, and so gnarled with veins and puckered skin, that he looked from his breast upward, like some old root in a fall of snow" (p. 39). He lives in darkness from choice, as symbolized not only by his den but also by his unwillingness to allow anyone to "enlighten" him by teaching him to read.

We think of Krook as mainly concerned with things, but at one point he displays an interest in a person too. When he first sees Ada, he says, "Hi! Here's lovely hair! I have got three sacks of ladies' hair below, but none so beautiful and fine as this. What colour, and what texture!" (p. 39). Since her hair had earlier twice been described as "golden" (pp. 23, 33), we realize that his desire is still to add to his hoard. But, since this appreciation comes in the middle of his comparison of himself to the Chancellor, we also realize an intended parallel with an earlier scene in Chancery in which Ada met the Lord Chancellor. Esther describes it: "That he had admired her, and was interested by her, even *I* could see in a moment. It touched me, that the home of such a beautiful young creature should be represented by that dry official place. The Lord High Chancellor, at his best, appeared so poor a substitute for the love and pride of parents" (p. 24). The question raised at the very beginning of the book is thus explicitly what relation guardians will have to their wards, and implicitly how far can an old man go in wishing to appropriate the treasure of a young woman?

Krook is further characterized in images which show him as an embodiment of the dark magician who is so appropriate an *alter ego* of that lawful "good" old man, the Lord Chancellor. At one point Krook stands "at his shop-door, in his spectacles . . . with his cat upon his shoulder, and her tail sticking up on one side of his hairy cap, like a tall feather" (p. 44). If not a witch with his familiar, Krook is clearly a wizard interchangeable with his beast: In a later description we are told that "Krook, who might have changed eyes with his cat, . . . casts his sharp glance around" (p. 106).

As indicated above, Dickens was quite straightforward in connecting Krook with the Lord Chancellor. One of the first things Krook says, for instance, is that "they call me the Lord Chancellor, and call my shop Chancery" (p. 39). The parallel is developed at some length (pp. 38–40) partly to give weight to Dickens' later outburst against the Lord Chancellor on the occasion of Krook's death. That death, by spontaneous combustion, is prepared for even in Krook's first appearance. His alcohol-sodden nature is given in an image that links him with the monster of Chancery. "He was short, cadaverous, and withered; with his head sunk sideways between his shoulders, and the breath issuing in visible smoke from his mouth, as if he were on fire within" (p. 39). That this creature is a fiery dragon out of a fairy tale is also indicated in the paragraph before, in which Richard compares Krook's warehouse to Chancery: "One had only to fancy . . . that yonder bones in a corner, piled together and picked very clean, were the bones of clients, to make the picture complete" (p. 39). The monster of Chancery is in one of its guises a dragon that hypnotizes its victims and lures them in to be devoured.

Dickens' handling of Krook's cat supports this symbolic pattern. She is bloodthirsty from the start, crouching on the parapet outside Miss Flite's room for hours. "I have discovered," says Miss Flite, fearing for her birds, "that her natural cruelty is sharpened by a jealous fear of their regaining their liberty" (p. 43). And Esther tells us that as she left the house the "cat looked . . . wickedly at me, as if I were a blood-relation of the birds up-stairs" (p. 44). This hint as to the possible range of the cat's appetite is developed when the mysterious character Nemo dies in one of Krook's rooms; to protect the body, the cat has to be driven out "licking her lips" (p. 109). But the full implications of the cat's place in the novel do not come out until the night of Krook's death: "She went leaping and bounding and tearing about, . . . like a Dragon, and got out on the house-top, and roamed about up there for a fortnight, and then came tumbling down the chimney very thin. Did you ever see such a brute? Looks as if she knew all about it, don't she? Almost looks as if she was Krook. Shoohoo! Get out, you goblin!" (p. 425). Krook, whom the cat "almost" resembles, had earlier been called a "Boguey" (p. 340), another name for goblin. And even earlier, upon examining an empty bottle of liquor, " 'I say!' he cries, like the Hobgoblin in the story, "Somebody's been making free here!' " (p. 216). With its taste for flesh and its similarity to a dragon, the cat joins Krook and the Lord Chancellor, reinforcing the image of selfish evildoers who collect everything to themselves without caring that they must live in filth and befoul the land which they plunder.

The cat's asserted resemblance to Krook touches again on the image of the magician and his destructive familiar. This image carried a high emotional charge for Dickens, as can be inferred from a letter written during the time when his hostility toward his wife was vying with his attraction to Ellen Ternan. "I am the modern embodiment of the old Enchanters, whose Familiars tore them to pieces. . . . I wish I had been born in the days of Ogres and Dragon-guarded Castles. I wish an Ogre with seven heads . . . had taken the Princess whom I adore . . . to his stronghold on the top of a high series of mountains, and there tied her up by the hair. Nothing would suit me half so well this day, as climbing after her, sword in hand, and either winning her or being killed."[18] In contrast to Dickens' notion quoted earlier of the novelist as the "Magician" who arouses "potent" spirits to "make them serve" his "purpose," we see Dickens here as the unfortunate human magician who is destroyed by his own *alter ego*, or who has set himself the impossible task of being the successful hero of a difficult adventure rather than accept the role of the enchanter who merely sets the beginning spell for the adventure. In other words, we could say of Dickens in his unfortunate liaison with Ellen Ternan that he mistook his role, gradually changing from fatherly helper to lover. And his characterization of Jarndyce in *Bleak House* indicates that he had recognized the problem five years

18. Johnson (p. 911) believes this letter is a comment on Dickens' relation with Ellen Ternan. For a Freudian analysis of the love and death dialectic in Dickens, see Leonard F. Manheim, "Thanatos: the Death Instinct in Dickens' Later Novels," *Psychoanalysis and the Psychoanalytic Review*, 47 (Winter 1960).

before it became his own and had solved it more or less successfully in art as he was unable to do in life.

In our effort to account for the beast images early associated with Jarndyce, we have looked at Dickens' own experience, and, in *Bleak House,* at the destructive or selfishly possessive actions of dark man-beasts. It is now time to scrutinize the later actions of Jarndyce for indications of base desires such as we have seen Dickens project for that other guardian, the Lord Chancellor, through his low *alter ego,* Krook. But surely Jarndyce always treats his wards in a considerate and helpful way? Out of love for Richard and Ada, for instance, he insists that they break off their understanding when Richard goes to Ireland. Perhaps it is our twentieth-century suspiciousness of motives that makes us feel Jarndyce acts too much like the heavy father in thus forcing his good intentions on his wards. Just because he calls Ada "my bird" at one point (p. 258) doesn't mean that we should connect him with the Chancellor who is said to keep Miss Flite's birds caged up. It is, after all, quite clear that Jarndyce wants to give his birds freedom.

Yet we must admit that he is not always open and aboveboard, especially in his dealings with Esther. She first becomes aware of something hidden in him fairly early in the book. "Said I, 'She blesses the Guardian who is a Father to her!' At the word Father, I saw his former trouble come into his face. He subdued it as before, and it was gone in an instant; but, it had been there, and it had come so swiftly upon my words that I felt as if they had given him a shock" (p. 181). This incident prepares for the un-fatherly love which is finally revealed after Esther is disfigured by smallpox.[19] Thinking she has lost all chance with Alan Woodcourt, she accepts Jarndyce's proposal of marriage.

Such a marriage would obviously violate not only the formula of popular fiction which Dickens both followed and shaped, but also the dominant role enacted by Jarndyce, that of the wise old man who wants not to possess but to free. That he should finally give Esther up to Woodcourt is standard Victorian nobility. But that he should send for her to come to Yorkshire where she knows he is visiting Woodcourt, that he should present her with a cottage named Bleak House, and that he should only then tell her that she will marry Woodcourt—these actions carry his authority a good way toward darkness. An exchange between Esther and Jarndyce hints at the danger. He says, "Full of

19. Just how far back Jarndyce's passion goes is indicated when he unites Esther with Woodcourt: "I sometimes dreamed when you were very young, of making you my wife one day" (p. 649).

curiosity, no doubt, little woman, to know why I have brought you here?" She responds, "Well, Guardian, . . . without thinking myself a Fatima, or you a Blue Beard, I am a little curious about it" (p. 647). Blue Beard is a slightly different type of fairy-tale character than we have encountered so far. His name points towards his hairy animal nature, which is cruel, potentially devouring.[20] His story concerns the dangers of marriage.

In her reply to Jarndyce, Esther could be taken as indicating her own unconscious realization that marriage to her Guardian Father would also be dangerous. Since Jarndyce had first appeared to her as a beast of whom she was slightly afraid, this connection is at least consistent. We may finally conclude that Jarndyce is at worst a sublimated Bluebeard—but then so is the Lord Chancellor. It is therefore worth remembering that in Dickens' opinion it was Ada's gold that the Chancellor and Krook really wanted, and it is Ada herself that Jarndyce finally gets. "To Ada and her pretty boy, he is the fondest father" (p. 664).

To recapitulate briefly, we have noticed how Dickens' use of *alter ego* characters is often given in a fairy-tale idiom and demonstrates his need to connect dark and light, man and beast, unconscious impulse and conscious thought. Easily traced at first in the overt linkage of the Lord Chancellor and the rag-dealer Krook, this emphasis on high and low becomes more complex with the addition of the destructive dragon and flesh-eating cat. Whereas Krook and his cat are only acting out what the Chancellor refuses to acknowledge in himself, with Jarndyce we observe high and low, beast and god in the same person. He is consequently a more complicated character. And if we have been a little hard on him, part of the fault is Dickens'. Despite what is *said* about Jarndyce, he is *presented* as human and fallible.

On the basis of his letter to Bulwer-Lytton, I asserted earlier that Dickens could be seen as a secular magician, the kind of writer who felt a need to release natural feelings from the prison of consciousness or who was fascinated with the results of repression. Besides Krook and the Lord Chancellor, we should consider two other complementary figures, though they are not *alter egos*, the lawyer Tulkinghorn and the detective Bucket. A model of repression, Tulkinghorn is not only "close," he is unhumane and anti-life. His rejection of the principles of

20. Dickens' first acquaintance with Bluebeard was in a vulgarized version, "Captain Murderer," told him by his nurse. For his account of the strong impression it made on him, see "Nurses Stories" in *The Uncommercial Traveler*.

warmth and growth favoured by Dickens is indicated in a comment he makes to Lady Dedlock: "My experience teaches me . . . that most of the people I know would do far better to leave marriage alone. It is at the bottom of three-fourths of their troubles" (pp. 440–41). His interest is elsewhere than in people.[21] As Lady Dedlock says at one point, "He is indifferent to everything but his calling. His calling is the acquisition of secrets, and the holding possession of such power as they give him, with no sharer or opponent in it" (p. 388). The law is, of course, a perfect vehicle for this calling; it allows him to be "the steward of the legal mysteries, the butler of the legal cellar, of the Dedlocks" (p. 9). He is, in fact the "high-priest of noble mysteries" (p. 443). The worship which gives such power is one we might have suspected from the blackness of his clothes. Dickens tells us that Tulkinghorn reads the letter which finally puts Lady Dedlock in his power "with a countenance as imperturbable as Death" (p. 368). Besides the Dedlock's "legal cellar," Tulkinghorn has his own much-frequented one, from which he "comes gravely back, encircled by an earthy atmosphere" (p. 232).

While he lives, the nature of his power is made manifest in a number of ways, for instance, in his sending of Bucket and Snagsby into "the pit" of Tom-All-Alone's. It is at his bidding that Bucket must keep warning Jo to move on. Bucket's response to the dehumanized role the law thrusts on him is to try to use his power for good, as in taking Jo to the hospital at one point. But, until Tulkinghorn dies, Bucket is a subordinate figure. Only after that death does the detective emerge as an imposing force to organize and control the action that follows. The most overt sign of this shift in power is Bucket's taking on the role of confidant to Sir Leicester. He interprets, insinuates, and takes over more openly than Tulkinghorn ever did, but for the human good of the marriage rather than its social dignity, to help Lady Dedlock rather than to demean her as Tulkinghorn did. The covert sign of this transfer of power is even more indicative of the underlying energy that Dickens was channelling.

Just as Tulkinghorn is, like the Lord Chancellor, a respectable member of a profession Dickens considered to be self-interested and pernicious, so Bucket, like Krook, is a member of a lower sphere which has its necessary contact with the upper. Where Krook has his demonic familiar in the form of his destructive cat, Bucket has a less sinister

21. On the implications of Tulkinghorn's refusal of sex, see Joseph Fradin's perceptive article, "Will and Society in *Bleak House*," *PMLA*, 81 (March 1966): 103–4.

familiar. As Dickens put it shortly after the murder of Tulkinghorn,

> When Mr. Bucket has a matter of this pressing interest under his
> consideration, the fat forefinger seems to rise to the dignity of a
> familiar demon. He puts it to his ears, and it whispers information;
> he puts it to his lips, and it enjoins him to secrecy; he rubs it over his
> nose, and it sharpens his scent; he shakes it before a guilty man, and
> it charms him to his destruction. The Augurs of the Detective Temple
> invariably predict, that when Mr. Bucket and that finger are in much
> conference, a terrible avenger will be heard of before long (p. 539).

He goes to Tulkinghorn's chambers, where "he and the Roman will be
alone together, comparing forefingers" (p. 539). The Roman is an
allegorical figure painted on Tulkinghorn's ceiling. Dickens had made
fun of it as removed from life, until the night of Tulkinghorn's death:
"For many years, the persistent Roman has been pointing, with no
particular meaning, from that ceiling" (p. 503). But this night he is
pointing at the murdered lawyer, so that Bucket's subsequent comparing of fingers is in the nature of a magician's attempt to discover
the truth.

Certainly the aura of magic surrounding Bucket is frequently emphasized by Dickens. Disguised as a doctor, he appears "to vanish by
magic" (p. 266) and be replaced by himself as detective when he has
located Gridley, a disturbed litigant in Chancery. Later Jo is unwilling
to pronounce Bucket's name because of a superstitious belief that the
detective may overhear. "Why, he is not in this place," remonstrates
Woodcourt. " 'Oh, ain't he though?' says Jo. 'He's in all manner of
places, all at wanst' " (p. 480). It is Bucket who later holds the handkerchief which might have the "enchanted power" (p. 581) to reveal
Lady Dedlock's whereabouts. Bucket does get on her trail, but his
magic is inferior to hers; by changing her clothes (or identity) as he
had earlier, she is able to elude him until her death.

Another ability Bucket has as detective-magician is indicated by his
name. He is, for instance, at one point able to "dip . . . down to the
bottom" (p. 234) of another character's mind and intuit what he wants
to know. Or as another character says, "Bucket is so deep" (p. 538).
This is meant in the same sense in which we are often told that Tulkinghorn is "close," that is, secretive and uncommunicative. But Bucket is
willing to talk when it is possible and convenient.

More important, unlike Tulkinghorn's aim, Bucket's is not to keep
everything locked up in a cellar but to bring the truth to light. Even if

Tulkinghorn had revealed Lady Dedlock's secret, it would have been for selfish reasons (disguised as the good name of the family) and after mental torture. Bucket acts from power, but with true impersonality, always in a professional capacity. Indeed, after the death of Tulkinghorn, he is even able to expand his previously marginal humanity to something like the role of a wise old man to Esther. Like Jarndyce, he takes her to a new destiny in a carriage ride. Where Jarndyce had tried, prematurely, to offer Esther royal food, Bucket is presumably able to make it stick when he tells her she is "a Queen." At least Esther reports his words to us and confesses she finds them "encouraging" (p. 606).

There is an ambiguity associated with Bucket as magician, which his role as detective helps clarify. The problem is crystallized in the scene in which Hortense is finally charged and arrested in front of Sir Leicester. She at first addresses Bucket as "my Angel," but as his questions become more pointed calls him "a Devil" (p. 558). When Bucket reveals the part his wife has played in trapping Hortense, we get the following exchange.

> "I would like to kiss her!" exclaims Mademoiselle Hortense, panting tigress-like.
> "You'd bite her, I suspect," says Mr. Bucket.
> "I would!" making her eyes very large. "I would love to tear her, limb from limb . . . you are a Devil still."
> "Angel and devil by turns, eh?" cries Mr. Bucket. "But I am in my regular employment, you must consider" (p. 562).

In the light of our analysis of the type of which Bucket is a variant, his last statement makes sense. His "regular employment" neutralizes him as a moral agent. He cannot be an angel, but neither is he ever really a devil. Hortense, who calls him one, is herself "tigerish," possessed of the same destructiveness we have seen in Krook's cat which had earlier "ripped at a bundle of rags with her tigerish claws" (p. 40). If this destructiveness is demonic, Bucket's apprehending her, even by dark and secret means, must be something else.

I would suggest that his powers make him a modern magician, not the kind that works by illusion, but one who penetrates the darkness for good. Bucket's "regular employment" as police detective is perhaps the one position from which in Dickens' opinion a person may do good impersonally. At the other pole from Tulkinghorn's selfish impersonality, Bucket's role allows him a wife and helpful insights and actions.

Whereas Tulkinghorn's power is associated with death, Bucket's is connected with life, as in the impressive and suggestive scene in which he arrests Hortense. "It is impossible to describe how Mr. Bucket gets her out, but he accomplishes that feat in a manner so peculiar to himself; enfolding and pervading her like a cloud, and hovering away with her as if he were a homely Jupiter, and she the object of his affections" (p. 563). Embellished though it is in the Dickensian grotesque manner, this description stands as another curve of the pattern we have followed of the old protector and the younger woman. Bucket is the one wise old man who can speak and act directly, and yet with impunity. Jarndyce frequently praises Esther, but usually indirectly. Bucket, as we have seen, is at once direct and impersonal. With Hortense, we may say, he is able to act as Jarndyce would like to with Esther, and as Zeus actually did with Io and Danaë. But his embrace is neutral, not a breaking of role likely to bother his conscience or make his wife jealous. Although he calls Hortense "my dear" and even "darling" (p. 562) twice each in this scene, he has already told her "I'm a married man, you know; you're acquainted with my wife. Just take my arm" (p. 560). Like the magician in Dickens' letter to Bulwer-Lytton, Bucket does not let any "potent spirit get the better" of him but works it so that an evil spirit like Hortense "serves [his] purpose."

Dickens' desire to alleviate social and psychological repression can be expressed in the adage which was in his mind as he began *Bleak House*: "Truth lies at the bottom of a well." In Chancery, he ranged the solicitors "in a long matted well (but you might look in vain for Truth at the bottom of it)" (p. 2). Unlike them, Bucket, as his name indicates, does use his office to find and bring to light the truth.[22] Consequently, I would urge that there are vital connections between Inspector Bucket and the roots of Dickens' sensibility, between Bucket as detective-magician and Dickens as writer-magician. We know that Dickens had a love of London at night, even its dangerous parts. In the articles on the new detective force in *Household Words*, there is a clear admiration for a detective's ability to roam freely among the potent and destructive characters of the underworld. Bucket is, of course, modelled on one of these detectives. The parallel between their power over the underworld, their painstaking solving of a case, and Dickens' power

22. Dickens' tendency toward figurative use of bucket and well is apparent in the second sentence of an essay called "The Ghost of Art," in which he described "a square court of high houses, which would be a complete well, but for the want of water and absence of a bucket."

over the potent spirit of his imagination, his painstaking working out of a plot (often a mystery) is not merely a fanciful one.

Another connection reinforces this parallel. Bucket is imaged as a god in the arrest scene. A magician can be compared to a god, especially if the god is spreading an earthly cloud around someone. More important, just as we have already seen Dickens writing to Bulwer-Lytton about the artist as magician, so he wrote to Lytton and to Wilkie Collins about the novelist as Providence.

In starting to follow this lead, we must distinguish between Dickens' notion of the author's relation to character on the one hand and to plot on the other. His advice to other writers on character analysis was consistent and emphatic. "The people do not sufficiently work out their own purposes in dialogue and dramatic action. You are too much their exponent; what you do for them, they ought to do for themselves" (*Letters*, II, 624). Or to Collins on *The Woman in White*: "The three people who write the narratives . . . have a DISSECTIVE property in common, which is essentially not theirs but yours; . . . my own effort would be to strike more of what is got *that* way out of them by collision with one another, and by the working of the story" (III, 145). This attitude might be described as authorial *laissez faire* and attributed to Dickens' feeling that he *saw* rather than *invented* his characters. But to this tendency must be contrasted his final working out of the plot.

Justifying the end of *A Tale of Two Cities* to Bulwer-Lytton, Dickens wrote, "Where the accident in such cases is inseparable from the passion and emotion of the character, where it is strictly consistent with the whole design, and arises out of some culminating proceeding on the part of a character, which the whole story has led up to, it seems to me to become, as it were, an act of divine justice" (III, 163). Or again to Collins, and even more significantly, "I think the business of art is to lay all that ground carefully, not with the care that conceals itself—to show, by a backward light, what everything has been working to—but only to *suggest*, until the fulfilment comes. These are the ways of Providence, of which all art is but a little imitation" (II, 124–25).[23]

---

23. At the end of *A Tale of Two Cities*, Dickens showed by "a backward light, what everything" had been working to when he referred to the "powerful enchanter, Time," as a "great magician who majestically works out the appointed order of the Creator" and "never reverses his transformations" (Book III, Chapter 15). Specially aimed at explaining the destruction of the French Revolution, this important generalization also casts light upon the positive transformation of a character like Sidney Carton.

To the picture of the novelist as powerful magician, we now can add the not incompatible one of him as a version of "Providence," his novel being a small universe in which he imitates the natural and moral laws that govern the larger one. The novelist must refrain from stepping in constantly to advise the reader. Dickens' objection to Thackeray's reference to his "puppets" would then be that Thackeray gave them no life, no free will to work out their own destinies. Dickens' own control came from his being outside the mystery, knowing what its outcome would be because he knew the nature of the character and created the laws by which that microcosm was to operate.

Similarly, Dickens the reformer could speak like a biblical prophet because he saw these same natural and moral laws working in society, and saw them, as he believed, objectively and with decent respect[24] The absence of Dickens' ego in his works may not be the first thing that strikes us about them, but it is certainly urged or strongly implied in all his advice on novel writing. This godlike attitude is quite different from the impersonality of Flaubert or Joyce, mainly because Dickens actually believed in the existence of a Christian God who had designed the world and whose mind and laws could be known. Dickens' reader, like the characters in one of his novels, might forget these laws of creation for a time, but the action and results of these laws would be evident to any interested person by the end of the novel.

Frequently Dickens' conception of the proper role of the novelist is also embodied in a certain type of character in the novels. This is the figure who can see and go anywhere, who can watch moved but un-swayed any action, and who can finally judge the result.[25] Bucket is such a figure, and his capture of Hortense aptly divine. Jarndyce is trying to be such a figure, and he succeeds in Dickens' eyes when he gives up Esther and becomes Ada's guardian. Dickens' ideal was to be such a figure too. We may doubt his success in controlling his own "potent spirit" in the conduct of his life, but we can hardly doubt his

24. By this standard, the characters Dickens identified with and whose sufferings he was most moved by are rightly the ones we today are least sympathetic with; he lost in that case what used to be called "aesthetic distance." Daniel Doyce, the inventor in *Little Dorrit*, may be taken as a kind of paradigm of the ideal: "He never said, I discovered this adaptation or invented that combination; but showed the whole thing as if the Divine artificer had made it, and he had happened to find it" (Book II, Chapter 8).

25. In 1849, two years before he began *Bleak House*, Dickens thought of organizing a magazine around the idea of "a certain SHADOW, which may go into any place . . . and be supposed to be cognizant of everything" (*Letters*, II, 178).

success as an artistic creator, as the black and white magician of potent narrative spells.

Being the kind of person he was, he could hardly help putting into his characters some of the potential of his own nature. In the character of Jarndyce, therefore, we may now find a complexity unsuspected before, and at the same time we may see that complexity as a meaningful extension of the fairy-tale method. Because of that method, even the simple character type of Cinderella becomes involved in complications which make her fate more interesting. Because of that method characters like Krook and Miss Flite stir deep and tangled forces inside the reader without benefit of a prominent part in the physical plot development.

Dickens' plots are sometimes objected to as mechanical and too full of coincidences. But these weaknesses can be seen as virtues when we realize that it was a world of meaning he aimed to create. And the meaning of the self-imposed darkness of Krook and his destructive familiar the cat is, for instance, in sharp contrast to the pitiful limitations of Miss Flite and the birds which she *must* keep caged. Freer than either of these, Jarndyce is enmeshed not by a greedy desire for power or by fear of it, but by the need for human relations and fear of their being corrupted by that power. Good though he is by conventional standards, he also must blunder in the dark which is part of every human heart. As social commentator, Dickens insisted that high and low, noble and baseborn cannot be separated; as psychologist, also, he saw the necessity of joining conscious and unconscious, sophisticated and naive, man and the beast within him. Looked at in this way, the fairy-tale element of his fiction offers as stable a base for permanent reader appeal as any literary form can pretend to.

Chapter Seven

The Return of the Native

Like Dickens, Hardy had a good eye for detail, but where Dickens exercised his in the city, Hardy's worked best in the country. In this respect Hardy is close to Emily Brontë before him and Joseph Conrad after him: all three deal with "nature" as the Romantic poets would have understood it. Separated from them at this level, Dickens is at one with them on another level; as indicated in the last chapter, he shares with them a penchant for romance as a means of illuminating the human psyche. Even more essential is the mode of vision of the four novelists: none of them can start to create a world until their imaginations have transformed what the physical eye can see. As the nineteenth century progressed, such artistic transformation became more and more difficult to achieve. We saw the difficulty Dickens faced in choosing the city as his world. We might think that Hardy's focusing on nature would have made his imaginative task easier. But we would be forgetting the advent of Darwin and his unromantic theory of natural selection.

Surely, after the appearance in 1859 of *The Origin of Species*, nature romanticism could only be an anachronism. If we remember that George Eliot published *Adam Bede* in the same year, we would have to see a turning of the tide toward realism, whether scientific or artistic. The argument seems all the stronger if we remember that in 1861, when *Great Expectations* appeared, Dickens used fairy-tale motifs as central to the *illusions* which Pip allows to dominate so much of his life. On the other hand, the psychological realities which were Dickens' primary concern were still shadowed forth in that novel not through artistic realism but by means of *alter ego* characters and other fairy-tale motifs of the sort we have discussed.[1] And, in *Silas Marner*, George Eliot herself made use of fairy-tale motifs for almost allegorical purposes (in the manner of Dickens' Christmas books).

But, having counter-stated this much, we must admit that the climate of Victorian opinion after 1859 was more conducive not only to artistic realism but also to artistic sophistication than it had been before. No major novelist after Dickens could confide to his readers in the preface of a novel that he had "purposely dwelt on the romantic side of familiar things." Yet, like Dickens, Thomas Hardy could not accept the realist doctrine of art. As he wrote in his notebook in 1890, "Art is a disproportioning—(i.e. distorting, throwing out of proportion)—of realities, to show more clearly the features that matter in those realities, which, if merely copied or reported inventorially, might possibly be observed, but would more probably be overlooked. Hence 'realism' is not Art."[2] Originally and finally a poet, Hardy was much influenced by Shelley (not to mention Coleridge, Wordsworth, Keats, and Byron, all of whom are often mentioned or quoted in the notebook entries in *The Life of Thomas Hardy*). A useful way of gauging the increasing sophistication of the novel by 1878 is to notice the varieties of romanticism in *The Return of the Native*, and Hardy's ambiguous attitude toward them.

I would like to distinguish three kinds of romanticism in the novel: first, the egocentric love romanticism of the Byronic hero, exemplified oddly but unmistakably in Eustacia Vye: second, an impersonal nature romanticism which Hardy associated with the four seasons and the practices by which his peasants indicated their relation to nature; third, an elemental romanticism in which we may see not only the heath and the peasants but even Eustacia integrated into the cosmic dance. We may say that each of these three fitted the mood of the age: love romanticism had an obvious appeal to the naive reader; nature romanticism satisfied the more sophisticated reader; and elemental romanticism fulfilled Hardy's need to voice his sense of universal flux.

From whichever direction we approach her, Eustacia Vye demonstrates the excess of subjective romanticism. Self-fulfilment is more important to her than nature, or society, or even the individuals with whom she is intimately connected. "Fidelity in love for fidelity's sake had less attraction for her than for most women: fidelity because of

1. See Harry Stone's article "Fire, Hand, and Gate: Dickens' *Great Expectations*," Kenyon Review, 24 (Autumn, 1962), 667.
2. Florence Emily Hardy, *The Life of Thomas Hardy* (London: Macmillan, 1962), p. 229. Hereafter cited as the *Life*.

love's grip had much." Until marrying Clym Yeobright she is relatively successful in ignoring or flouting the conventions of the heath dwellers, but she is not able simply to ignore the heath itself. "Egdon was her Hades, and since coming there she had imbibed much of what was dark in its tone, though inwardly and eternally unreconciled thereto." Her dislike is directed not only at the heath but also at the realities of human life. "She could show a most reproachful look at times, but it was directed less against human beings than against certain creatures of her mind, the chief of these being Destiny, through whose interference she dimly fancied it arose that love alighted only on gliding youth."[3] As the phrase "creatures of her mind" indicates, Hardy does not share her sense of persecution.

The best place to see the illusions fostered by Eustacia's romantic outlook is in her relations with Clym. At one point, just after she has met him in her mummer's disguise, she herself sees the danger. "What was the use of her exploit? She was at present a total stranger to the Yeobright family. The unreasonable nimbus of romance with which she had encircled that man might be her misery" (II, 6). Needless to say, Hardy in all his work shows a considerable insight into "the unreasonable nimbus of romance."

The word *nimbus* has a special meaning in the relations of Clym and Eustacia. When she first sees him, Clym is characterized in romantic fashion: "As is usual with bright natures, the deity that lies ignominiously chained within an ephemeral human carcase shone out of him like a ray. The effect upon Eustacia was palpable" (II, 6). Even before she sees him, Hardy reports that Clym's "influence was penetrating her like summer sun" (II, 4). His connection with the sun is balanced by Eustacia's connection with the moon. The chapter describing her is called "Queen of the Night," and contains a number of passages associating her with the moon. In making this connection, Hardy was working for more than conventional romantic associations, however. He wanted a romantic symbolism which could contain within itself the means of its own dissolution.

As the romance of their marriage is tempered by the realities of Clym's becoming a partial invalid and refusing to move to Paris,

3. There being so many editions of *The Return of the Native,* I shall give Book and Chapter numbers instead of page numbers. These quotations are all from Book First, Chapter 7. Future citations in the text will be on the model (I, 7). Unless otherwise cited, all ellipses are mine. The edition actually used is the Macmillan, St. Martin's (London, 1958).

Eustacia regresses to reproachfulness. "Do you remember how, before we were married, I warned you that I had not good wifely qualities?" Clym replies "You mock me to say that now. On that point at least the only noble course would be to hold your tongue, for you are still queen of me, Eustacia, though I may no longer be king of you" (IV, 2). If we have been prepared to see Eustacia as queen, we are soon shown how Clym was a king. His title grows as much out of his connection with the sun as Eustacia's did out of hers with the moon. Clym comments, "I suppose when you first saw me and heard about me I was wrapped in a sort of golden halo to your eyes—a man who knew glorious things, and had mixed in brilliant scenes—in short, an adorable, delightful, distracting hero?" (IV, 3). But he has spoken true in implying that he is king of her no longer.

Eustacia's gaining dominance over Clym is indicated both in the fact and the imagery of his letting her go gipsying alone. "Go and do whatever you like. Who can forbid your indulgence in any whim? You have all my heart yet, I believe; and because you bear with me, who am in truth a drag upon you, I owe you thanks. Yes, go alone and shine" (IV, 3). And shine she does, as romance leads her away from the subservient role of housewife to new adventures. When she reaches the grounds where the late-summer dance is to be, the sun has "quite disappeared," but this makes "little difference either to Eustacia or to the revellers, for a round yellow moon was rising before her, though its rays had not yet outmastered those from the west" (IV, 3). Then she begins dancing with Damon Wildeve. "The pale ray of evening lent a fascination to the experience. There is a certain degree and tone of light which tends to disturb the equilibrium of the senses, and to promote dangerously the tenderer moods; added to movement, it drives the emotions to rankness, the reason becoming sleepy and unperceiving in inverse proportion; and this light fell now upon these two from the disc of the moon. All the dancing girls felt the symptoms, but Eustacia most of all" (IV, 3). Hardy further remarks of the dancers that "for the time Paganism was revived in their hearts, the pride of life was all in all, and they adored none other than themselves" (IV, 3). The difference is that for the others it is only a temporary revival, for Eustacia, and for Wildeve, it is the beginning of the end of their respective marriages.

Eustacia is in several ways an alien on the heath. Not only did she grow up on the sea at Budmouth, but "her father was a romantic wanderer—a sort of Greek Ulysses" (III, 6). In revising the novel to make the father come from Corfu,[4] Hardy was undoubtedly bringing Eustacia's heritage in line with one of the "philosophic" themes of the novel. As expressed at the beginning of Book Third, that theme involves a variation on the same problem of beauty that had come up in the very first chapter of the novel. "A long line of disillusive centuries has permanently displaced the Hellenic idea of life, or whatever it may be called. . . . That old-fashioned revelling in the general situation grows less and less possible as we uncover the defects of natural laws, and see the quandary that man is in by their operation" (III, 1). In other words, pagan enjoyment of life must be replaced by scientific appraisal of life.

Such an appraisal was still yielding Hardy the following conclusion three years after the publication of *The Return of the Native*. "The emotions have no place in a world of defect, and it is a cruel injustice that they should have developed in it" (*Life*, p. 149). This reads curiously like a justification of Eustacia's romantic outburst just before her death. "O, the cruelty of putting me into this ill-conceived world! I was capable of much; but I have been injured and blighted and crushed by things beyond my control! O, how hard it is of Heaven to devise such tortures for me, who have done no harm to Heaven at all!" (V, 7). Though it is not all of the truth, this cry has truth in it. Its logical faults are well expressed by M. A. Goldberg. "Natural law, or 'Fundamental Energy,' as Hardy calls it in his introduction to *The Dynasts,* may appear as a malignant and destructive force, conflicting with human aims—but only when, like Eustacia Vye or Susan Nunsuch, the reader assumes the inherent evil or goodness of the universe, instead of an inherent neutrality."[5] Leaving aside for the moment the unasked question whether Susan Nunsuch can somehow bend that "Fundamental Energy" to her will, we may take it that Goldberg has effectively answered Eustacia's accusations.

Are we then to take as Hardy's view the reasonable attitude of Thomasin on the stormy heath? "To her there were not, as to Eustacia, demons in the air, and malice in every bush and bough. The drops which lashed her face were not scorpions, but prosy rain; Egdon in the mass was no monster whatever, but impersonal open ground. Her fears of the place were rational, her dislikes of its worst moods reasonable.

---

4. As shown by Patterson, *The Making of "The Return of the Native"* (Berkeley: University of California Press, 1960), pp. 109–11.
5. "Hardy's Double-Visioned Universe," *Essays in Criticism,* 7 (Oct. 1957): 382.

At this time it was in her view a windy, wet place, in which a person might experience much discomfort, lose the path without care, and possibly catch cold" (V, 8). If Hardy agreed with this common-sense view, he was undercutting his own conception of the setting, the conception on which the development of his novel was based.[6]

The heath, we were informed in Chapter 1, responded to dark tempests, "for the storm was its lover, and the wind its friend. Then it became the home of strange phantoms; and it was found to be the hitherto unrecognized original of those wild regions of obscurity which are vaguely felt to be compassing us about in midnight dreams of flight and disaster, and are never thought of after the dream till revived by scenes like this." Notice that Hardy knows not "seems"; he says flatly that the heath "was found to be" the original of a certain kind of dream, the kind in fact which comes true when Eustacia is finally involved "in midnight . . . flight and disaster." Even if we take Eustacia's death as suicide (and I do), this passage suggests that the heath is responsible. We have already seen that "she had imbibed much of what was dark in its tone." But, if we insist on entering the world of delayed causality, we must investigate the effigy sacrificed by Susan Nunsuch, as well as Eustacia's own prefigurative dream. And before we can approach these matters we need to make a fresh approach to the vexed question of Hardy's realism and romanticism.

One critic has already given the question a just, though limited, answer: As "a product of the province of Dorset," Hardy can be seen as "the inheritor of a traditional moral wisdom older and more durable than the wisdom of romantic philosophy and profoundly skeptical of it. The Dorset peasant, at least in Hardy's picture of him, was incapable of romantic disillusion because he had never been corrupted by romantic illusion."[7] If we move beyond the area of the romantic ego-ideal, however, we may question how far the "skepticism" of either Hardy or a Dorset peasant extends. In 1890, Hardy asked his anthropologist friend, Edward Clodd, "why the superstitions of a remote Asiatic and a Dorset labourer are the same." Clodd replied that "The attitude of a man . . . at corresponding levels of culture, before like phenomena, is pretty much the same, your Dorset peasants representing the persistence of the barbaric idea which confuses persons and

6. Hardy may simply have held both views. He often expressed an awareness of having both rational and irrational views. See *Life*, pp. 403, 408.
7. Patterson, p. 132.

things, and founds wide generalizations on the slenderest analogies."
Hardy's significant comment on this explanation was that "this barbaric
idea which confuses persons and things' is, by the way, also common
to the highest imaginative genius—that of the poet" (*Life,* p. 230).
In short, Hardy's ambivalent feelings about romantic egoism aside, it
appears evident that the kind of incident which stimulated his imagination was rooted in unrealistic folk beliefs, superstitions, primitive
animism. In its spiritual form, such animism might produce scientific-
ally untenable concepts such as Eustacia's antipathetic "Destiny" or
Hardy's crude "President of the Immortals" (borrowed from Aeschylus
at the end of *Tess of the d'Ubervilles*). In this form, the result would
be either a character's illusion or the author's poetic licence. But, in
the form Hardy used and knew best, animism did not contradict the
reasoning of at least two men whom he respected, John Stuart Mill
and Edward Clodd.

In 1885 Clodd wrote in *Myths and Dreams* that the "artificial"
division "between the inorganic and the organic" was being replaced
by a "growing conception of unity."[8] More important, there appeared
in 1874, four years before Hardy wrote *The Return of the Native,*
Three Essays on Religion, a posthumous publication by J. S. Mill,
whom Hardy later described as "one of the profoundest thinkers of the
last century" (*Life,* p. 330). In "Theism" Mill voiced a position similar
to Clodd's. "The scientific view of nature" shows it "as one connected
system, or united whole, united not like a web composed of separate
threads in passive juxtaposition with one another, but rather like the
human or animal frame, an apparatus kept going by perpetual action
and reaction among all its parts."[9] Both men were obviously influenced
by evolutionary thinking.

So was Hardy, and his concern with the concept as Mill phrased
it was a lasting one. In 1886, he wrote in his notebook, "The human
race to be shown as one great network or tissue which quivers in every
part when one point is shaken, like a spider's web if touched" (*Life,*
p. 177). And, in 1890, "Altruism, or The Golden Rule, or whatever
'Love your Neighbour as Yourself' may be called, will ultimately be
brought about I think by the pain we see in others reacting on ourselves, as if we and they were a part of one body. Mankind, in fact,

8. Edward Clodd, *Myths and Dreams* (London, 1885), pp. 160–61.
9. John Stuart Mill, *Three Essays on Religion* (London: Longmans, Green,
1874), p. 133.

may be and possibly will be viewed as members of one corporeal frame" (*Life,* p. 224). Similar jottings were made in 1909 and 1910; the idea is central to *The Dynasts,* and important in most of the novels, including *The Return of the Native.* But, whereas by 1891, in *Tess of the d'Ubervilles,* the spirit of pity was strong in Hardy, in *The Return of the Native* he was concerned to explore more impersonally the idea not just of mankind but of all nature, animate and inanimate, as "one corporeal frame" —Mill's "united whole," an "animal frame . . . kept going by perpetual action and reaction among all its parts."

A simple version of this conception is evident at the end of Chapter 2 of *The Return of the Native,* when Hardy comments on the person atop the barrow. "Such a perfect, delicate, and necessary finish did the figure give to the dark pile of hills that it seemed to be the only obvious justification of their outline. Without it, there was the dome without the lantern; with it the architectural demands of the mass were satisfied. The scene . . . amounted . . . to unity. Looking at this or that member of the group was not observing a complete thing, but a fraction of a thing" (I, 2). Acutely aware of the discredited medieval view of man as the crown of nature, Hardy went on to develop a potentially optimistic evolutionary view. "The form was so much like an organic part of the entire motionless structure that to see it move would have impressed the mind as a strange phenomenon. Immobility being the chief characteristic of that whole which the person formed portion of, the discontinuance of immobility in any quarter suggested confusion." When we remember that the figure is Eustacia and that she is giving up her position as "lantern" on the "dome" to go to her bonfire, we can better understand Hardy's later comment, that to her "a blaze of love, and extinction, was better than a lantern glimmer of the same which should last long years" (I, 7). To remain part of the whole, however, the individual must be content with a glimmer only.

The animated whole which set this pace is, of course, the heath, which has a "quality of repose" thus characterized by Hardy: "Not the repose of actual stagnation, but the apparent repose of incredible slowness. A condition of healthy life so nearly resembling the torpor of death is a noticeable thing of its sort" (I,2). Hardy notices even more. Focusing on the sounds of the heath in Chapter 6, he again brings in the notion of death. One sound made by the wind "was the united products of infinitesimal vegetable causes."

They were the mummied heath-bells of the past summer, originally tender and purple, now washed colourless by Michelmas rains, and dried to dead skins by October suns. . . . Yet scarcely a single accent among the many afloat to-night could have such power to impress a listener with thoughts of its origin. . . .

"The spirit moved them." A meaning of the phrase forced itself upon the attention; and an emotional listener's fetichistic mood might have ended in one of more advanced quality. It was not, after all, that the left-hand expanse of old blooms spoke, or the right-hand or those of the slope in front; but it was the single person of something else speaking through each at once (I, 6).[10]

Clearly Hardy is encouraging the reader to move beyond both a literal and a merely "fetichistic" attitude to "one of more advanced quality" in which he imagines "the single person" of nature as an organic whole. Egdon Heath as "a character in the novel" can thus be taken as Hardy's imaginative expression of the quasi-scientific insight into nature as "one corporeal frame." The romanticism of this conception lies in its attempt at unifying man, his natural environment, and its basic elements into an interrelated whole.

Some indication of the part played by the peasants in the frame of nature is given in the first description of them after they displace Eustacia on top of the barrow. "Every individual was so involved in furze by his method of carrying the faggots that he appeared like a bush on legs till he had thrown them down. The party had marched in trail, like a travelling flock of sheep; that is to say, the strongest first, the weak and young behind" (I, 3). As these comparisons suggest, the peasants are well adapted to the heath; in harmony with its moods, they will go their usual ways when outsiders and alienated natives are dead or subdued. The immediate action they plan is not, however, in absolute harmony with the heath. But, when we contrast the nature

10. Rather than trace this notion of a "single person" in nature, to Schopenhauer (whom Hardy had evidently not read at this date), we may turn to Comte: "The conception among the ancients of the Soul of the universe, the modern notion that the earth is a vast living animal, and in our own time, the obscure pantheism which is so rife among German metaphysicians, is only fetichism generalized and made systematic" (*The Positive Philosophy,* London: Kegan Paul, 1853, II, 189). Closer in tone and idiom is Edward Tylor's statement: "The result of carrying to their utmost limits the animistic conceptions which among low races and high pervade the philosophy of religion, is to reach an idea of as it were a soul of the world, a shaper, animator, ruler of the universe" (*Primitive Culture,* London: John Murray, 1871, Chapter 17).

of the fire they light with Eustacia's fire, we see that theirs is only a gesture, and as Hardy emphasizes, a traditional one.

> It was as if these men and boys had suddenly dived into past ages, and fetched therefrom an hour and deed which had before been familiar with this spot. . . . Indeed, it is pretty well known that such blazes as this the heathmen were now enjoying are rather the lineal descendants from jumbled Druidical rites and Saxon ceremonies than the invention of popular feeling about Gunpowder Plot.
>
> Moreover to light a fire is the instinctive and resistant act of man when, at the winter ingress, the curfew is sounded throughout Nature. It indicates a spontaneous, Promethean rebelliousness against the fiat that this recurrent season shall bring foul times, cold darkness, misery and death. Black chaos comes, and the fettered gods of the earth say, Let there be light (I, 3).

To the extent that man has spontaneous impulses of "a more advanced kind" than the rest of nature, he will be out of harmony. The peasants are generally sheeplike, but a character like Eustacia insists on making "Promethean rebelliousness" a permanent trait. To put it another way, her fire represents an individual act, with a particular end in view. Their fire has only general meaning for them.

The peasants have a series of traditions which they act out, as it were unconsciously. For instance, of the midwinter one, the mummer's play, Hardy tells us that "like Baalam and other unwilling prophets, the agents seem moved by an inner compulsion to say and do their allotted parts whether they will or no. This unweeting manner of performance is the true ring by which . . . a fossilized survival may be known" (II, 4). The unconsciousness of the actors here can be distinguished from that engendered in the dancers at the late-summer festivity in which Eustacia later takes part. But, if we remember "the demoniac measure" of the dance round the November bonfire, we can appreciate Hardy's general point in commenting on the spring maypole late in the novel. "The symbolic customs which tradition has attached to each season of the year were yet a reality on Egdon. Indeed, the impulses of all such outlandish hamlets are pagan still: in these spots homage to nature, self-adoration, frantic gaieties, fragments of Teutonic rites to divinities whose names are forgotten, seem in some way or other to have survived mediaeval doctrine" (VI, 1). We realize that Hardy has in fact provided us with a communal tradition for each season: the maypole with its symbols of fertility for Spring, the gipsying with its abandoned dancing for Summer, the bonfire with its defiant light for Fall, and the Mummers' play ushering in the new year for winter. The symbolism of these rites we will investigate further.

Turning our attention to the four seasons as they circumscribe the world Hardy has created, we find further indications of natural animism in a series of correspondences at the beginning of Book Fourth.

> The July sun shone over Egdon and fired its crimson heather to scarlet. It was the one season of the year, and the one weather of the season, in which the heath was gorgeous. This flowering period represented the second or noontide division in the cycle of those superficial changes which alone were possible here; it followed the green or young-fern period, representing the morn, and preceded the brown period, when the heath-bells and ferns would wear the russet tinges of evening; to be in turn displaced by the dark hue of the winter period, representing night.

These connections of a plant, a season, and a time of day function more than casually in the novel. We have for instance already seen the emphasis on the heath-bells in the fall. In Chapter I, we were told that the heath was "a near relation of night" and further that "ever since the beginning of vegetation its soil had worn the same antique brown dress, the natural and invariable garment of the particular formation." We can understand then why, in the paragraph above, Hardy speaks of "those superficial changes which alone were possible" on the heath. We can also appreciate the implications of Clym's becoming a furze cutter. "This man from Paris was now so disguised by his leather accoutrements, and by the goggles he was obliged to wear over his eyes, that his closest friend might have passed by without recognizing him. He was a brown spot in the midst of an expanse of olive-green gorse, and nothing more" (IV, 2). His harmony with the heath is underlined in the subsequent paragraph. "His daily life was of a curious microscopic sort, his whole world being limited to a circuit of a few feet from his person. His familiars were creeping and winged things, and they seemed to enroll him in their band."

A further implication of the imagery used by Hardy to characterize summer on the heath comes out in a passage describing Clym's closeness even to the rabbits. They "sun themselves upon hillocks, the hot beams blazing through the delicate tissue of each thin-fleshed ear, and firing it to a blood-red transparency in which the veins" are visible. Just as heather in summer is "fired . . . scarlet," so the ears of the rabbits are *fired* "blood-red." Only in summer is this passion of blood encouraged on the heath, although in winter, when man burns his fire to assert his active nature, Hardy calls our attention to "red suns and tufts of fire ... flecking the whole country round. ... Some ... glowing scarlet-red from the shade, like wounds in a black hide" (I, 3). Rather than being mere similes, I take this series—red sun, blood-red, wound, scarlet-red, fire—as part of Hardy's sometimes-overt, sometimes-covert vision of nature as a corporeal frame. Characteristically, the heath prefers to hide its vitality under a dark skin. But the "Fundamental Energy" is there; it appears in summer; and it can be brought out at other times by those who are knowing enough in what Hardy calls in Chapter I the "primitive" ways of the heath.

In the concluding chapter of *Folkways in Thomas Hardy,* Ruth Firor makes an interesting comparison of magic and science. "Even when magic employs spirits, personal agents of the kind assumed by religion on a far greater scale, the believer in magic treats these agents as impersonal, inanimate, absolute forces, coercing and constraining them by setting them to work out some given effect from a fixed sequence of given causes. ... Modern science ... owes to magic the fundamental assumption that there are certain invariable and necessary sequences of cause and effect, independent of personal will or caprice."[11] Eustacia tries personal will and fails; Christian Cantle calls on a personal God to protect him from Satan (Diggory Venn in Chapter 3), but he is the self-confessed "rames of a man." At the other end of the scale of assertion is Susan Nunsuch, whose husband was the "son of a witch" (I, 3). Superstitious herself, she sticks Eustacia with a stocking needle, we are told, "so as to draw her blood and put an end to the bewitching of Susan's children" (III, 2).[12] Susan's most decisive use of folk magic is, of course, the burning of an effigy of Eustacia just before the latter actually dies. In that scene, Hardy not only followed the traditions of magic as he knew of them in Dorset, but also included a ritual that taps the sources of natural energy already presented in the novel.

11. Ruth Firor, *Folkways in Thomas Hardy* (New York: A. S. Barnes & Co., 1962), p. 305.
12. Using the publisher's manuscript, John Patterson argues convincingly that Eustacia was originally conceived as even more of a witch than she appears now. Susan Nunsuch might also be termed a witch, but it should be noted that her steps against Eustacia are counteractions only, and are not like Eustacia's for her own individual gain.

As a base for her modelled image, Susan uses part of a "yellow mass" of wax, "the produce of the bees during the foregoing summer" (V, 7). When she has completed her image, she thrusts into it approximately fifty long yellow pins "with apparently excruciating energy." Finally, she rakes the turf fire which is "dark and dead on the outside" until "the inside of the mass showed a glow of red heat." Then she holds yellow image to red heat until "a long flame arose from the spot, and curling its tongue round the figure ate still further into its substance. A pin occasionally dropped with the wax, and the embers heated it red as it lay." As far as Susan will be concerned, the magic is successful this time. What Miss Firor calls the "necessary sequences of cause and effect" will have worked themselves out.

More logical spirits may object that it is a case of *post hoc, ergo propter hoc*. I do not believe that Hardy was one of these; the image and the death do, after all, make a perfect example of "the barbaric confusion of persons and things" which Hardy appreciated as the bond between the peasant and the poet. More pious souls may, on the other hand, object that Susan's backward repetition of the Lord's Prayer is simply a satanic inversion of Christianity. Although technically they have a point, what is important is that her incantation comes out not as human speech but as "a strange jargon." As such, it clearly belongs in Miss Firor's category of primitive magic, with its "impersonal, inanimate, absolute forces." Helpfully, this characterization also applies to the heath as we have seen Hardy present it. If "inanimate" is too strong, we have at least seen organic beeswax combust into elemental fire. In any case, the parallel between the "dark and dead" turf from which Susan rakes a fire and the year-earlier bonfires like "wounds in a black hide" seems to me strong enough to justify some attempt to connect folk magic, natural energy, and the heath.

The most impressive case of a charcter not only close to the heath and its ways, but also willing and able to use its latent energy is Diggory Venn. Just as Susan acts like a witch in trying to obtain what Hardy called "unhallowed assistance against an enemy," so Diggory Venn is associated with the devil without being actually in league with him.[13] If both are connected with "the powers of darkness," it is again the primitive heath rather than the Christian devil that Hardy apparently meant. Although he characterized Diggory as a "Mephistophelian

13. See J. O. Bailey, "Hardy's 'Mephistophelian Visitants'," *PMLA,* 61 (Dec. 1946).

visitant," Hardy quickly made his real point: "A child's first sight of
a reddleman was an epoch in his life. That blood-coloured figure was
a sublimation of all the horrid dreams which had afflicted the juvenile
spirit since imagination began" (I, 9). If "blood-coloured" is not
enough, a further indication of his connection with the energy normally
hidden under the heath comes when Eustacia is out walking. "She
beheld a sinister redness arising from a ravine a little way in advance—
dull and lurid like a flame in sunlight, and she guessed it to signify
Diggory Venn" (II, 7).

How has Diggory, the son of a dairy farmer, became associated with
such images and such an occupation? The answer is simple: being
rejected by Thomasin Yeobright, he has given up thoughts of marriage
and chosen the role of outcast, "isolated and weird" as Hardy later
characterized him (VI, 4). In his chosen role, Diggory "is a curious,
interesting, and nearly perished link between obsolete forms of life and
those which generally prevail" (I, 2). By giving up civilized ways, he
gains a closeness with primitive nature. "To many persons," the heath
also "was a place which had slipped out of its century generations ago,
. . . an obsolete thing" (III, 2). This sense of the primitive past is, as
we have seen, an important part of Hardy's conception. Clym later
imagines "forgotten Celtic tribes . . . standing beside the barrows which
swelled around, untouched and perfect as at the time of their erection"
(VI, 1). Most important for our purpose is the analogue to Diggory
created by Clym's thinking of those primitive men as "dyed bar-
barians." Though their colour was blue, and Diggory's is red, the connection is possible because of Diggory's closeness to the heath. Hardy
underlined that closeness in several striking ways.

The most innocuous-appearing of these is the scene in which Diggory
eavesdrops on Eustacia and Wildeve, before either is married. Taking
two "large turves," he "dragged them over him till one covered his
head and shoulders, and the other his back and legs. . . . The turves,
standing upon him with the heather upwards, looked precisely as if
they were growing. . . . Approaching thus, it was as though he
burrowed underground" (I, 9). The symbolism of a red Diggory under
dark turves is obvious enough if we remember Susan's turf fire "dark
and dead on the outside." And it adds further import to Hardy's later
description of Eustacia in the storm, "gradually crouching down under
the umbrella as if she were drawn into the Barrow by a hand from
beneath" (V, 7). Not that the hands are Diggory's, but that Eustacia,
in setting her will at odds with that of the heath, will go under. Those

who can give their will over to the heath win out in the long run. Whereas Eustacia is concerned with the desires of her ego, both Diggory in his concern for Thomasin and Susan in hers for her children can use the powers of the heath effectively, but in a non-social way. Speaking of Susan's belief that Eustacia is a witch, Hardy says, "It was one of those sentiments which lurk like moles underneath the visible surface of manners" (V, 2). Noting that the mole burrows underground like Diggory, we need to remember also that it is blind.

The place where Diggory's closeness to the heath is most clearly underlined is in the gambling scene, through a contrast with Wildeve. Just as the heath had earlier been characterized as having "the apparent repose of incredible slowness," in contrast to Eustacia's rapid descent off the barrow, so, in Chapter 8 of Book Third, Diggory's lack of motion is contrasted with Wildeve's nervousness. The latter "writhed, fumed, shifted his seat; and the beating of his heart was almost audible. Venn sat with lips impassively closed and eyes reduced to a pair of unimportant twinkles; he scarcely appeared to breathe. He might have been an Arab, or an automaton." The word "automaton," and the concept behind it fascinated Hardy. (See *Life*, pp. 140, 152, 260, 315; also 148, 168; and 184, 186, 416). Diggory is like an automaton because he does not appear to act from his volition. And like a mole he seems to have given up his sight: "eyes reduced to a pair of unimportant twinkles." A clue to the importance of this odd condition can be found in the later description of Clym on the heath. First, we must remember that Clym's regaining harmony with his native heath followed the partial failure of his eyesight. Second, we can look at a suggestive description of the grasshoppers who "leaped over his feet, falling awkwardly on their backs, heads, or hips, like unskilful acrobats, as chance might rule" (IV, 2). The grasshopper cannot see the end of his jump; he has to let chance rule. Man, on the other hand, may choose to let chance rule or not; he may even bend it to his own will, as Wildeve does the weak-willed Christian when he wins the guineas from him. Christian calls the dice "them wonderful little things that carry my luck inside 'em" (III, 7). Wildeve is made of sterner stuff. But Diggory abnegates his human stuff entirely, becomes a "red automaton," and "Fortune" falls "in love with the reddleman" (III, 8). Or we might say, "unlucky in love, lucky in dice." Certainly the irony of this saying must have been in Hardy's mind all through this sequence. Christian, whom no woman will marry, has won "a gown-piece" fit for a man's "wife or sweetheart if he's got one" (III, 7). Wildeve, who has presumably begun to regret his marriage, wants the money that should belong to his wife. Diggory, of course, having lost Thomasin, wants the money for her.

The rationale behind Hardy's conception can be seen clearly enough in what he voiced a number of years later as the only two sympathetic explanations of the imperfections of nature: "that she is blind and not a judge of her actions, or that she is an automaton, and unable to control them" (*Life,* p. 315). The attributes of blindness and automatism exhibited by Diggory put him in harmony with that nature which Hardy had early seen as more limited than man its creature. Whereas Hardy the aspiring romantic is sympathetic when Eustacia and Clym are cut down to size, Hardy the folk romantic portrays the power that can come from voluntary self-limitation. By giving up sight (or foresight) and will (or ego), Diggory is able to achieve harmony with the heath for the paradoxical purpose of changing the future and achieving his personal aim, that is getting the money and giving it to Thomasin.

The general philosophy of the peasants, "'Tis nature" (I, 4) keeps them in harmony; we see it in their sheep-files and their "unweeting manner of performance" in mumming. Whether Hardy's attitude was one of sympathy for his peasants or anger against "a dominant power of lower moral quality than" man's (VI, 1), we are confronting the same central insight which we have already noted in his use of superstition, forebodings, and folkways in his fiction.

But, if the folk are fatalistic, Hardy was not, for all that his necessitarianism was so strongly flavoured with chance. The first chapter of *The Return of the Native* again provides the key. The heath "was at present a place perfectly accordant with man's nature—neither ghastly, hateful, nor ugly: neither commonplace, unmeaning, nor tame; but, like man, slighted and enduring; and withal singularly colossal and mysterious in its swarthy monotony." Of course the "at present" leaves room for a change out of accordance with man's nature; it could even be argued that, if the First Cause is of lower moral quality than man, then any talk of accordance between man and the heath (as nature) is illusory. But let us take up the possibility that such accordance is not treated as an illusion in the novel. Let us look at, say, the comment Hardy makes about Eustacia in the storm before she dies. "Never was harmony more perfect than that between the chaos of her mind and the chaos of the world without" (V, 7). We remember the imminence of "black chaos" which called forth the November bonfires. They remind man that the winter to come can be endured because the cycle of nature will bring back light and warmth.

Winter chaos is the product not just of the heath's darkness but of "the storm" which is the heath's "lover." The passage in Chapter 1 about "wild regions of obscurity" common to storms and dreams is in fact rephrased in the paragraph just before the one comparing Eustacia's mental chaos with that of nature. Primitive man fortified himself to live through the nightmare of winter, to resist the forces of disintegration which must ultimately rule him. But Eustacia, having liberated herself from the limited community around her, has no protection from winter chaos when it reinforces her own. From this point of view, we could still affirm that nature is accordant with man's nature, as long as we understand that statement to mean that all the impulses in nature have a counterpart in man, and that his problem arises from consciousness, which bids him try to regulate his internal microcosm. Hardy's romanticism lies in his stress on the correspondence; his uniqueness lies in his tempering that view of nature with varying amounts of irony, pity, and austerity.

As already emphasized, Hardy's fascination with folkways was not simply the product of nostalgia or a quaint antiquarian interest in local colour. And his insistence on the "unweeting" (unknowing) way the mummers did their parts takes on importance when we contrast it with Eustacia's very knowing desire to be part of the play. Mumming had its own customs which Eustacia violated, first by eavesdropping on the rehearsal, and second by taking part in a play the cast of which was supposed to be entirely male. Unlike Eustacia, the mummers give up their will to something older than they are. In fact, as Ruth Firor notes, this kind of drama traces back to a primitive ritual the intent of which is still easily discernible, both from the season in which it is given and from the structure of the play, in Hardy's version especially. It is a death and revival drama connected not only with the end of one year and the beginning of the next, but also with the death of life in winter and the hoped-for coming of spring (Firor, pp. 197–207).[14]

It does not matter that the "unweeting manner of performance" indicates what Hardy himself called "a fossilized survival," that is, an act which has lost its religious significance and is no longer consciously

14. See also Louis Crompton, "The Sunburnt God: Ritual and Tragic Myth in *The Return of the Native,*" *Boston University Studies in English,* 4 (Winter 1960), 233.

understood. It has survived precisely because the actors give them-selves unconsciously to the impersonal pattern.[15] Eustacia, as her last name indicates, refuses to submit, demands to live as an individual. Unlike those who give up their wills to the communal ritual, she will be rewarded as an individual, for in Hardy's typical ironic fashion she will suffer the fate of the character she impersonates, the dark Turkish Knight who is singled out as the scapegoat in the ritual pattern. In fact, when we view the events of the novel with a cosmic eye, we discover in the pattern of the seasonal rituals a dislocation which matches exactly the usual dislocation in a Hardy plot.

What Theodore Gastner calls "the Seasonal Pattern' can itself be seen as falling into a kind of archetypal plot.

> First come rites of MORTIFICATION, symbolizing the state of suspended animation which ensues at the end of the year, when one lease of life has drawn to a close and the next is not yet assured.
>
> Second come rites of PURGATION, whereby the community seeks to rid itself of all noxiousness and contagion, both physical and moral, and of all evil influences which might impair the prosperity of the coming year and thereby threaten the desired renewal of vitality.
>
> Third come rites of INVIGORATION, whereby the community at-tempts, by its own concerted and regimented effort, to galvanize its moribund condition and to procure that new lease of life which is imperative for the continuance of the topocosm.
>
> Last come rites of JUBILATION, which bespeak men's sense of relief when the new year has indeed begun and the continuance of their own lives and that of the topocosm is thereby assured.[16]

In Hardy's parallel folk pattern, we have the November bonfires, the Christmas mumming, the spring maypole, and the summer dancing.

---

15. It could further be argued that their passive submission to it is very much in tune with the religious spirit which originally lay behind the ritual. As Joseph Campbell asserts, it is a misrepresentation "to describe the seasonal festivals of so-called native peoples as efforts to control nature. . . . [T]he dominant motive in all truly religious (as opposed to black-magic) ceremonial is that of sub-mission to the inevitables of destiny—and in the seasonal festivals this motive is particularly apparent." *The Hero with a Thousand Faces*, p. 384.

16. *Thespis* (Garden City: Doubleday & Co., 1961), p. 26. In defining "topocosm," Gastner reveals how close his reading of the primitive mind is to Hardy's: "the entire complex of any given locality conceived as a living organism" (p. 17).

Significantly, however, in Hardy's plot their sequence in time is marred by the maypole's coming not in the first year with the other three rites, but in the third year of the story. Keeping strictly to the folk level, it is not hard to see why. Eustacia tries to disrupt the first ceremony by using her fire as a personal signal instead of an impersonal gesture. That she is functioning as a witch is suggested by the power she exercises over Johnny Nunsuch. " 'Put in one stick more.' The little slave went on feeding the fire as before. He seemed a mere automaton, galvanized into moving and speaking by the wayward Eustacia's will" (I, 6). Where Diggory, the later "automaton," does the heath's will, Johnny does Eustacia's will. But his mother becomes aware of this and takes steps in church.

Eustacia's part in the second seasonal ritual is even more disruptive; by breaking the taboo against female participation, she endangers "that new lease of life" which should be the next stage in the cycle. Consequently, the third ritual of invigoration is missing. Although the heath gives its sign, in the "great animation" of Eustacia's pond, Clym does not respond. "He had been standing there with another person quite silently and quite long enough to hear all this puny stir of resurrection in nature; yet he had not heard it" (III, 3). This missed step bodes ill, at least for these two characters, and those who love them. Clym is partially blinded, which is punishment enough to bring him back into harmony with the heath. Eustacia goes off alone to take part in the last rite in the sequence. Her "jubilation" at the dance is marred by only one circumstance: she is celebrating with another woman's husband. It is therefore appropriate that her death and Wildeve's are both part of the following "mortification" rite. At the same time, in Susan's death-by-fire ritual, we also have the second step in the next cycle, "purgation," in which a member of "the community" seeks to get rid of an "evil influence" which threatens "the desired renewal of vitality."

According to this "logic" we finally witness in the third spring the communal invigoration which was left out during the first year. The added Book Sixth of the novel justifies itself in this scheme, despite Hardy's own misgivings about it (expressed in a footnote, VI, 3). Diggory, who had gone underground because of Thomasin's refusal of him, reemerges to marry her as a proper fulfilment of his role.

In the spirit of Hardy's complaint about the rehabilitation of Diggory, John Patterson has pointed out that Venn's newly whitened face is characterized as "an ordinary Christian countenance," and has argued that he undergoes "a species of Christian conversion."[17] But the change is not so complete as the word "conversion" makes it seem. Pallid and tame, Diggory may fit the picture Hardy liked to give of a certain kind of Christian, but he still has an important pagan connection, as demonstrated when he sets up the maypole in front of the house in which Thomasin is staying. A different kind of vitality flows from it than ever did from the energetic reddleman:

> The next morning, when Thomasin withdrew the curtains of her bedroom window, there stood the Maypole in the middle of the green, its top cutting into the sky. It had sprung up in the night, or rather early morning, like Jack's bean-stalk. She opened the casement to get a better view of the garlands and posies that adorned it. The sweet perfume of the flowers had already spread into the surrounding air, which, being free from every taint, conducted to her lips a full measure of the fragrance received from the spire of blossoms in its midst (VI, 1).

Diggory has risen from the underground to transmit its energy in a new way. The erected maypole not only asserts his desire to create new life, it ensures Thomasin's acquiescence, her re-entry into the cycle.

Hardy's concern with the primitive rhythms of man in nature is a romantic concern, focusing as it does upon the individual and his chances for harmony with nature. But Hardy's is a new form of romanticism. Egocentric Eustacia does not, for instance, get the sympathy that the Byronic hero did in his alienation from mankind and its conventional ways. She is in conflict not with modern social conventions but with primitive traditions which are themselves romantic for Hardy and later times (see James Frazer and Carl Jung) because they connect man's spirit with nature and the cosmos. On the one hand these primitive traditions seem to be based on the facts of nature (such as seasonal changes and their effect on man), while on the other hand they are really no more than an author's subjective imaginings. Brooded on by an imagination as powerful as Hardy's, such traditions, patterns, and cycles offer the basis of a strong and convincing vision of inner and outer reality.

If we must admit that Eustacia loses sympathy by the part she plays in the cyclic pattern of Hardy's novel, we may still assert that she

---

17. *"The Return of the Native* as Antichristian Document," *Nineteenth Century Fiction,* 14 (Sept. 1959), 120.

regains it by the part she plays in an equally strong pattern based on the four elements of nature. Paradoxically, the impersonal elements enhance the very personal qualities of Eustacia. Though connected with the four seasons in Hardy's economically constructed universe, the four elements function sympathetically to Eustacia in intensifying her elevated or depressed moods.

Hardy matches seasons with appropriate elements. Summer, as we have seen, is connected with fire. Diametrically opposed is the dark earth of Winter in which the bare heath is at its most characteristic. The element connected with Spring is water, which symbolizes renewal in man, just as dark earth is connected with death or at least sleep. The winds of Autumn suggest dissolution. These correlations are of course only tendencies of a particular element to dominate in a particular season. But we shall discover that as tendencies they aid Hardy in achieving his artistic aim. "Consider the Wordsworthian dictum (the more perfectly the natural object is reproduced, the more truly poetic the picture). This reproduction is achieved by seeing into the *heart of a thing* (as rain, wind, for instance), and is realism, in fact, though . . . pursued by means of imagination" (*Life*, p. 147). Like Dickens', Hardy's "seeing to the heart" catches both the essence and the pertinent details of a scene. The imaginations of both men are concerned with the forces in conflict outside and inside man.

From what we have seen so far, we would expect fire to be the element most often connected with Eustacia.[18] In fact, Hardy told us as much: "Assuming that the souls of men and women were visible essences, you could fancy the colour of Eustacia's soul to be flame-like" (I, 7). But she cannot burn freely on the heath; its darkness inhibits her flame. Referring to her hair, Hardy indicated her dilemma: "Her appearance accorded well with this smouldering rebelliousness, and the shady splendour of her beauty was the real surface of the sad and stifled warmth within her." One way out of the darkness is to throw on more fuel and fan the fire until it flames high. Such "a blaze of love, and extinction," as we have seen, would suit Eustacia better than "long years" of "a lantern glimmer." But her connection with another

18. Many of the fire and heat images connected with Eustacia were late additions by Hardy. See Patterson's book, *The Making of "The Return of the Native."* See also another article of his, "The Poetics of *The Return of the Native*," *Modern Fiction Studies*, 6 (Autumn 1960). He connects fire with "the Promethean theme" but without much differentiation.

element indicates the possibility of another kind of escape from the dark and oppressive earth of the heath.

The other element strongly connected with Eustacia's actual experiences, as well as her inner dreams, is water. Soon after Clym first confesses his love for her, she complains that he has an easier time when they are apart than she does. "To me, who can do nothing, it has been like living under stagnant water" (III, 4). She has even earlier first shown her aversion to such water: "I am managing to exist in a wilderness, but I cannot drink from a pond" (III, 3). But she confesses, "my grandfather calls it water enough." He claims, in fact, to have lived "more than twenty years at sea on water twice as bad as that" (III, 3). The captain further reveals, "I lived seven years under water on account of " the French Revolution and its aftermath (II, 1). In contrast to him, Eustacia again shows herself unwilling to bow to the dictates of necessity. Yet, as the captain has discovered, and as Hardy insists, there is life under stagnant water. In the spring "the pool outside the bank of Eustacia's dwelling, which seemed as dead and desolate as ever to an observer who moved and made noises in his observation, would gradually disclose a state of great animation when silently watched awhile" (III, 3).

This "stir of resurrection in nature," as Hardy called it, is in contrast with a description of Eustacia's well given earlier. Some neighbours are helping to retrieve the bucket which has fallen. "Strange humid leaves, which knew nothing of the seasons of the year, and quaint-natured mosses were revealed on the well-side as the lantern descended. . . . They pulled with the greatest gentleness, till the wet bucket appeared about two yards below them, like a dead friend come to earth again" (III, 3). But it drops again with a sound like "the beating of a falling body." Hardy's intimations here about escaping the seasons and possible resurrection can be taken as one of many premonitions that Eustacia will escape her bondage to the crude cycle of life above ground only by going underwater. But, before she will accept such a fate, she must be offered pure water, as in her dream.

Her attraction to such water is evident in her insistence on lowering, against Clym's warning, the bucket he has attached to the well rope. It gets away from her but is stopped by Clym, who then looks at her hands. "One of them was bleeding; the rope had dragged off the skin." Eustacia comments, "This is the second time I have been wounded to-day." Clym's sympathy causes her to draw up her sleeve and disclose the earlier wound, caused by Susan's needle, on "her round white arm. A bright red spot appeared on its smooth surface, like a ruby on Parian marble." Both these woundings are the result of Eustacia's refusal to be content with what the heath has to offer.

Fire, as we have seen, symbolizes passion for Eustacia, as it does in summer on the heath. But in the late fall, when man's fires are a sign of his Promethean will, the element in its animate form of blood becomes associated with death on the heath, as in the "wounds in a black hide." It functions similarly, we realize, in Eustacia's two woundings, as well as in Mrs Yeobright's snakebite and her vision of the sun in August "like some merciless incendiary, brand in hand, waiting to consume her" (IV, 6). The activity of nature's energy makes it easily able to pass from the pleasant fire that warms mammals to the deadly one that burns or subdues them. The implication for man is again that balance and control are necessary, that those non-natives who do not learn to get in harmony with nature cannot expect longevity.

Like fire, water also has a dual function. Eustacia prefers deep pure well water to the contaminated pond water of the surface. Heated by the sun, the "shallower ponds" will in summer decrease "to a vaporous mud amid which the maggoty shapes of innumerable obscure creatures could be indistinctly seen, heaving and wallowing with enjoyment" (IV, 5). Away from the sun, the well is dark and cool, its water untouched by surface life. Figuratively speaking, it is in such a realm that Eustacia makes her first search for a true hero (in her dream), as well as her last effort to recoup her earthly fortunes. In water lies both an escape and a kind of justification for this romantic protagonist.

Eustacia's dream is not only elaborate but very convincing, whether compared with our own dreams or judged on the principles laid down by Freud. It is an important dream, what Jung calls a "big dream," that is one which in its clarity and impact impresses the dreamer as saying something significant. "Such an elaborately developed, perplexing, exciting dream was certainly never dreamed by a girl in Eustacia's situation before. It had as many ramifications as the Cretan labyrinth, as many fluctuations as the Northern Lights, as much colour as a parterre in June, and was as crowded with figures as a coronation" (II, 3). The labyrinth is an elaborate man-made construction, as is the coronation, in another sense, both to be contrasted with the Northern Lights. The parterre, with its arranged flowerbeds, is of course a shaping of nature, and some such mixing of nature and man's designs is evident in the dream episode Hardy gives us.

There was . . . gradually evolved from its transformation scenes a less extravagant episode, in which the heath dimly appeared behind the general brilliancy of the action. She was dancing to wondrous music, and her partner was the man in silver armour who had accompanied her through the previous fantastic changes, the visor of his helmet being closed. The mazes of the dance were ecstatic. Soft whispering came into her ear from under the radiant helmet, and she felt like a woman in Paradise. Suddenly these two wheeled out from the mass of dancers, dived into one of the pools of the heath, and came out somewhere beneath into an iridescent hollow, arched with rainbows. "It must be here," said the voice by her side, and blushingly looking up she saw him removing his casque to kiss her. At that moment there was a cracking noise, and his figure fell into fragments like a pack of cards (II, 3).

"The mazes of the dance" can be connected with the "Cretan labyrinth" above, and both bear some relation to the "transformation scenes" which characterize the dream. The motion, change, and mystery of them speak to something in Eustacia's nature. Her highest moment in waking life comes in the scene most nearly parallel to this "ecstatic" dream dance. Hardy reports of Eustacia that at the gipsying, "the enchantment of the dance surprised her." Like the dream dance, it is described as a "maze of motion." The result is interesting. "Eustacia floated round and round on Wildeve's arm, her face rapt and statuesque; her soul had passed away from and forgotten her features, which were left empty and quiescent, as they always are when feeling goes beyond their register" (IV, 3). This intimation of a higher sphere is also present in the dream, where the "Northern Lights" of Hardy's prologue can be matched with the rainbows in the dream episode. Both lights and rainbow are clearly connected with the idea of "Paradise."

The odd thing to waking consciousness (though perfectly fitting in the dream world) is the fact that Eustacia dives *down* to come *up* in an "iridescent hollow, arched with rainbows," her paradise. In any case, the climax of the dream follows: her partner with "the radiant helmet" says "It must be here," which Eustacia in the dream understands immediately: "Blushingly looking up she saw him removing his casque to kiss her." Freud aside, we outside the dream may be permitted to wonder why her partner says "must," with its sense of necessity, and also whether we can really be so sure what "it" refers to.

Tantalizingly, the dream ends before Eustacia sees her partner's face; waking, however, she quickly decides the man would have turned out to be Clym (whom she had heard without seeing that evening). In her daydreams, therefore, Paris becomes heaven or paradise, and Clym, as he says ironically later, becomes "wrapped in a sort of golden halo" like "an adorable, delightful, distracting hero." Her most obviously mistaken action is taking the part of knight in armour to find a partner who in her dream had appropriately worn the armour and been the initiator himself. Nor are Eustacia's distortions of the dream our only clues.

In folk tradition, as Ruth Firor notes, (pp. 35–36), there are several omens embodied in the dream. Three good omens at its beginning are matched by three bad omens at the end. The most obvious of the latter is the figure of the man falling "into fragments like a pack of cards." The overtones in Hardy's use of cards become clear in a later variation on the image. Cooling down after his impetuous decision to marry Eustacia, Clym has second thoughts: "but the card was laid, and he determined to abide by the game" (III, 5). The reference in the dream can also be taken as the ending of a game of cards. A more likely image would seem to be to armour made out of cards, like a card house falling down. But, if we allow the connection with a game of chance to take us to the dicing on the heath, we can connect the crack in the die which ends Wildeve's gamble with the crack in the figure which ends Eustacia's game. Just as we saw that Wildeve loses out to the heath, so we can see the intimation that Eustacia will too, when the impingement of reality with its coincidences (bad fortune) destroys for her the possibility of finding a "distracting hero." In this light, the assertion, "It must be here" will take on a more sinister meaning.

The mazes of the dance on the heath turn for Eustacia into a labyrinth from which she cannot escape. Unlike Mrs. Yeobright, who was physically unable to evade the overpowering vitality of the heath, Eustacia is vulnerable because of the psychological limitations of her romantic ego. Of her possible saviour, Wildeve, she moans, "He's not *great* enough for me to give myself to" (V, 7). Mrs. Yeobright, in her exhaustion, sees an ironic reminder of human limitations:

> While she looked a heron arose on that side of the sky and flew on with his face towards the sun. He had come dripping wet from some pool in the valleys, and as he flew the edges and lining of his wings, his thighs, and his breast were so caught by the bright sunbeams that he appeared as if formed of burnished silver. Up in the zenith where

he was seemed a free and happy place, away from all contact with the earthly ball to which she was pinioned; and she wished that she could arise uncrushed from its surface and fly as he flew then (IV, 6).

The heron can also be taken as an image of Eustacia's dreams, his silver like that of her knight, his movement toward the zenith reminiscent of rising to her heaven, and his wet body undaunted by the pool from which he has come.

But Eustacia's reality is different. Shortly before her death, Hardy tells us that "the wings of her soul were broken by the cruel obstructiveness of all about her" (V, 7). Unable to fly out or, as a realist might say, no longer able to sustain the romantic illusions that have made life tolerable for her, Eustacia decides that "it must be here," that she will force her destiny by diving into eternity through one of the pools on the heath, as in her dream. Hearing a splash, Clym and Wildeve rush to the pool.

> The light from Yeobright's lamp shed a flecked and agitated radiance across the weir-pool, revealing to the ex-engineer the tumbling courses of the currents from the hatches above. Across this gashed and puckered mirror a dark body was slowly borne by one of the backward currents.
> "O, my darling!" exclaimed Wildeve in an agonized voice; and, without showing sufficient presence of mind even to throw off his great-coat, he leaped into the boiling caldron (V, 9).

The only reminder of the dream imagery here is the radiance shed by Clym's lantern. One other image is worth comment, though, "the boiling caldron."[19] This phrase harks back to the November bonfires a year earlier: "Some were Maenades, with winy faces and blown hair. These tinctured the silent bosom of the clouds above them and lit up their ephemeral caves, which seemed thenceforth to become scalding caldrons" (I, 3). This description unites fire and water through the image of the witch who uses both elements in her magic spells. But, where the fire transforms by destroying, as Susan's does by consuming the image offered to it, water transforms by at once killing and preserving. Eustacia in her waking life is concerned mainly with the fire of passion. But, in her dream and in her death, she is much more involved with water, being able finally to triumph through it:

19. As Patterson points out in his book, the word "caldron' was a late (1912) revision. See his comment on the deaths of Eustacia and Wildeve (p. 146).

> Eustacia, . . . as she lay there still in death, eclipsed all her living phases. Pallor did not include all the quality of her complexion, which seemed more than whiteness; it was almost light. The expression of her finely carved mouth was pleasant, as if a sense of dignity had just compelled her to leave off speaking. Eternal rigidity had seized upon it in a momentary transition between fervour and resignation. Her black hair was looser now than . . . before, and surrounded her brow like a forest. The stateliness of look which had been almost too marked for a dweller in a country domicile had at last found an artistically happy background (V, 9).

The light in Eustacia's face, connected as it is with *phase* and *eclipse,* reminds us of the earlier moon imagery associated with her. Then "she was given . . . to sudden fits of gloom, one of the phases of the night-side of sentiment which she knew too well for her years" (I, 7); now she has transcended darkness.

The moon is also connected with water, the more so in Hardy's scheme by the transformations connected with both. Eustacia's soul "passed away from . . . her features" in the gipsying dance. But, its "wings" broken by her environment, she cannot hope for it to carry her upward in life. Rather she must achieve in death the "perfection" of which she thought herself capable.[20] That perfection, as indicated at the very beginning of the "Queen of the Night" chapter, was at no less a level than "divinity." Eustacia is not the first romantic protagonist, nor will she be the last, to exchange imperfect life for the perfection of death.

20. Patterson notes (p. 87) that in the manuscript, Eustacia in her last outburst says "I was capable of perfection," rather than simply "of much."

Chapter Eight

Artist and Magician

As a novelist concerned with the irrational, Joseph Conrad had affinities with both Hardy and Dickens. Perhaps because he was a religious skeptic like Hardy, he was preoccupied as Hardy was with those who are close to nature, sharing the primitive religious apprehensions of uncivilized man. Similarly, because he was concerned, like Dickens, with the craft of the novel, Conrad was fascinated by the same primitive figure that Dickens used, the magician who controls the mysteries of the craft. Confessedly influenced by Dickens, Conrad may well have picked up some of his own interest in fairy-tale motifs from "the master."[1] Other similarities are more obviously temperamental: Dickens confided to Bulwer-Lytton, "If you were the Magician's servant instead of the Magician, these potent spirits would get the better of you; but you *are* the Magician, and they don't, and you make them serve your purpose" (*Letters,* III, 218). Conrad spoke of the dangers of being a literary magician in the preface to *A Personal Record*. Then he commented. "In order to move others deeply we must deliberately allow ourselves to be carried away beyond the bounds of our normal sensibility. . . . But the danger lies in the writer becoming the victim of his own exaggeration" (pp. xix-xx). This he pledged not to do.

On the other hand, like Dickens, Conrad is quite willing to use a superstition to give resonance to both theme and plot, as we shall dis-

1. *A Personal Record* (1912). Volume Nine of the Twenty-Volume Medallion edition of the Works of Joseph Conrad (London: The Gresham Publishing Co., 1925), p. 124. This edition was printed from the same plates as the Dent Collected Edition (1923). All citations to works by Conrad will be to this edition, except those to *Lord Jim.*

cover in considering *The Nigger of the Narcissus*. Whereas Dickens could justify his tight plotting and coincidences with references to Providence, Conrad, like Hardy, had to resort to devices such as ritual and folklore to achieve the same effect. These effects are important because they are allied with the strong bent toward the archetypal that Conrad shared with Dickens and Hardy. I shall approach the archetypal level later in this chapter and in the two that follow, but, as an introduction to it, we need to turn our attention to Conrad's notion of the kind of imagination he had. Toward the end of his life he stated, "The romantic feeling of reality was in me an inborn faculty. This in itself may be a curse but when disciplined by a sense of personal responsibility and a recognition of the hard facts of existence shared with the rest of mankind becomes but a point of view from which the very shadows of life appear endowed with an internal glow. And such romanticism is not a sin. It is none the worse for the knowledge of truth. It only tries to make the best of it, hard as it may be; and in this hardness discovers a certain aspect of beauty."[2] In this important confession lies a paradigm first of Conrad's sea life, begun in the glamour of Marseilles and ending in the mastery of a craft, and second of his fiction with its constant testing of romantic ideals by the realism of hard work.

His attempt to give full due to the demands of inner and outer nature fulfilled a strong need in Conrad; it was an attempt to harmonize two poles of interest which were in his case quite antithetical. The tension of balancing the demands of romantic ego with the demands of the physical world and the community of man gave Conrad his characteristic fictional problem and allowed him to achieve his characteristic successes. Part of his achievement lay in shaping this tension so that it informed the very structure of his three early masterpieces, *The Nigger of the Narcissus* (1897), *Heart of Darkness* (1899), and *Lord Jim* (1900). Tentatively in the first and consummately in the next two, he used a narrator committed to the world and society as a commentator on the almost completely self-absorbed characters of James Wait, Mr. Kurtz, and Lord Jim.

Captain Marlow, the narrator of *Lord Jim*, is practically an incarnation of the human values Conrad had enshrined in the preface to *The Nigger of the Narcissus*. There Conrad had twice extolled the virtues of "solidarity," his term for the force "which binds men to each other

2. Author's Note (1920) to *Within the Tides* (1915), pp. vii–viii.

and all mankind to the visible world." Similarly, Marlow speaks of the "fellowship of the craft" of the sea, of "the feeling that binds a man to a child," and of "the solidarity of the craft."[3] More important for his relation to Jim, Marlow believes that "the real significance of crime is in its being a breach of faith with the community of mankind" (p. 135). Jim's desertion of the *Patna* is, of course, a crime in exactly those terms. But Jim's determination to face up to the consequences of his deed, his attempt to uphold, somehow, his integrity in the face of the evidence, shakes Marlow. In talking with Jim, Marlow comes to realize, he had "hoped for the impossible—for the laying of what is the most obstinate ghost of man's creation, of the uneasy doubt uprising like a mist, secret and gnawing like a worm, and more chilling than the certitude of death—the doubt of the sovereign power enthroned in a fixed standard of conduct" (p. 43). Only faith can overcome doubt, and Marlow is sophisticated enough to realize that there is no objective validating of a belief. Later in the novel, speaking of the bond with the home land, Marlow suggests that Jim also "felt confusedly but powerfully, the demand of some such truth or some such illusion—I don't care how you call it, there is so little difference, and the difference means so little" (p. 192). This is the pragmatist Marlow's version of a philosophic concern to which we shall return both in this chapter and in the next.

As seaman, Conrad shared Marlow's allegiance to solidarity. Even as artist, in some moods he could agree. But in other moods he saw the question differently. First of all, as he argued the case in his "Familiar Preface" to *A Personal Record,* there is no easy way of judging what goes on when "an artist" starts "pursuing . . . a creative aim. In that interior world where his thought and his emotions go seeking for the experience of imagined adventures, there are no policemen, no law, no pressure of circumstance or dread of opinion to keep him within bounds." On the other hand, being internal, the adventures and temptations of the artist cannot be judged by law. As a result "all intellectual and artistic ambitions are permissible, up to and even beyond the limit of prudent sanity." But, wondered Conrad, "is it such a very mad presumption to believe in the sovereign power of one's art, to try for other means, for other ways of affirming this belief in the deeper appeal of

3. *Lord Jim* (New York: Rinehart and Co., 1957), pp. 111, 113. Robert B. Heilman, the editor of this edition, has used the text of the collected edition, but consulted three other editions. See his Textual Note, pp. 365–69.

one's work?" (p. xx). To the mariner's necessary belief in "the sovereign power enthroned in a fixed standard of conduct" we may then add the artist's necessary belief in "the sovereign power of one's art." Hedged though this second power is within the realm of the imagination, it is yet capable of encompassing more than the standard of conduct. Or so Conrad asserted at the end of Chapter 1 of *A Personal Record*. "Only in men's imagination does every truth find an effective and undeniable existence. Imagination, not invention, is the supreme master of art as of life" (p. 25).

As a writer Conrad did not find the task of tapping the imagination an easy one. Nor did he believe it should be. In a letter written at the very beginning of his own career as novelist, he had counselled another beginner that, to give his work imaginative life, the writer must squeeze out of himself "every sensation, every thought, every image,—mercilessly, without reserve and without remorse: . . . must search the darkest corners of [his] heart, the most remote recesses of [his] brain." The result will, of course, be that at the end of a day's work the writer feels "exhausted, emptied of every sensation and every thought, with a blank mind and an aching heart, with the notion that there is nothing" left in him.[4] From Conrad's complaints and the nature of his fiction, we may speculate that at its best his labour had such an aim and such an effect, both on him and on the work produced. In a letter to Edward Garnett in 1920, Conrad gave to this state the appropriate name of "creative darkness."[5]

Conrad did not enter his creative darkness for purposes of comfort or self-deception. As he wrote his friend John Galsworthy, in a passage of advice very like some of Dickens' advice to Wilkie Collins, "in a book you should love the idea and be scrupulously faithful to your conception of life. There lies the honour of the writer, not in the fidelity to his personages. You must never allow them to decoy you out of yourself. As against your people you must preserve an attitude of perfect indifference, the part of creative power" (*Life and Letters*, 1, 301). In practice Conrad was much more aloof than Dickens, in life and in art. "I have a positive horror of losing even for one moving

---

4. Letter to Edward Noble, October 28, 1895. G. Jean-Aubry, ed., *Joseph Conrad Life and Letters,* in two vols. (New York: Doubleday, Page & Co., 1927), I, 183. Future citations in the text will be to *Life and Letters*.

5. Edward Garnett, ed., *Letters from Joseph Conrad 1895–1924* (New York: The Bobbs-Merrill Co., 1962), p. 273. This edition is printed from the plates of the original 1928 edition.

moment that full possession of myself which is the first condition of good service" (*Personal Record,* xix). Therefore he would not, or so he claimed, become Dickens' kind of magician. "Yes! I, too, would like to hold the magic wand giving that command over laughter and tears which is declared to be the highest achievement of imaginative literature. Only, to be a great magician one must surrender oneself to occult and irresponsible powers, either outside or within one's breast" (xviii). While there can be no doubt of Conrad's sense of responsibility, neither can there be of the strength of his imagination. Subjects and incidents in his fiction often border on the occult.

Just as Dickens was aware that an author can function as a magician or as providence, so Conrad was aware not only of the temptation to be a magician, but also, because of his Catholic background, of the mediation possible between the individual spirit and some greater realm. In a letter written in 1908 to his friend E. V. Lucas, Conrad referred both to the secular character of a writer and to the religious nature of his most serious work. " 'A man should not be tame' says the Spanish proverb, and I would say: An author is not a monk. Yet a man who puts forth the secret of his imagination to the world accomplishes, as it were, a religious rite" (*Life and Letters,* II, 89). Eleven years earlier, in his first serious work, *The Nigger of the Narcissus,* Conrad had forced his title character, James Wait, into an experience which several critics have seen as involving not only a ritual but a probing of religious experience.[6]

Although I would like to begin by noting Conrad's scorn of conventional religious motives in that novel, we shall end by examining the primitive initiation rite he favoured over the suspect Christian one. *The Nigger of the Narcissus* contains Conrad's first definitive attempt to work out the central theme of his best work, the plight of egocentric man in a ruthless universe. Doomed to die, Wait refuses to accept his fate and manages by the force of his ego to enlist the sympathy of most of the crew in his resistance. The scene in which they rescue him from the cabin where he has been trapped below water is crowded with images suggesting birth and a kind of parody of resurrection, grave robbing: "Belfast plunged in head and shoulders and groped viciously . . . 'I've got 'im!' [But] he stuck half-way, . . . we

6. Notably Vernon Young and Albert J. Guerard whose views on the novel are included in *The Art of Joseph Conrad: A Critical Symposium,* ed. by R. W. Stallman (1960).

swung him up. His breath whistled" (p. 70). "He was screaming and
knocking below us with the hurry of a man prematurely shut up in a
coffin" (p. 66). "He was as quiet as a dead man inside a grave" (p. 69).
"On the very brink of eternity we tottered all together with concealing
and absurd gestures, like a lot of drunken men embarrassed with a
stolen corpse" (p. 71). Later, the ship righted and Wait obviously
dying, the crew cannot gainsay his assertions that he will live; they wait
on him assiduously. "He was so utterly wrong about himself that one
could not but suspect him of having access to some source of supernatural knowledge. . . . We had the air of being initiated in some infamous mysteries. . . . We lied to him with gravity, with emotion, with
unction, as if performing some moral trick with a view to an eternal
reward" (p. 139). If Conrad is working at a ritual here it is a parody
of the one that offers man salvation through following the pattern of
Christ's experience.

   This parody, which might be taken as a means merely of derogating
Wait, also reflects an anti-Christian bias in the novel. That bias is
evident at the beginning of Chapter 4: "On men reprieved by its dis-
dainful mercy, the immortal sea confers in its justice the full privilege
of desired unrest. Through the perfect wisdom of its grace they are not
permitted to meditate at ease upon the complicated and acrid savour
of existence" (p. 90). Clearly Conrad's "immortal sea" bears little
resemblance either to a benevolent God or to earlier Romantic pantheism. Despite the hostility of the environment which dominates the
novel, Conrad did provide an example of a viable relation to it in the
person of the taciturn and stoical Singleton. But, before looking at the
positive side of that relation, we must examine the negative. Halfway
through the novel, Singleton becomes aware that he has reached old
age: "he looked upon the immortal sea with the awakened and groping
perception of its heartless might: he saw it unchanged, black and foam-
ing under the eternal scrutiny of the stars" (p. 99). The conception is
that of Conrad the realistic Victorian mechanist.

   The same theme appeared in several letters Conrad wrote to his
friend R. B. Cunninghame Graham, shortly after *The Nigger of the
Narcissus* was published. In an effort to break through Graham's
idealist attitude toward this novel, and toward life, Conrad developed
his pessimist-materialist views in a manner worthy of Hardy. Imagining
the universe as a machine, he scorned Cunninghame Graham's supposed "celestial oil" as a means of making it run right. He continued,
"The most withering thought is that the infamous thing has made

itself: made itself without thought, without conscience, without foresight, without eyes, without heart. . . . It knits us in and it knits us out. It has knitted time, space, pain, death, corruption, despair and all the illusions,—and nothing matters. I'll admit however that to look at the remorseless process is sometimes amusing" (*Life and Letters,* I, 216). Exaggerated though this view may be for the purpose of pricking Cunninghame Graham, it emphasizes the immortal and impersonal nature of the cosmos, as Conrad also did in *The Nigger of the Narcissus*; it seems to me fair then to take it as a heavily underlined version of Conrad's actual philosophic position.[7]

Like Hardy, Conrad was too perceptive to deny the partial truth of Victorian science, rationalism, and materialism. Like Hardy also, he responded both with a romantic heart and an austere eye to these insights of the second half of the nineteenth century. The parallel can be carried further: just as Conrad with *The Nigger of the Narcissus* in 1897, so Hardy with *The Return of The Native* in 1876, for the first time tried to express fully his view of man's place in the cosmos. The results are surprisingly similar. Both writers felt obliged to withhold or withdraw sympathy from the characters with pronounced egos and individuality. Instead, both gave sympathy to those without individuality or self-consciousness, Hardy to his peasants, Conrad to his seamen. And both reacted so because of the view they took of nature as a hard, impersonal force which has no room for soft illusions. Though both in later novels went on to deal admirably with the efforts of an individual to develop his highest capacities, in these early novels both were interested not in evolving consciousness, but in unconscious harmony with the patterns of nature.

Like Hardy, Conrad drew from the folklore of his environment, the sea, a pattern that gives shape to his narrative. Further, he insisted like Hardy on the unconscious nature of anyone who is in tune with such a pattern. In *The Nigger of the Narcissus* the unconscious person is Singleton and the kind of folklore is a particular superstition of the sea: that a mortally sick man will linger until the land is sighted, after which the ship will not get a favourable wind until he dies. Behind this folklore of the sea lies an impersonal acceptance of death that scorns Wait's hysterical inability to face his mortality. Not only Singleton but Conrad judges Wait and the crew that comes under his spell.

7. For his continuing assertion of the position to his friend see *Life and Letters,* I, 222 and 226.

Although Wait is a more prominent character, Singleton is equally central to Conrad's theme and is first in his allegiance. In his reply to Cunninghame Graham's comment on the novel Conrad is unequivocal: "You say: 'Singleton, with an education.' . . . what education? If it is the knowledge of how to live, my man essentially possessed it. He was in perfect accord with his life. . . . Would you seriously, of malice prepense, cultivate in that unconscious man the power to think? Then he would become conscious,—and much smaller,—and very unhappy. Now he is simple and great like an elemental force" (*Life and Letters,* I, 214–15). That this defence is not just an after-the-fact development is clear from several passages in the novel. The key word, "unconscious," for instance, is twice applied to Singleton. And early in the book Conrad indicates the kind of knowledge Singleton possesses. "He said, with unmoved face,—'Ship! . . . Ships are all right. It is the men in them!' He went on smoking in the profound silence. The wisdom of half a century spent in listening to the thunder of the waves had spoken unconsciously through his old lips" (p. 24, ellipses Conrad's). Later, in his second attempt to enlighten the crew about Wait, Singleton's primitive role is made even clearer: "He was old enough to remember slavers, bloody mutinies, pirates perhaps. . . . His moustache and beard stirred. He chewed words, mumbled behind tangled white hairs; incomprehensible and exciting, like an oracle behind a veil. . . . —'Stop ashore—sick.—Instead—bringing all this head wind. Afraid. The sea will have her own.—Die in sight of land. Always so. They know it'. . . . He seemed to wake up from a dream. . . . He radiated unspeakable wisdom, hard unconcern, the chilling air of resignation . . . profound and unconscious" (pp. 129–30).

As oracle, Singleton suspends his individuality, and this enables him, like Diggory Venn during the gambling scene in *The Return of the Native,* to make contact with the impersonal forces that finally control man's destiny. Interestingly, he even shares with Venn distinctive bodily ornamentation: "Old Singleton, the oldest able seaman in the ship, set apart on the deck right under the lamps, stripped to the waist, tattooed like a cannibal chief all over his powerful chest and enormous biceps. Between the blue and red patterns his white skin gleamed like satin. . . . With his spectacles and a venerable white beard, he resembled a learned and savage patriarch, the incarnation of barbarian wisdom serene in the blasphemous turmoil of the world" (p. 6). Conrad's attitude toward "barbarian" wisdom is similar to Hardy's notion that the "barbaric idea which confuses persons and things" is "common to the highest imaginative genius—that of the poet" (*Life of Hardy,* p. 230). In *The Mirror of the Sea,* Conrad voiced a similar observation: "Looking back after much love and much trouble, the instinct of primitive man, who seeks to personify the forces of Nature for his affection and for his fear, is awakened again in the breast of one civilized beyond that stage even in his infancy" (p. 71). Conrad's own philosophy also contained a belief similar to that from which Singleton acts. "I think that the proper wisdom is to will what the gods will without, perhaps, being certain what their will is" (*Personal Record,* xxi). The seaman works hard, of course, to manage what he can see and use around him, but he knows that his experience will always be of the surface of the sea; below it lie depths and forces that his conscious will cannot fathom.

This depth contains what Jung called the archetypes. Reading certain myths and fairy tales, Jung claimed, we will find elements that strike us as having "a distinctly numinous character which can only be described as 'spiritual', if 'magical' is too strong a word."[8] Why these terms might apply to an archetypal image (as opposed to the simple memory image of, say, a sunny day at the beach) becomes understandable in Jung's elaboration of primitive thought processes:

> It is not enough for the primitive to see the sun rise and set; this external observation must at the same time be a psychic happening: the sun in its course must represent the fate of a god or hero who, in the last analysis, dwells nowhere except in the soul of man. All the mythologized processes of nature, such as summer and winter, the phases of the moon, the rainy seasons, and so forth, are in no sense allegories [conscious elaborations] of these objective experiences; rather they are symbolic expressions of the inner, unconscious drama of the psyche which becomes accessible to man's consciousness by way of projection—that is, mirrored in the events of nature. The projection is so fundamental that it has taken several thousand years of civilization to detach it in some measure from its outer object.[9]

Again we can remember Hardy's connection of the primitive religious view with the artistically imaginative one. Jung's perspective suggests that Hardy may have been striving to heal a breach he felt modern

8. "On the Nature of the Psyche" in Vol. 8 of Jung's *Collected Works.* Quoted here from *The Basic Writings of C. G. Jung,* p. 75.
9. "Archetypes of the Collective Unconscious," from *The Basic Writings,* p. 289.

man had made in his own nature by centering his conception of himself in his conscious will and intellect.

Just as Clym Yeobright foolishly sought to bring modern philosophy to the heath, only to be pulled down into the natural sphere, so Conrad had come to follow the will of the gods "without, perhaps, being certain what their will is." Both Hardy and Conrad were concerned to put their human characters in contact with the ancient, primitive side of nature to discover what would happen. In both *The Return of the Native* and *The Nigger of the Narcissus,* the unsophisticated toiler who accepts his fate and labours within it provides a ground bass for the painful thrashings of too-conscious and too-vocal modern man. This opposition, which is actually a confrontation in the two novels, presents a conflict which undoubtedly went on in the minds of the two writers, concerned as both were with the opposition between conscious and unconscious thought, conscious as each was that he had lost touch with a desirable "natural" (unconscious) ability to relate to the feelings and religious impulses of less sophisticated types with whom each had been associated.

Writing during the nineties, neither Hardy nor Conrad appears to have been aware that Freud was publishing his discovery of the unconscious, although Hardy knew Von Hartmann's book *The Philosophy of the Unconscious* (1869).[10] Yet both novelists can be taken as examples of an attempt to rectify the dilemma that resulted when conscious rejection of organized religion robbed experience of its spiritual overtones. Without culturally supported symbols, they had to rely on those which the culture considered beneath it (pagan rituals, oracles) or on Christian symbols transposed (rebirth confused with grave robbing). Conrad especially seems to have been aware that there were secrets to be discovered inside man's nature, and that those who possessed esoteric knowledge were often willing to pass it on.

We can take as an example Singleton in his role not only as oracle but as mentor, or what Jung called wise old man. Both oracle and wise old man give good advice, but the latter also acts as a person and a practical guide. "Tall and fatherly" (p. 14), Singleton teaches young Charley knots, yells "Look out for yourselves!" (p. 57) when the *Narcissus* is about to be hit by a huge wave, and stays at the wheel

10. Hardy mentions Von Hartmann in a letter in 1902 (p. 315 of *Life*). See Lancelot Whyte, *The Unconscious Before Freud* (Garden City: Doubleday and Co., 1962).

throughout the period when the ship is heeled over. In these actions he shows his affinities not only with numerous characters in Conrad's later novels but also with the character in Conrad's own youth who served as a model for most of them.

As characterized by G. Jean-Aubry in *Life and Letters*, Dominic Cervoni was "Conrad's true initiator into the life of the sea.... Dominic was the mentor of this young Telemachus; a mentor of a rather unusual kind, with a contempt for law, an ardent, romantic scepticism and a love of adventure which found an echo in the restless heart of his pupil" (I, 36). The validity of Aubry's portrayal is attested to not only by his friendship with Conrad but also by Conrad's own picture of Cervoni in *The Mirror of the Sea*, in which the concept of initiation and the image of Ulysses are both important. In Conrad's portrait, Cervoni as mentor is played down, while Cervoni as initiated magician is played up. "On board the *Tremolino*, wrapped up in a black *caban*, the picturesque cloak of Mediterranean seamen, with those massive moustaches and his remorseless eyes set off by the shadow of the deep hood, he looked piratical and monkish and darkly initiated into the most awful mysteries of the sea" (p. 164). At a key moment in the adventure of the *Tremolino*, Cervoni realizes that the only way to escape the Spanish coast guard is to smash the ship with its cargo of contraband arms. This suggestion takes the young Conrad aback. " 'Can you?' I murmured, fascinated by the black hood turned immovably over the stern, as if in unlawful communion with that old sea of magicians, slave-dealers, exiles, and warriors, the sea of legends and terrors, where the mariners of remote antiquity used to hear the restless shade of an old wanderer weep aloud in the dark. 'I know a rock,' whispered the initiated voice within the hood secretly" (p. 176). With the two safe on shore, at the end of the chapter Conrad sums up with a comparison of Cervoni to Ulysses that again brings up the initiate theme.

> Dominic Cervoni takes his place in my memory by the side of the legendary wanderer on the sea of marvels and terrors, by the side of the fatal and impious adventurer, to whom the evoked shade of the soothsayer predicted a journey inland with an oar on his shoulder, till he met men who had never set eyes on ships and oars. It seems to me I can see them side by side in the twilight of an arid land, the unfortunate possessors of the secret lore of the sea, ... surrounded by silent and curious men: even as I, too, having turned

my back upon the sea, am bearing those few pages in the twilight, with the hope of finding in an inland valley the silent welcome of some patient listener (p. 183).

Elaborate though it is, this threefold comparison provides some important insights into Conrad, the artist of memory and imagination.

As one who had been initiated, Conrad tried to pass on not just Marlow's respectable doctrine of hard work and fidelity, but also here explicitly Cervoni's unrespectable knowledge of "the secret lore of the sea," the fruit of "unlawful communion with that old sea of magicians." The possessor of such secrets is doomed because after a life of adventure he has knowledge which makes it difficult if not impossible for him to lead a normal life. Ulysses faced the dangers and seductions of the legendary Mediterranean, and even journeyed to Hades. Cervoni was a pirate and smuggler, and knew what it was to smash a brave ship on a hidden shoal. Conrad had also adventured to the romantic places of the world, smuggled and smashed a ship with Cervoni, and had also found it hard to settle on land.[11]

Nor does Conrad's relation to Cervoni and Ulysses exhaust the list of paradigms. In his confessed identification with another older man, the fictional Don Quixote, we can discover a slightly different initiation into the realm of the imagination. For wanting to go to sea, Conrad was, at the age of fifteen, termed "an incorrigible, hopeless Don Quixote" (*A Personal Record,* p. 44). Several paragraphs in *A Personal Record* are concerned with the Don. One characteristic attributed to him could well apply to Conrad's Lord Jim: "After reading so many romances he desired naively to escape with his very body from the intolerable reality of things" (p. 36). As mentor, however, the Don more obviously had an importance to Conrad himself: "He rides forth, his head encircled by a halo—the patron saint of all lives spoiled or saved by the irresistible grace of imagination" (p. 37).

Of the numerous examples that might be given of Don Quixote's desire to escape the unimaginative, material reality around him, we may focus on the episode of "The Cave of Montesinos" (Part II, Chapter 22). In that episode, Don Quixote is lowered into a *sima,*

11. Conrad wrote of at least one character who had a similar problem, Peyrol of *The Rover* (1923). Based on Cervoni, Peyrol has also more than a little of the older Conrad in him. As the Prospero, in this last of Conrad's novels, he functions as the aging magician, ambivalent toward his power and his knowledge. In another mode, Stein figures as a similar character in *Lord Jim.*

that is a "deep cavern, an abyss, a chasm."[12] There he dreams that he meets chivalric heroes connected with the past of the area and also that he sees his lady Dulcinea in her enchantment. By one of her followers he sends her his vow to persist in his efforts to free her from the spell she is in. At this point he is hauled back up, asleep, and when awakened by his friends insists that what he dreamed really happened. He is angry with them for taking him away from that marvellous place: "Now truly do I understand how it is that all the pleasures of life pass away like a shadow or a dream" (p. 655). As the editor comments, this lament contains a reference to Calderon's famous epigram, "La vida es sueño y sueño de sueño"—life is a dream and dream of a dream (p. 1001). This concept and Calderon's phrasing of it were both favourites of Conrad's. In *A Personal Record,* after referring again to the charge of quixotism levelled against him in his youth and to the long hard years he put in at sea, Conrad concluded that he had the right to assert "that all these years [at sea] have not been altogether a dream" (p. 110).

As irony this statement effectively understates Conrad's past labour in the British Merchant Marine. But, in the light of the theme of imagination, which we have seen in both *The Mirror of the Sea* and *A Personal Record,* Conrad's intent may be paraphrased more solemnly: No, those years at sea were not altogther a dream, but they seem like one now; if that seaman has managed to justify his existence, it has been by the labour of his mind and pen, putting down on paper a truth so individual and subjective that it could have life in no other way.

Professing not to be a magician, Conrad yet found it necessary to write of visits to the other world in *Heart of Darkness*[13] and, as we shall see, in *Lord Jim.* Put more prosaically, Conrad learned not only the external craft of the sea, but also the deeper art of internal scrutiny, which the lonely sea encourages in its conscious initiates. The positive benefits of this knowledge he then voiced in the early letter of advice already quoted from. The writer should "treat events only as illustrative of human sensation, —as the outward sign of inward feelings, . . . imagination . . . should be used to create human souls: to disclose

12. Miguel de Cervantes Saavedra, *Don Quixote,* trans. by Samuel Putnam (New York: Viking Press, 1949), pp. 654 and 1001, footnote 12.

13. Cf. articles by Lillian Feder, and Robert O. Evans in *The Art of Joseph Conrad.* See also Albert J. Guerard, *Conrad the Novelist* (Cambridge: Harvard University Press, 1958), Chapter 1, "The Journey Within."

human hearts" (*Life and Letters*, I, 183). In Conrad's mind there existed a distinction betwen the heart, to which he thought art should be directed, and the emotions, which he believed it should not exploit. "An historian of hearts is not an historian of emotions, yet he penetrates further, restrained as he may be, since his aim is to reach the very fount of laughter and tears" (*Personal Record,* xxi). The literary magician seeks to play on emotions, the true artist seeks to move hearts. The magician gives us thrills, easy tears, and superficial characters. The artist may not make us cry, but he shows us more of the characters he creates. The same writer can, of course, be both artist and magician, as Dickens was. Similarly, in the second half of *Lord Jim,* it can be argued that Conrad himself became a magician as well as an artist. Marlow gives us the clue in his mistrust of the sensational world of Patusan. The characters in that land "exist as if under an enchanter's wand. But the figure round which all these are grouped—[Jim] lives, and I am not certain of him. No magician's wand can immobilise him under my eyes. He is one of us" (pp. 286–87). In the next chapter, we shall see how Conrad, with the mixed feelings of both artist and magician, created Patusan as another world in which to give his hero full scope to work out his romantic destiny.

Chapter Nine

Lord Jim

Of the four novelists closely considered in this book, Conrad was the most self-consciously artistic. Partly this was historical: he lived during a time when the novel was beginning to be taken seriously as a literary form. But more to the point, as we saw in the last chapter, Conrad was temperamentally self-conscious, obliged to scrutinize motives and methods. The first sentence of the preface to *The Nigger of the Narcissus* could be said to stand as a paradigm not only of his aesthetics but of his psychology and philosophy: "A work that aspires . . . to the condition of art should carry its justification in every line." Conrad himself, we may gloss, carried the burden of justifying his life from the time of his escapades in Marseilles (see below, p. 000, n. 8). Thematically and artistically, his work was the highest expression of this need to justify. *Lord Jim* seems to me of all these attempts the most ambitious—"the most satanically ambitious" as Conrad confided to a friend. Any work of art is satanic insofar as it attempts to create another universe, especially one operating on laws different from God's. Conrad as a lapsed Catholic would have been well aware of this view. In fact, I would like to suggest that he tried to embody the dilemma in his novel. In the first half of *Lord Jim*, he presented us with an egoist trying to cope with the social world. In the second half, he allowed the egoist to withdraw into himself, satanically to set up his own kingdom. Then he asked, Can such a world of romance stand up on its own terms, transcending the conventional world? Conrad had doubts that he had successfully asked the question or presented the problem. We may therefore expect to have to exert ourselves if we want to understand what is going on in *Lord Jim*.

Our first task is to try to understand the opposed conceptions of

the first and second halves of the novel. The *Patna* episode demonstrates that the beliefs men share govern their fate, while the Patusan
sequence tests the possibility that one man's imagination can determine
his fate. The Western world of the *Patna* is dominated by Marlow's
moral principles; the Eastern world of Patusan appears to function
according to Jim's application of Stein's romantic prescription. Marlow
delivers his code in Chapter 5, immediately after his introduction.
Jim, he says, as "one of us" should have "that inborn ability to look
temptations straight in the face—a readiness unintellectual enough,
goodness knows, but without pose—a power of resistance . . . —an
unthinking and blessed stiffness before the outward and inward terrors
. . . backed by a . . . belief in a few simple notions" (p. 36).

For Marlow, as we saw in the last chapter, the central notion is
fidelity to 'the craft of the sea . . . the craft whose whole secret could
be expressed in one short sentence, and yet must be driven afresh
every day into young heads till it becomes the component part of every
waking thought—till it is present in every dream of their young sleep!"
(p. 37). The implications of this statement are far reaching. A good
sailor must be alert and conscious of detail. In fact he must reshape
his unconscious life to the image of his consciousness of the outside.
Formulated in this way, Marlow's belief stands directly opposed to
Stein's basic principle that "a man that is born falls into a dream like
a man who falls into the sea" (p. 184). Stein, an initiate into the secret
lore of adventure, advises living from the dream. Marlow, speaking for
responsibility but also for Western materialism, emphasizes the need to
understand and master outside reality. Of the situation that precipi-
tated Jim's jump from the *Patna*, Marlow says, "It was all threats, all a
terribly effective feint, a sham from beginning to end, planned by the
tremendous disdain of the Dark Powers whose real terrors, always on
the verge of triumph, are perpetually foiled by the steadfastness of
men" (p. 105).

Human solidarity is only one part of Marlow's code; the bond with the
visible universe is equally important. Simply, a sailor must be responsive
to the elements and to his ship. Jim is unable to give his full attention to them. "He had to bear the criticism of men, the exactions of
the sea, and the prosaic severity of the daily task that gives bread—
but whose only reward is in the perfect love of the work. This reward
eluded him" (p. 7). Instead of showing a concern for the demanding
but necessary routine of the ship or for his duty to the passengers, Jim
spends his time in daydreams of heroism. These dreams are intensified

when he arrives in the East. He is lulled by "the softness of the sky, the languor of the earth, the bewitching breath of the Eastern waters. There were perfumes in it, suggestions of infinite repose, the gift of endless dreams" (p. 9).

Appropriately enough, those who live in the East have evolved a religion which includes this gift of the region. The eight hundred Moslem pilgrims stream on to the *Patna* "urged by faith and the hope of paradise." They journey "at the call of an idea . . . the unconscious pilgrims of an exacting belief" (p. 11). These pilgrims have made the dream their reality. They are as true to it as Marlow is to the demands of his reality and are therefore as successful in achieving their goal. The opposition between Western and Eastern man can be seen initially, then, as the opposition already mentioned between conscious and unconscious. In fact the pilgrims' way of life embodies one version of Stein's philosophy; they have so far submitted to the unconscious as to be identified with the sea. They "spread on all sides over the deck, flowed forward and aft, overflowed down the yawning hatchways, filled the inner recesses of the ship—like water filling a cistern, like water flowing into crevices and crannies, like water rising silently even with the rim" (p. 11). Western man, on the other hand, rises above the sea, as seen in one of several contrasts Conrad makes between the Western and Eastern ways of life. "The Arab standing up aft, recited aloud the prayer of travellers by sea. He invoked the favour of the Most High upon that journey, implored His blessing on men's toil and on the secret purposes of their hearts; the steamer pounded in the dusk the calm water of the Strait; and far astern of the pilgrim ship a screw-pile lighthouse, planted by unbelievers on a treacherous shoal, seemed to wink at her its eye of flame, as if in derision of her errand of faith" (p. 12).

The lighthouse is the epitome of Western man, symbolizing as it does his attempt to penetrate the darkness, to enable himself to steer a safe course through the dangerous unknown, to safeguard the future by rearranging the materials of nature and giving them conscious shape through the light of reason. It winks in derision at the faith of the pilgrims because, where they give themselves up to an inscrutable God (the word *Islam* means "submission"), Western man sets out to subdue the unknown, to impose the light of conscious reason on all dark and treacherous realms.

Balancing the demands of the inner and outer worlds was a preoccupation with Conrad. In 1903, for instance, he wrote to a Polish

friend of his artistic aim, "It is difficult to depict faithfully in a work
of imagination that innermost world as one apprehends it, and to
express one's own real sense of that inner life (which is the soul of
human activity)."[1] Conrad believed in human activity, but as something done physically. In his writing he was always concerned to give
expression to those patterns of the inner self which are the shaping
spirit of such activity.

Jim, from this point of view, has the wrong type of soul to grapple
effectively with the problems raised by the crisis on the *Patna.* Conrad
therefore presents him with Patusan, a world ordered according to
Stein's romantic philosophy. Even Marlow says of Patusan that there
"the haggard utilitarian lies of our civilisation wither and die, to be
replaced by pure exercises of imagination, that have the futility, often
the charm, and sometimes the deep hidden truthfulness, of works of
art" (p. 244). As I see Conrad's aim in the second half of *Lord Jim,*
it was to present a picture of the land of the imagination, to give a
true rendering of the large and autonomous forces that reign there.

In fact, I believe that Conrad constructed Patusan on principles
strikingly similar to those later used by Jung to analyse the structure
of what he called the collective unconscious. Briefly, Jung believed that
where psychic energy can not "flow into life at the right time [it]
regresses to the mythical world of the archetypes, where it activates
images which, since the remotest times, have expressed the non-human
life of the gods, whether of the upper world or the lower."[2] Jung saw
these images as unconscious personas, "certain types which deserve the
name of dominants. These are archetypes like the anima, animus,
wise old man, witch, shadow, earth-mother, . . . and the organizing
dominants, the self, the circle, and the quarternity, i.e., the four functions
or aspects of the self or of consciousness" (*Symbols of Transformation,*
p. 391). As an empiricist, Jung admitted that these figures are a metaphorical way of talking about mental processes, but he also insisted
that whether by definition or by observation unconscious processes
cannot be known except through metaphor (as they are expressed, for
instance, in dreams). In any case, we can see these traditional personified forms as part of a pattern which throws considerable light on Jim's
experience in Patusan.

1. *Conrad's Polish Background: Letters to and from Polish Friends,* ed. by
Zdzislaw Najder, trans. by Halina Carroll (London: Oxford University Press,
1964), p. 240.
2. *Symbols of Transformation,* p. 308.

First we should note the presence of a Jungian figure that we have already met, the wise old man. Although *Lord Jim* has a number of helpful, fatherly figures, only one, Stein, fits the following description by Jung:

> Often the old man in fairy tales asks questions like who? why? whence? and whither? for the purpose of inducing self-reflection and mobilizing the moral forces, and more often still he gives the necessary magical talisman, the unexpected and improbable power to succeed, which is one of the peculiarities of the unified personality in good or bad alike. But the intervention of the old man—the spontaneous objectivation of the archetype—would seem to be equally indispensable, since the conscious will by itself is hardly ever capable of uniting the personality to the point where it acquires this extraordinary power to succeed.[3]

Stein sees immediately that Jim is romantic, thinks of Patusan as the place to send him, and gives him the ring which is "the necessary magical talisman" that opens up Patusan for Jim's improbable success. In contrast, Marlow, representing the strength of the conscious mind, comes to realize that, for all his fatherly good intentions, the opportunities he has given Jim were "merely opportunities to earn his bread" (p. 173).

In a letter to Edward Garnett, Conrad voiced agreement with his friend's criticism of *Lord Jim*: "I've been satanically ambitious, but there's nothing of a devil in me, worse luck."[4] In fact, however, Conrad was well aware that he had at least a daimon inside him, an *alter ego* which had long known adventures in the interior world. Patusan seems to me the equivalent of that world, and Stein the magician who makes it come alive for Jim. In the same letter to Garnett, Conrad admitted that he had "wanted to obtain a sort of lurid light out (of) the very events" in *Lord Jim* (p. 172). The word "lurid" is exactly the right word to characterize the tone of the second half of the novel. Conrad's conception of Patusan was, as I see it, intentionally romantic and archetypal. The nature of the action there is thus clearly to be con-

---

3. "The Phenomenology of the Spirit in Fairy Tales" in *Psyche and Symbol*, pp. 75–76.

4. *Letters from Joseph Conrad*, p. 172. The same letter is printed in *Life and Letters*, I, 299. For other references to the devil inside, see *Life and Letters*, I, 220, Garnett's Letters, p. 99, and *A Personal Record*, p. 12. The word "devil" runs almost like a refrain through *Lord Jim*.

trasted with, but not necesarily judged by, the more realistic action of the first part of the novel.

As a preliminary to an archetypal analysis of Patusan, let us consider Stein's romantic prescription. "A man that is born falls into a dream like a man who falls into the sea. If he tries to climb out into the air as inexperienced people endeavour to do, he drowns." So "the way is to the destructive element submit yourself, and with the exertions of your hands and feet in the water make the deep, deep sea keep you up" (p. 184). As noted already, this approach is the opposite of Marlow's realistic desire to drive "the craft of the sea" into the minds of young seamen "till it is present in every dream of their young sleep" (p. 37). Marlow would make the inner world over to the demands of the outer; Stein would keep asserting the inner until it works in the outer, "to follow the dream, and again to follow the dream" (p. 185).[5]

Stein's own past offers a good illustration of this process. A hunter of butterflies, he had long looked for a specimen of a certain rare species. "I took long journeys and underwent great privations; I . . . dreamed of him in my sleep" (p. 181), but he never found one until he gave himself over to the life of a native state in which he went as a Western trader. He became a close friend of the ruler, took his sister as wife, and had a daughter by her. Then riding alone he was ambushed by his friend's enemies. Still acting as a man engaged in that life (rather than in the Western one of laws), Stein immersed himself in the destructive element by feigning death, waiting until his attackers drew near, then killing three of them. As he looked at the third "for some sign of life I observed something like a faint shadow pass over his forehead. It was the shadow of this butterfly" (p. 181). It is the rare one, and he catches it.

The parallel with Jim's experience in Patusan is evident. He also gives himself to the life of the native state to which Stein sends him. He conceives a plan to help Stein's old "war-comrade" (p. 201), Doramin, by defeating the destructive force of Sherif Ali. Just after convincing Doramin's followers to follow his plan, he has to face a plot on his life. "Jim's slumbers were disturbed by a dream of heavens like brass resounding with a great voice, which called upon him to Awake!

5. For a closely reasoned scrutiny of all Stein's comments on the dream and their relation to his experiences and Jim's, see Kenneth B. Newell's persuasive article, "The Destructive Element and Related 'Dream' Passages in the *Lord Jim* Manuscript," *Journal of Modern Literature,* 1 (1970).

Awake! so loud that, notwithstanding his desperate determination to sleep on, he did wake up in reality" (p. 256). He is warned of the coming attempt on his life by the stepdaughter of Cornelius, the treacherous man with whom he is staying. When he refuses her advice to flee to Doramin, she leads him to the storeroom in which he thinks the assassins may be hiding. At first the room appears empty; then from under the mats emerges a man with a sword; "his naked body glistened as if wet" (p. 261). Confidently, Jim withholds his fire so long that when he shoots the man falls dead "just short of Jim's bare toes." Immediately, Jim finds "himself calm, appeased, without rancour, without uneasiness, as if the death of that man had atoned for everything" (p. 261). Then another assassin crawls out of the mats. "You want your life?" Jim said. The other made no sound. 'How many more of you?' asked Jim again. 'Two more, Tuan,' said the man very softly, looking with big fascinated eyes into the muzzle of the revolver. Accordingly two more crawled from under the mats, holding out ostentatiously their empty hands" (p. 262). He takes the three to the river, where (unconsciously) he makes them enact his own earlier desertion of duty. " 'Jump!' he thundered. The three splashes made one splash, a shower flew up, black heads bobbed convulsively, and disappeared; . . . Jim turned to the girl, who had been a silent and attentive observer. His heart seemed suddenly to grow too big for his breast . . . and the calm soft starlight descended upon them, unchecked" (pp. 262–63).[6] Just as Stein has found his treasure after immersing in the destructive element and following his dream where it led him, so Jim under parallel circumstances finds his in the girl to whom he gives a name "that means precious, in the sense of a precious gem—jewel" (p. 240). And Jewel she is called.

   This name is responsible for a mistake which illustrates Marlow's comment that the native mind replaces "the haggard utilitarian lies of our civilisation" with "pure exercises of imagination that have . . . sometimes the deep hidden truthfulness of works of art" (p. 244). During a conversation with a man on the coast south of Patusan, Marlow hears about "a mysterious white man in Patusan who had got hold of an extraordinary gem—namely, an emerald of an enormous

6. Since only three are made to jump, perhaps they stand for the other three officers on the *Patna*. Jim in this case does not jump. But the fourth member of the native group is the brave one, and he is dead. Is Jim killing his past or himself? For more on the problem of destruction see my article "Pure Exercise of Imagination: Archetypal Symbolism in *Lord Jim,*" *PMLA,* 89 (1964): 146–47.

size, and altogether priceless" (pp. 242–43). More, "such a jewel—it
was explained to me by the old fellow from whom I heard most of this
amazing Jim-myth . . . is best preserved by being concealed about the
person of a woman." If there were such a woman, always close to
Jim, "there could be no doubt she wore the white man's jewel concealed upon her bosom" (p. 243). Looking at the "Jim-myth" from
a Jungian point of view, Jewel is clearly the anima.

The anima is Jung's term for a conception "for which the expression
'soul' is too general and too vague" ("Aion," *Psyche and Symbol,*
p. 12). For a man it stands as the feminine counterpart of his consciously masculine nature. "The anima personifies the total unconscious so long as she is not differentiated as a figure from the other
archetypes. With further differentiations the figure of the (wise) old
man becomes detached from the anima and appears as an archetype
of the 'spirit' " (*Symbols of Transformation,* p. 437). The situation
which causes these manifestations to appear is lack of inner harmony.
Once faced the problem may be resolved. "If this situation is drama-
tized, as the unconscious usually dramatizes it, then there appears
before you on the psychological stage a man living regressively, seeking his childhood and his mother, fleeing from a cold cruel world
which denies him understanding" ("Aion," p. 10). Since the last part
of this statement obviously suits Jim, let us see if the first part about
regression toward the mother does.

Conrad certainly goes out of his way to indicate a quality of childish-
ness in Jim in Patusan. Chapter 34 ends with Cornelius' biased comment on him, "No more than a little child—a little child." But Chapter
35 ends with a similar comment by Marlow; as he sails away, Jim
appears "no bigger than a child." And earlier, Marlow's description
of Jim with Jewel strikes the same odd note. " 'Hallo, girl!' he cried,
cheerily. 'Hallo, boy!' she answered at once. . . . This was their usual
greeting to each other" (p. 278). A clue to the reason for such behaviour is also given by Jung; it is that a person regresses, or goes back
toward childhood, in order to start again. But before he can start again
he must be reborn.

We may see Jim's second chance really beginning just after he
makes his two jumps into the real life of Patusan: In the first he goes
"like a bird" over the stockade in which he has been a prisoner of the
Rajah, and in the second he jumps across the creek which separates
him from Doramin, landing "in an extremely soft and sticky mudbank" (p. 220).

The higher firm ground was about six feet in front of him. "I thought I would have to die there all the same," he said. He reached and grabbed desperately with his hands, and only succeeded in gathering a horrible cold shiny heap of slime against his breast—up to his very chin. It seemed to him he was burying himself alive, and then he struck out madly, scattering the mud with his fists. It fell on his head, on his face, over his eyes, into his mouth. . . . He arose muddy from head to foot and stood there, thinking he was alone of his kind for hundreds of miles, alone, with no help, no sympathy, no pity to expect from any one (pp. 220–21).

He is wrong, however; as soon as he produces the ring, he is accepted by Doramin and his followers, who give him the sympathy and aid that a helpless child needs. "He was safe. Doramin's people were barricading the gate and pouring water down his throat; Doramin's old wife, full of business and commiseration, was issuing shrill orders to her girls. 'The old woman,' he said, softly, 'made a to-do over me as if I had been her own son. They put me into an immense bed—her state bed— and she ran in and out wiping her eyes to give me pats on the back" (pp. 221–22). As Jung puts it, "He who stems from two mothers is the hero: the first birth makes him a mortal man, the second an immortal half-god" (*Symbols of Transformation,* p. 322). On the simplest archetypal level, then, Jim's heroic success-to-come with the assassins, with Jewel, with Sherif Ali's force can all be accounted for by his having found the right way to begin his second chance.

Jim's jump into the mud bears some resemblance to the mythical hero's plunge into darkness as well as to the rejuvenation process of many fairy tales.[7] We have already seen the youth in "Iron Hans" dip his hair in the well of purity. In the similar Norwegian tale of "The Widow's Son," as in the Russian "Fire-Bird," the hero plunges into a boiling cauldron and emerges young, fresh, and strong. That Conrad knew of such tales is evident from a letter he wrote Hugh Walpole during World War I. "I have been (like a sort of dismal male witch) peering (mentally), into the cauldron into which *la force des choses* has plunged you bodily. What will come of it? A very subtle poison or some very rough-tested Elixir of Life? Or neither?" (*Life and Letters,* II, 194). We can find in fairy tales all three of these motifs of magical peering, plunging, and drinking. The latter along with the

7. For the plunge into the monster, see Joseph Campbell, *The Hero with a Thousand Faces,* Chapter 1, Part V, "The Belly of the Whale."

key word, "elixir," makes an appearance in *Lord Jim,* in an ironic metaphoric description by Marlow of Jim's reaction to the "legend of strength and prowess, forming round his name" in Patusan (p. 150). "Felicity, felicity—how shall I say it?—is quaffed out of a golden cup. . . . He was of the sort that would drink deep, . . . flushed with the elixir at his lips" (p. 151). But the second motif of "plunging into" is the one that applies best to Jim's jump. If Conrad had plunged Jim in water instead of mud, he would not only have come closer to the conventional model of heroic transformation, he would also have made the incident fit better Stein's prescription, "in the destructive element immerse" (p. 185). Why did he choose this other way?

The most obvious explanation is an experience of Conrad's own. According to his wife, when he was in the Congo, in 1890, he was involved in a terrifying accident. Running a steamboat on the river,

> he had sent his boys ashore to cut wood. . . . After a time he heard shots and sounds of quarrelling. Seizing his rifle—and his whistle, which he hung round his neck, he started to look for them. Almost before he had gone ten yards from the bank his feet sank into a deep bog, he fired all his cartridges without attracting any attention from the two men left on board the steamer, and sank steadily deeper and deeper. He was already as deep as his armpits, when he bethought himself of the whistle. At the third shrill note he saw two men running towards him with boughs and he swooned. His next recollection was finding himself strapped to a chair on the bridge and the steamer already underway.[8]

Conrad told the anecdote after Mrs. Conrad found the whistle, still on its string. We might remember that it is on a string round his neck that Jim puts the ring which will save his life in Patusan (p. 203).

8. Jessie Conrad, "Conrad as an Artist," *The Saturday Review of Literature* 2 (1926): 700. If the incident was only a tall tale for his wife's benefit, it still as fantasy is equally revealing. (Note it is the third whistle that brings help; the successful third try is ubiquitous in fairy tales.) Conrad's earlier brush with death is better known. He claimed to have been shot in a youthful duel in Marseilles, but recent evidence suggests he attempted suicide instead. Jocelyn Baines in his *Joseph Conrad: A Critical Biography* (London: Weidenfeld & Nicolson, 1959) gives good reasons for accepting that evidence. On the other hand, Albert Guerard in *Conrad the Novelist* makes out a plausible case for not accepting the suicide evidence. This early brush with death added to Conrad's morbid boyhood, spent with mother and father exiled and slowly dying in Northern Russia, certainly helps to explain his concern with the necessity and difficulty of being born again.

Conrad's accident can help to explain the overtones of burial and death noticeable when rebirth is suggested not only in *Lord Jim,* but also in *The Nigger of the Narcissus* and in *Heart of Darkness.*

But there is more to this thematic cluster than can be seen in one accident in Conrad's life. The other possibilities come out interestingly in the letter to Edward Garnett on *Lord Jim.* "I admit I stood for a great triumph and I have only succeeded in giving myself utterly away. Nobody'll see it, but you have detected me falling back into my lump of clay I had been lugging up from the bottom of the pit, with the idea of breathing big life into it. . . . The *Outcast* is a heap of sand, the *Nigger* a splash of water, *Jim* a lump of clay. A stone, I suppose will be my next gift to the impatient mankind—before I get drowned in mud to which even my supreme struggles won't give a simulacrum of life" (*Letters to Garnett,* pp. 171–72). The phrase, "drowned in mud" provides an obvious connection with the accident described by Mrs. Conrad, while the images of birth restore the connection between such an immersion and life. What in Jim's experience is connected with rebirth is in Conrad's connected with creation. Nor is the psycho-analytic correlation far to seek. As the phrases "heap of sand," "lump of clay," and "a stone" indicate, Conrad's gifts to mankind are of an anal nature. Rather than a cause for outrage, however, we may take that nature as a compliment to his readers. Although one obvious use of anal imagery is aggressive and destructive, another use is also recognized in psychiatry. This second use is creative, perhaps in males a substitute for the female's ability to give birth.[9] As Jung comments, in myths, "the first men were made from earth or clay. The Latin *lutum,* which really means 'mud,' also had the metaphorical meaning of 'filth' " (*Symbols of Transformation,* p. 191).

If we now look again at Jim's action in the mudbank we can appreciate an important passage not quoted before. Jim made efforts "culminating into one mighty supreme effort in the darkness to crack the earth asunder, to throw it off his limbs—and he felt himself creeping feebly up the bank. He lay full length on the firm ground and saw the light, the sky" (p. 220). Although he then goes on to Doramin's wife still "beplastered with filth out of all semblance to a human being" (p. 221), he has already been born, has thrown off the earth and moved

9. Freud and Jung appear to agree on this point, as on the connection of dung and gold, an important fairy-tale motif. See *Symbols of Transformation,* pp. 189–90.

from darkness to light on his own. As Jung notes, in this process of self-transformation into the hero, the individual becomes more intimately connected with the mother, but becomes independent of and equal to the father. In Jungian terms, the hero assimilates the archetype of the wise old man in the process of becoming "his own father and his own begetter" (*Symbols of Transformation*, p. 333). Where, before, Jim had been grateful for and followed the advice of such father figures as Marlow and Stein, after his rebirth he himself becomes the advice-giver, the planner, the law-giver. He overshadows all fathers: Cornelius ("in-law"), the Rajah (political), Sherif Ali (religious), and even Doramin, whose son becomes Jim's brother.

As we know, however, it is Doramin who shoots Jim at the end of the novel. How are we to treat as a hero someone whose life ends as Jim's does? One answer lies within the archetypal framework through which we have approached his experience. In our analysis so far we have omitted one important figure, the shadow, which in Jung's system stands for all the unfavourable characteristics of an individual which are repressed from conscious knowledge. Rather than disappearing, these unacknowledged dark traits tend to take on a life of their own. "The shadow is a moral problem that challenges the whole ego personality, for no one can become conscious of the shadow without considerable moral effort. To become conscious of it involves recognizing the dark aspects of the personality as present and real" ("Aion," p. 7). It is here that Jim's weakness lies. He cannot admit his kinship with the disreputable characters whom he accompanies in deserting the *Patna*. He stands trial in the hope of distinguishing himself from them, but his failure in analysis is precisely moral, in Marlow's opinion. Although Marlow grants that Jim is trying to "save from the fire his idea of what his moral identity should be" (p. 69), he comes to believe that Jim "had no leisure to regret what he had lost, he was so wholly and naturally concerned for what he had failed to obtain" (p. 71). Marlow tries unsuccessfully to make Jim aware of his moral failure. Stein, however, without concerning himself with that side of the problem, simply sends Jim into a situation in Patusan where he can obtain his desired heroism. Jim's success is therefore achieved without his ever coming to terms with his shadow.

According to Jungian theory, this move simply strengthens the shadow. Unrecognized within, it appears without as an *alter ego* which will isolate the individual from his environment. The person who takes on this role in Jim's life is Gentleman Brown. He is obviously a villain, but as Jim's shadow he is able to hit with uncanny accuracy on the words which immobilize Jim and keep him from dealing effectively with that villainy. As Marlow characterizes Brown's verbal approach to Jim, it contains "a vein of subtle reference to their common blood, an assumption of common experience; a sickening suggestion of common guilt, of secret knowledge that was like a bond of their minds and of their hearts" (p. 337). This dark, private bond, which is the inverse of public solidarity, culminates in Brown's act of treachery—which, in Marlow's evaluation, has its inverse morality. "It was a lesson, a retribution—a demonstration of some obscure and awful attribute of our nature which, I am afraid, is not so very far under the surface as we like to think" (p. 352).

In killing Dain Waris, the son of Doramin, Brown disrupts the harmony that Jim created and maintained in his archetypal land. Jim has two choices. He can flee with Jewel and a few followers, or he can maintain the pledge he made to Doramin, to "answer with his life for any harm" (p. 342) that Brown and his men might do if allowed to go free. In keeping his word, Jim has to give up the authority he has exercised in Patusan. He gives it back to Doramin, from whom he had taken it. But what he activates in doing so is a side of Doramin's nature which had lain dormant as long as Jim was in command.

In Marlow's first description of Doramin, we hear that he has a "throat like a bull" (p. 224). When his son's body is brought to him, Doramin is silent until shown Jim's silver ring, which was on the forefinger of Dain Waris because Jim had sent it to him as "a token" of the importance of giving Brown a clear passage down the river. At sight of the ring, Doramin gives "one great fierce cry, deep from the chest, a roar of pain and fury, as mighty as the bellow of a wounded bull" (p. 358). Then when Jim confronts him, "the unwieldy old man, lowering his big forehead like an ox under a yoke, made an effort to rise, clutching at the flintlock pistols on his knees. From his throat came gurgling, choking, inhuman sounds, and his two attendants helped him from behind. People remarked that the ring which he had dropped on his lap fell and rolled against the foot of the white man, and that poor Jim glanced down at the talisman that had opened for him the door of fame, love, and success" (pp. 361–62). In one sense, then, Jim dies a sacrifice to the subhuman side of human nature as represented in Doramin's destructive animality, and in that of Brown, whom Marlow had described as "bowed and hairy . . . like some man-beast of folklore" (p. 324). Since Brown is Jim's *alter ego*, we realize that Jim, the idealist who dresses in pure white, is the victim of his own repressed brute nature.

But, from Jim's point of view, he sacrifices himself to gain the higher goal he has desired. As Marlow puts it, after Brown's act Jim determines that "the dark powers should not rob him twice of his peace" (p. 356). Jim had known such a state on the *Patna,* the "high peace of sea and sky" which allowed his thoughts to "be full of valorous deeds" (p. 16). In such an atmosphere, "the eternity beyond the sky seemed to come down nearer to the earth, with the augmented glitter of the stars" (p. 17). Conrad had himself experienced this same feeling when he first went to sea: "In my early days, starting out on a voyage was like being launched into Eternity. . . . An enormous silence, in which there was nothing to connect one with the Universe but the incessant wheeling about of the sun and other celestial bodies, the alternation of light and shadow, eternally chasing each other over the sky. The time of the earth, though most carefully recorded by the half-hourly bells, did not count in reality."[10] Earth and its time were exactly what Jim left behind when he dropped the clock he was mending and jumped out of the Rajah's stockade. Here is Conrad's description of the second jump: "The earth seemed fairly to fly backwards under his feet" (p. 219). And here is Marlow's preview of Jim achieving success in Patusan: "Had Stein arranged to send him into a star of the fifth magnitude the change could not have been greater. He left his earthly failings behind him and . . . there was a totally new set of conditions for his imaginative faculty to work upon" (pp. 188–89).

But, when those earthly, animal failings intrude even into this world, Jim chooses to "prove his power in another way and conquer the fatal destiny itself" (p. 357). He must move on to yet another world and find his anima or soul in an eternal realm where no shadows exist. Marlow speculates, "it may very well be that in the short moment of his last proud and unflinching glance, he had beheld the face of that opportunity which, like an Eastern bride, had come veiled to his side" (p. 362).

Like Eustacia Vye, Jim may be seen as having found through death "an artistically happy background." But Conrad, like Hardy, felt quite ambiguous about his self-centered hero. Whereas Hardy expressed his reservations in direct comments, Conrad demonstrated his by creating a narrator with an outlook diametrically opposed to Jim's. Needless to

10. "Well Done," in *Notes on Life and Letters,* p. 182.

say, Marlow's temperament has its effect in the characterization not just of Jim but of Stein and Jewel, and of Patusan. Marlow puts his position most graphically in the form of an opposition between images. In Patusan he watches the moon rise

> like an ascending spirit out of a grave; its sheen descended, cold and pale, like the ghost of dead sunlight. There is something haunting in the light of the moon; it has all the dispassionateness of a disembodied soul, and something of its inconceivable mystery. It is to our sunshine, which—say what you like—is all we have to live by, what the echo is to the sound: misleading and confusing whether the note be mocking or sad. It robs all forms of matter—which, after all, is our domain—of their substance, and gives a sinister reality to shadows alone (p. 213).

The images present here—"grave" and "ghost," "spirit" and "shadow" —Marlow uses many times to characterize Jim, Jewel, and Stein. The aim of this use is to undercut the validity of Jim's life in Patusan, and of the romanticism which made Jim's heroism possible.

The process of undercutting begins in Marlow's original conversation with Stein. Just before Stein delivers his romantic prescription, Marlow describes him: "His tall form, as though robbed of its substance, hovered noiselessly over invisible things with stooping and indefinite movements; his voice, heard in that remoteness where he could be glimpsed mysteriously busy with immaterial cares, was no longer incisive, seemed to roll voluminous and grave" (p. 184). It is from this recess, "out of the bright circle of the lamp into the ring of fainter light" (p. 184), that Stein discusses the value of the dream. The bright light is equivalent to the sun, the fainter light to the moon of Marlow's allegorical description of Patusan. The opposition between "concrete" and "immaterial" is again emphasized.

It is in such a context that Stein propounds his solution for Jim's problem. And, as he finishes it, Marlow gives us his reaction. "The light had destroyed the assurance which had inspired him in the distant shadows. . . . The whisper of his conviction seemed to open before me a vast and uncertain expanse, as of a crepuscular horizon on a plain at dawn—or was it, perchance, at the coming of the night? One had not the courage to decide; but it was a charming and deceptive light throwing the impalpable poesy of its dimness over pitfalls—over graves" (p. 185). For a third time we have dim light connected with graves. Then Jim is mentioned, and something similar occurs when

Stein suggests Patusan as a place to send him. Thinking of Jewel's mother, he says, "and the woman is dead now." Marlow comments, "Of course I don't know that story; I can only guess that once before Patusan had been used as a grave for some sin, transgression, or misfortune. It is impossible to suspect Stein" (p. 189).

When Marlow visits Patusan, he puts quite a bit of emphasis on this grave, and the relation of Jewel and Jim to it. Although the two lovers keep it up well, her mother's grave seems to Marlow to have a sinister appearance in the light of the moon. "It threw its level rays afar as if from a cavern, and in this mournful eclipse-like light the stumps of felled trees uprose very dark, the heavy shadows fell at my feet on all sides, my own moving shadow, and across my path the shadow of the solitary grave perpetually garlanded with flowers. . . . The lumps of white coral shone round the dark mound like a chaplet of bleached skulls" (p. 279). In view of these associations, it is not surprising that Marlow views Patusan as an unhealthy place for Jim to be, or that his final attitude toward Jim's decision to sacrifice himself is a suspicious one. "We can see him, an obscure conqueror of fame, tearing himself out of the arms of a jealous love at the sign, at the call of his exalted egoism. He goes away from a living woman to celebrate his pitiless wedding with a shadowy ideal of conduct" (p. 362).

If we look back as far as the *Patna* with Marlow's key images in mind, but without forgetting the later "Jim-myth," we can begin to see another possibility of interpreting those images. The sun, which Marlow takes as an image of what man has to live by, is not only present in the *Patna* episode; it is personified. "Every morning the sun, as if keeping pace in his revolutions with the progress of the pilgrimage, emerged with a silent burst of light exactly at the same distance astern of the ship, caught up with her at noon, pouring the concentrated fire of his rays on the pious purposes of the men, glided past on his descent, and sank mysteriously into the sea evening after evening" (p. 12). This early part of the novel is narrated by an impersonal voice presumably closer to Conrad's own than is Marlow's. In line with Conrad's impersonal philosophy, this voice describes the ship as suffering under the sun "as if scorched by a flame flicked at her from a heaven without pity. The nights descended on her like a benediction" (p. 13). In the night, "the propeller turned without a check, as though its beat had been part of the scheme of a safe universe" (p. 13). Though the universe is not safe, Jim mistakenly identifies with the night world rather than the day, and is betrayed when the *Patna* strikes a mysterious submerged object in the dark.

After he jumps, Jim looks back up at the *Patna*. "'She seemed higher than a wall; she loomed like a cliff over the boat. . . . I wished I could die,' he cried. 'There was no going back. It was as if I had jumped into a well—into an everlasting deep hole. . . .' " (ellipses Conrad's, p. 96). The wall, the cliff, and the hole are all images that reappear in the novel. Marlow picks them up immediately. "He had indeed jumped into an everlasting deep hole. He had tumbled from a height he could never scale again. By that time the boat had gone driving forward past the bows. It was too dark just then for them to see each other, and, moreover, they were blinded and half drowned with rain. He told me it was like being swept by a flood through a cavern" (pp. 96–97). If we remember that Marlow had described the moon in Patusan as throwing "its level rays afar as if from a cavern" (p. 279), we can realize that in his opinon Jim, unlike Don Quixote, never does get out of the hole; he is buried there. As Jim himself puts it, "after the ship's lights had gone, anything might have happened in that boat. . . . We were like men walled up quick in a roomy grave" (p. 104). The question then becomes whether he can climb out.

Or as Conrad seems to have conceived it: can a man, once he has been buried, reappear *and live*? James Wait is rescued from his tomb in the *Narcissus,* but he must die and be committed to the deep before the ship reaches land. Kurtz is taken on board Marlow's ship in *Heart of Darkness* more dead than alive. Marlow says, "You should have heard the disinterred body of Mr. Kurtz." Later, "I looked at him as you peer down at a man who is lying at the bottom of a precipice where the sun never shines." Then he really dies, and Marlow is aware that "the pilgrims buried something in a muddy hole." (pp. 115, 149, 150). Though Marlow is more intimately involved in the adventures of *Heart of Darkness,* Kurtz is a less sympathetic egoist than Jim; we must therefore simply note that a similar problem is posed in *Lord Jim.*

Before the *Patna* inquiry, we have a picture of Jim passing "days on the verandah, buried in a long chair, and coming out of his place of sepulture only at meal-times or late at night, when he wandered on the quays all by himself, detached from his surroundings, irresolute and silent, like a ghost without a home to haunt" (pp. 70–71). The word "sepulture" should make us aware of the ironic allusion to Christ which is implicit in the experience of Jim, as it was in the rescue of

James Wait. At first glance, this reference does not help us solve the problem because, although Christ rose from burial, like Wait and Kurtz, also like them he did not remain on earth long or substantially afterward. Jim does live long, but not, according to Marlow, substantially.

The Christ reference does provide a helpful clue, however, if we wish to connect Conrad's use of the sun with the various father figures in Jim's life. In *The Nigger of the Narcissus* Conrad referred to "the immortal sea" which in "its grace" insists that man labour rather than rest in peace. In *Lord Jim* he substitutes the sun as an image of God, but again it is "a heaven without pity." Sea and sun work together, however, in an interesting scene while Jim and the crew of the *Patna* are isolated in the life boat. Marlow reports that even Jim's "few mumbled words were enough to make me see the lower limb of the sun clearing the line of the horizon, the tremble of a vast ripple running over all the visible expanse of the sea, as if the waters had shuddered, giving birth to the globe of light, . . . I could imagine under the pellucid emptiness of the sky these four men imprisoned in the solitude of the sea, the lonely sun, regardless of the speck of life, ascending the clear curve of the heaven as if to gaze ardently from a greater height at his own splendour reflected in the still ocean" (p. 106). Lack of pity is still evident; it is joined by another characteristic.

The sun gazing "ardently . . . at his own splendour reflected in the still ocean" is presumably acting as the author of nature may. But we have quite a different situation when Marlow very soon after pictures for us a youth like Jim, just starting his career and "looking with shining eyes upon that glitter of the vast surface which is only a reflection of his own glances full of fire" (p. 111). Unlike the author of nature, the youth sees not reality but, according to Marlow, an "illusion" which is very "wide of reality" (p. 111). Although we have to take most of what Marlow reports as good evidence, we do not have to accept his interpretation of it. Accepting his view of the sun, we may ask ourselves whether it has to be the only standard of value. Why can we not see the hero, if he is brave enough and self-sufficient enough, becoming autonomous, born again to a cosmic destiny?

Something like this at any rate is what seems to happen after the sun had risen on the *Patna* lifeboat. Jim describes it. " 'The sun crept all the way from east to west over my bare head, but that day I could not come to any harm, I suppose. The sun could not make me mad. . . .'

His right arm put aside the idea of madness. . . . 'Neither could it kill me. . . . ' Again his arm repulsed a shadow. . . . '*That* rested with me' " (ellipses and italics Conrad's, p. 109). He sums up, "I didn't bother myself at all about the sun over my head. I was thinking as coolly as any man that ever sat thinking in the shade" (p. 109). Jim has outfaced the sun, denied its authority, its right to punish him with the death that he suspects is its penalty for his crime. The result, however, seems to be that he is able to think on his own, "as coolly as any man that ever sat . . . in the *shade*." In other words, accepting Jim's testimony, we may want to see him as giving off his own light—see him as author, say, of the new life of Patusan. But we should see him as shining in areas not previously illumined, darkness being a figurative necessity for his assertion of authority.

Perhaps, then, we should not try to see Jim getting out of the hole into which he has jumped. Perhaps we should make a virtue of necessity and take the other image Jim offers us, the well, as offering something positive. James Wait was also in such a place; we are told that his rescuers "longed to abandon him, to get out of that place deep as a well" (*The Nigger*, p. 67). This in itself is only an indication, but from Conrad's other writing it is evident that for him, as for Dickens, the image of the well had a special meaning.[11] Conrad wrote in *A Personal Record* that fiction "after all is but truth often dragged out of a well and clothed in the painted robe of imaged phrases" (p. 93). Some indication of the location of this well came out in an ironic passage of a letter to John Galsworthy. "I shall keep the lid down on the well of my emotions. It's a question whether I even could lift it off. The hot spring boils somewhere deep within" (*Life and Letters*, II, 112). We have already seen Conrad's contention that it is the artist's duty to "squeeze out" of himself "every sensation, every thought, every image" so that he finishes the day "*emptied* of every sensation and every thought," with "nothing left in" him (*Life and Letters*, I, 183). I would urge, therefore, that the saying "Truth lies at the bottom of a well" can be taken as a more or less conscious epigraph for Conrad's aim and method as a writer.

To find the truth at the bottom of Jim's well will require, however, a little further digging. A well is often important in fairy tales. In "The Frog Prince" a princess loses her golden ball down a well, and finds there her husband-to-be. In "Iron Hans" we saw a young lad set to

11. See *Typhoon*, pp. 23 and 70 (also 82–83). Treasure appears at the bottom of a well at the end of *The Rover*, p. 283.

guard a well which gilds everything that is dipped in it. Similarly in
"The Goose Girl at the Well," its water is associated with her golden
hair that shines like sunbeams when she washes at the well. Most
common, however, is the use of the well as a means to descend to
another world, as in "Toads and Diamonds" or the similar "Mother
Holle." In the latter it is again associated with gold, the good girl
being showered with gold as she finally leaves this lower world into
which she has jumped in despair. All of these tales are in Grimm, as
is another common fairy-tale type, the three princesses abducted
underground. In "The Gnome" the youngest of three huntsmen is
lowered down a well by his two brothers. After defeating three
dragons, he has the three princesses raised back up the well, but is
treacherously stranded below by his brothers. He finds a flute, and
when he blows it some elves appear; they take him back to the upper
world where he is finally able to marry the youngest princess.

In *Lord Jim* Patusan is obviously the land at the bottom of the well
where Jim, like the huntsman, can become the hero who rescues and
destroys. But we must notice a crucial difference. In the fairy tale,
despite serious obstacles, both to the rescue of the three princesses
and to his return, the huntsman is able to accomplish both. Jim, however, is able to accomplish only the rescue. In his failure to return
from the other world he breaks the pattern of the traditional hero of
myth, fairy tale, or epic.

Jim succumbs to the danger expressed by Jung. If "regression
occurs in a young person, his own individual life is supplanted by the
divine archetypal drama, which is all the more devastating for him
because his conscious education provides him with no means of recognizing what is happening, and thus with no possibility of freeing himself from its fascination" (*Symbols of Transformation,* p. 308). In Marlow's view, this is exactly what happens to Jim. "All his conquests,
the trust, the fame, the friendships, the love—all these things that
made him master had made him a captive, too. He looked with an
owner's eye" at these things, "but it was they that possessed him and
made him their own to the innermost thought, to the slightest stir of
blood, to his last breath" (pp. 214–15). We have to admit the perti-
nence of this insight. Not only does "his last breath" push us ahead to
Jim's death, but "stir of blood" suggests that we associate that death
with an image immediately prefiguring it. "The sky over Patusan was
blood-red, immense, streaming like an open vein" (pp. 359–60).
Jim's death is a direct result of his giving over authority to one of the

archetypal figures in that land. This act can now be seen not only as suicidal (so that in Patusan he is both self-born and self-destroyed) but also as a sacrifice to the sun as the ultimate author of life. For it is the sun which makes the sky "blood-red," the same "western sun" which Marlow claims makes "the coast" of Patusan look "like the very stronghold of the night" (p. 362).

But suppose, being satisfied that Jim fails because he is in some way not strong enough, we are still not willing to take Marlow's analysis at face value. Suppose we feel that a "satanically ambitious" Conrad must have intended a stronger romanticism than Marlow condemns. In that case we must switch our critical perceptions to a closer study of Marlow's own character.

Marlow is aware that his motives for getting involved with Jim were suspect. He hoped through a "miracle" to discover behind the obvious fact of Jim's dereliction of duty some means of meeting "the doubt" it seems to cast on Marlow's own code, "the sovereign power enthroned in a fixed standard of conduct" (p. 43). As indicated by the words "fixed" and "enthroned," Marlow means a standard established and upheld by public authority. His condemnation of Jim for upholding a personal and hence "shadowy ideal of conduct" is therefore understandable. Marlow must, of course, be given high marks for his persistent attempt to be sympathetic while telling Jim's story. But the fact is that he lacks the one quality necessary to a real understanding of Jim. Marlow confesses, "As to me, I have no imagination (I would be more certain about him to-day, if I had)" (p. 193).

Remembering Marlow's evocation of the sun over the *Patna* lifeboat or the moon over Patusan, we may be inclined to doubt this statement. In fact it brings up the inevitable question of how much of himself an author puts into a narrator. My belief is that much of Marlow's negative imagining (of which we are about to see more) expresses Conrad's own unconscious fears.[12] But I also believe that Conrad

12. Conrad's difficulty in portraying women and describing love scenes in his novels is well known. For a thorough Freudian analysis of its relation to his artistic career, see Thomas Moser, *Joseph Conrad: Achievement and Decline* (Cambridge: Harvard University Press, 1957). In dealing with *Lord Jim*, Moser tends to focus on Jewel as the threatening woman. In reality the witch figures are motherly: Jewel's mother, Doramin's wife (pp. 225 and 238), and an "old hag" who hovers around while Jim faces his assassins (257, 259, 260). For a study of Conrad's own psychic problems, as they can be seen in his novels, and in "unarmed" heroes such as Jim, see Bernard Meyer, *Joseph Conrad: A Psychoanalytic Biography* (Princeton: Princeton University Press, 1967).

consciously characterized Marlow as having an intellectual ability to construct favourable explanations of Jim's conduct which his emotions cannot accept.

In any case, right after denying his own imaginative faculty, Marlow goes on to give what seems to me quite clearly a warning to the reader. "He existed for me, and after all it is only through me that he exists for you. I've led him out by the hand; I have paraded him before you. Were my commonplace fears unjust? I won't say—not even now. You may be able to tell better, since the proverb has it that the onlookers see most of the game" (p. 194). One of the things that makes *Lord Jim* a great novel is the use to which Conrad put that insight, the number of characters whose views we are invited to absorb before coming to our own conclusions. That side of the novel concerns us, however, only as it applies to the principal narrator, Marlow. Conrad has him chivy his conventional listeners, as he did so successfully in *Heart of Darkness*. But in *Lord Jim* Marlow does not gain a deep emotional revelation, as he did in that shorter novel; rather Marlow specifically refuses a chance for involvement and possible enlightenment in the latter part of *Lord Jim*.

On the question of race, religion, and colour, the narrating voice of the early chapters is sympathetic to the dark Moslem pilgrims from the East. Marlow is much less so (as is the friend to whom he writes, see p. 294); he can speak only condescending praise of Jim's friendship for Dain Waris. But he does give us a clue when he mentions Dain Waris' "great reserves of intelligence and power. Such beings open to the Western eye, so often concerned with mere surfaces, the hidden possibilities of races and lands over which hangs the mystery of unrecorded ages" (p. 227). In *Heart of Darkness,* Marlow's active commitment to these "mere surfaces" saves him from "the reality" and "the inner truth, luckily, luckily" (p. 93). Marlow has no direct encounter with the barbaric tribes of the Congo; he learns vicariously through Kurtz. But in *Lord Jim,* the natives are not so barbaric, nor is it their truth which will corrupt Jim. In Patusan, therefore, Marlow's "mere surface" carries less dramatic and thematic weight than it did in the Congo. Marlow's clinging to it is consequently much less of a virtue in Patusan, as the comment on Dain Waris indicates.

The test of Marlow's clear-sightedness comes in his confrontation with Jewel, which is to the second half of the novel what his meeting with Jim is to the first. Ironically, in the first part of the confrontation Marlow may be compared to Jim approaching his destiny, the jump from the *Patna* into his hole. Looking into Jewel's eyes, Marlow seems to see "a faint stir, such as you may fancy you can detect when you plunge your gaze to the bottom of an immensely deep well. What is it that moves there? you ask yourself. Is it a blind monster or only a lost gleam from the universe? It occurred to me—don't laugh—that all things being dissimilar, she was more inscrutable in her childish ignorance that the Sphinx propounding childish riddles to wayfarers" (p. 266). Like Jim, Marlow is offered a chance to find truth at the bottom of a well. And, as in Marlow's relation to Kurtz in *Heart of Darkness,* this chance comes in a vicarious form, through another person. Jewel, like the Sphinx, asks a basic question about her man. Less flattering to Marlow, she propounds an answer, one that upsets him considerably. She suggests that Jim will prove unfaithful to her. Marlow's reaction is to feel insecure. "The very ground on which I stood seemed to melt under my feet" (p. 273).

Although all of Marlow's emphasis is on Jewel's irrational state, the beginning of the scene makes it clear that Marlow has a problem, too. All Jewel has to do is tell him the one reservation she had in giving her love to Jim, and Marlow begins to feel threatened. "I didn't want to die weeping," she says (p. 270). " 'My mother had wept bitterly before she died,' she explained. An inconceivable calmness seemed to have risen from the ground around us, imperceptibly, like the still rise of a flood in the night, obliterating the familiar landmarks of emotions. There came upon me, as though I had felt myself losing my footing in the midst of waters, a sudden dread, the dread of the unknown depths" (p. 271). The description of the death that Jewel then goes on to give is too much for Marlow.

> It had the power to drive me out of my conception of existence, out of that shelter each of us makes for himself to creep under in moments of danger, as a tortoise withdraws within its shell. For a moment I had a view of a world that seemed to wear a vast and dismal aspect of disorder, while, in truth, thanks to our unwearied efforts, it is as sunny an arrangement of small conveniences as the mind of man can conceive. But still—it was only a moment: I went back into my shell directly. One *must*—don't you know?—though I seemed to have lost all my words in the chaos of dark thoughts I had contemplated for a second or two beyond the pale. These came back, too, very soon, for words also belong to the sheltering conception of light and order which is our refuge (pp. 271–72).

At least three points here need comment.

First of all, we should notice that the sun has been reduced to a Polyanna adjective connected with "small conveniences." Marlow's irony in doing so is not really confident understatment, as his situation indicates. Second, we should notice that "words," like "light" and "order," have become a "refuge" rather than a means to truth.[13]

And third, we should notice the image Marlow uses to describe his act of seeking refuge from the truth, "as a tortoise withdraws within its shell." This image appears only one other time in the novel, when Jim is in the lifeboat facing the sun. The other three deserters have "crept under" a boat-sail spread on the gunwales (p. 108). After a while, the captain of the *Patna* "poked his big cropped head from under the canvas and screwed his fishy eyes up at me. 'Donnerwetter! you will die,' he growled, and drew in like a turtle" (p. 109). I don't believe the parallel is fortuitous, but even if it is, the larger parallel of the two incidents will hold. Faced with the threat of sinking in stormy waters or in a panicking sea of "unconscious pilgrims," the officers of the *Patna* take refuge in a lifeboat. Faced with the possibility of losing his mental "footing in the midst of dangerous waters" and "unknown depths," Marlow withdraws into "that shelter each of us makes for himself to creep under in moments of danger."

The only person to vary the pattern is Jim. He elects to sit outside the shelter, to face the trial, to go to the bottom of the well. He is not interested in "sunny" arrangements and "small conveniences." He is interested in words, light and order, but not as a "sheltering conception." Marlow himself finally puts Conrad's case directly: "The point, however, is that of all mankind Jim had no dealings but with himself, and the question is whether at the last he had not confessed to a faith mightier than the laws of order and progress" (p. 294). Jim's own faith obviously is "mightier" in the sense that he follows it with complete confidence at the end. Conrad expressed his own faith twelve years later in *A Personal Record*: "Only in men's imagination does every truth find an effective and undeniable existence. Imagination, not invention, is the supreme master of art as of life" (p. 25).

We may find it harder to accept Jim's desertion of Jewel. Marlow

13. Again it seems to me that Marlow's irony hides self-deception. The reader of *Heart of Darkness* may remember how Marlow there charges women with an inability to face harsh truth. Though Conrad may have occasionally agreed, he usually admitted that it is men who are the hopeless idealists. Clearly Jewel is much more willing to face the truth about Jim than is Marlow.

is willing before the end to face even that. "She had said he had been driven away from her by a dream,—and there was no answer one could make her—there seemed to be no forgiveness for such a transgression. And yet is not mankind itself, pushing on its blind way, driven by a dream of its greatness and its power upon the dark paths of excessive cruelty and of excessive devotion? And what is the pursuit of truth, after all?" (p. 303). The truth Jim is after does not lie in the "mere surfaces" usually scanned by "the Western eye" (p. 227). Rather it lies deep in his own sense of himself. If he discovers a flaw there which calls in doubt the harmony of that order, his decision to abide by the code he has established is at worst equivocal. A minor moral of the novel could certainly be that it is not for those who (like Marlow) are afraid to dip into the well of truth to condemn those who (like Jim) are drowned in the attempt to plumb its depths.

Perhaps Stein's original advice would have been clearer if it had begun "A romantic when he is born falls into a dream. . . . " From this point of view, we can understand why it is necessary for Jim to plunge in, and why it is not necessary for Marlow. We need also to remember that such a plunge was necessary for Conrad—as witness the late preface from which we have already quoted: "The romantic feeling of reality was in me an inborn faculty." Given a second chance after his misfortunes in Marseilles, Conrad, like Stein, settled down to the hard business of Western life. Then he gave himself a third chance, allowing the same imaginative faculty that had revelled in the adventures of his youth to create new and more lasting fictional adventures. Conrad's ambition was satanic in more than one way. As a writer who was at once romantic, realist, and impressionist, he aimed to create an ordered and almost tangible world of his own. And in his pride he wished to be honoured for his efforts.

The contrast between the man of action and the man of words was almost second nature to Conrad by the time he began his writing career. The man of action has to know the physical world, its necessities and its recalcitrance. He has to know how to work with other men, how to respect his bond with them. To this substantial world, and to the deserving people who populate it, Conrad naturally paid homage in description and in theme. But, in addition and behind this, in the very act of conception, he attempted "to depict faithfully" in each "work of imagination that innermost world . . . that inner life (which is the soul of human activity)."

In the light of such a confession, we should not be surprised if in one novel he not only chose a dreamer as his hero, but put him into a dream world to allow him to fight out there the very real conflicts which go on inside all of us. Nor is it improbable that, having chronicled Jim's failure, Conrad should yet have left open the likelihood that his hero had the right to make the choice he did.

Chapter Ten

The Well of Truth

Throughout this study I have used the term "romance" as synonymous with such examples of pure fantasy as dream and fairy tale. But, in the view of Richard Chase, romance comprehended more than this subjective area. He used a statement from the Introduction to *The Scarlet Letter* as a basis for a provocative distinction. Hawthorne wished to find for fiction

> "a neutral territory, somewhere between the real world and fairyland, where the Actual and the Imaginary may meet, and each imbue itself with the nature of the other." Romance is, as we see, a kind of "border" fiction, whether the field of action is in the neutral territory between civilization and the wilderness . . . or whether . . . the field of action is conceived not so much as a place as a state of mind—the borderland of the human mind where the actual and the imaginary intermingle. Romance does not plant itself, like the novel, solidly in the midst of the actual. Nor when it is memorable, does it escape into the purely imaginary (*The American Novel and its Tradition*, pp. 18–19).

Adapting Chase's point to the novels we have examined, we could say that different geographical areas tend to become associated with or symbolic of different states of mind. The irrational in *Wuthering Heights, The Return of the Native* and *Lord Jim* is associated with the moor, the heath, and uncivilized Patusan. Jim brings the rational standards of honesty and consistency to Patusan but is destroyed by an unscrupulous Satanic outcast from the civilized world. Clym Yeobright attempts to bring enlightenment to the dark heath and is severely chastised by it for his pains. As children and as spirits, Cathy and

Heathcliff come to terms with the irrational, though not even they can manage it during adulthood.

The moors are not much disturbed by the advent and exit of civilized outsiders like Lockwood. But the heath insists on doing away with all non-natives, Wildeve the engineer, cultured Mrs. Yeobright, and discontented Eustacia. Although Hardy and Emily Brontë use the world of affairs as ballast, their interest and sympathy is clearly with the uncivilized. Conrad's case is more ambiguous; he is suspicious of Patusan as an alien country; in contrast the also uncivilized moor and heath are at least populated by English people. For Conrad, Patusan and England are opposite poles, but the sea often provides him with a meeting place of East and West, dream and reality, the borderland where the imaginary and the actual meet to test their equally strong claims.

An important difference between Dickens and the three novelists just discussed is that Chase's notion of the borderland does not work for a novel like *Bleak House*. When we ask ourselves how Dickens, dealing so much with urban life, manages not to write realistic novels totally devoted to the actual, the answer is that Dickens transcends Chase's distinction. In focusing on London, Dickens worked with the world he knew best; but that world, unlike the moors or the heath of Emily Brontë or Hardy, was also one that his readers knew well, one about which there was no developed attitude of nature romanticism. Yet Dickens stubbornly insisted that the city not only could but must be seen with an imaginative eye. "A nation without fancy, without some romance, never did, never can, never will, hold a great place under the sun" (*Household Words,* Oct. 1, 1853). His achievement lay exactly in choosing an area of England to which his readers could not easily extend poetic belief, in forcing them to give credence to scenes which might purport to originate in their everyday experience, and in trans-forming these into an imaginative experience. Small wonder that literal-ists complained, or that Dickens was touchy about his lack of realism. Small wonder that the fastidious were often offended at the vulgarity of that world, or that Dickens' tone should often be strident and theatrical. He needed not only an active imagination but a strong will to persevere in the task he set himself.

I do not wish to imply that Dickens simply invented out of his divine imagination all the materials that went into the making of his fictional universe. We know that he drew on various traditions, not only the eighteenth-century novelists but the world of the theatre, where he found many types to take over as characters for his novels. He appropriated such types, however, not just because he found them ready to hand and easy to manipulate, but also because he himself tended to see people that way. And, if this way of seeing had its defects, it also had its virtues.

At the beginning of this book, we looked at Ian Watt's conception of personal identity as something which the eighteenth-century novel helped contribute to fiction. Admitting that this is a valuable concept for approaching the novels of Jane Austen and George Eliot, I suggested that it is somewhat less so for understanding the novels we have been considering. The reason is that our novelists characteristically place their protagonists in a tension of which the need to develop a *personal* identity is only half. The other equally necessary half of the character's identity we might label as *archetypal*. These two terms can be correlated with the ones Chase borrowed from Hawthorne, personal identity relating to the actual world, archetypal identity to the imaginary.

The tension between the two identities can be resolved in favour of either. In *The Mysteries of Udolpho,* the personal is tested against seemingly supernatural experiences, but once these have proved Emily St Aubert's character, the archetypal level is jettisoned by her Augustan author. In *The Monk*, on the other hand, Ambrosio has never had strictly personal experiences from which to build up an identity. Raised in a monastery, he knows only the theory of life, which he preaches winningly in public, until privately corrupted to the life of sensations by Rosario-Matilda. But, as we saw, these "sensations" are very much connected with daydreams and nightmare, moving toward an archetypal level. The difference between *The Mysteries of Udolpho* and *The Monk*, which we earlier suggested as being between sensibility and sensation, can also be seen as the difference between Mrs. Radcliffe's concern with the stability of her heroine's identity and Lewis's revelling in the disintegration of his hero's identity. Being children of the eighteenth century, Lewis and Mrs. Radcliffe were agreed in seeing the indulgence of daydreams and superstitions as a giving in to the irrational, which was considered demonic—demonic but attractive.

The Romantics tended to accept this analysis, but tried to alter their judgment or conclusion from it, changing *demon* (the evil one) into *daimon* (the *alter ego* of the conscious self). By this process the archetypal became not a lurid realm of demonic sensation so much as a higher realm of individual enlargement. The moors serve as this realm for the young Heathcliff and Cathy in *Wuthering Heights,* just as it does in the posthumous union of their spirits. And their achievement of archetypal identity is neatly balanced in the worldly realm of personal identity by the mutual adjustment of Catherine's too-high nature to Hareton's too-low one. In *Bleak House,* the archetypal realm is present negatively in Krook, positively in the imagery associated with Esther Summerson. Whereas Emily Brontë discriminated and balanced archetypal and personal in her two pairs of lovers, Dickens, as we might expect, tried to relate the two, so that Esther's willingness to sacrifice her identity, in the Christian doctrine of helpfulness and duty, finally results in her having thrust on her a very solid personal identity.

Lacking the comfort of traditional Christianity and of traditional social conventions, Hardy and Conrad were not hopeful about the possibility of achieving an identity. Both admired the simple labourer on land or sea whose identity flowed from involvement through hard work in the lasting process of nature. But both saw that such an impersonal identity was not for them or any thinking modern man. Both celebrated it anyhow, as preferable to the new middle-class "personal" identity located in things, in cities, in progress. Like the romantics they preferred the simple life of nature, though deprived by Darwin of some of the more comforting earlier romantic ideas about man's place in nature.

The exceptional individual of romanticism also presented himself as an ambiguous hero to Hardy and Conrad. But Hardy in his later works was able to come to some sort of terms with this avenue for achieving a personal identity. *Tess of the d'Urbervilles,* especially, seems to me a very impressive attempt to present the struggles of an exceptional individual to find herself in a concrete environment which is at the same time permeated by cosmic patterns.[1] Although almost the same could be said of Hardy's treatment of Eustacia Vye and Clym Yeobright in *The Return of the Native,* the fact is that in that earlier novel Hardy was so bound up with the archetypal level that he never really gave his characters a chance to develop a personal identity.

Heathcliff and Eustacia resolved their lives in favour of an archetypal identity through death; Conrad had Lord Jim do likewise. But

1. See my article, "Darwinism and Initiation in *Tess of the d'Ubervilles,*" *Nineteenth-Century Fiction,* 18 (December 1963).

the circumstances created by Conrad were quite different from either of the earlier two. Like Emily Brontë, Conrad was trying to balance the two possible areas for finding identity. But, unlike any English novelist since Monk Lewis, Conrad actually plunged his hero into the archetypal world. Yet, where *The Monk* is no more than romance, *Lord Jim* is a novel, containing both the world of the actual, in the *Patna* episode, and the world of the imagination, in Patusan. Jim is thus given a chance to work out his identity in two ways, a personal identity in his job and failing that, an archetypal identity in a land corresponding to his daydreams. Conrad could allow this second chance because he knew the importance of the interior world, and he knew that a born romantic could not cope effectively with the outside world until he had mastered the interior one.

Jim lets someone else pull the trigger of the gun which provides him with an entrance to this final world; so we may presume Eustacia Vye lets the storm on Egdon Heath drive her into the weir whose noise should be warning enough. Like Jim in Patusan, she has "tried and tried to be a splendid" person, but "destiny has been against" her (*Return,* V, 7). Therefore, rather than flee with someone she is not married to, she decides, still like Jim, to follow her own personal dream in the only way left open to her. She plunges into the archetypal world where her beauty is fully revealed.

Cathy Linton of *Wuthering Heights* also achieves in death what she could not in life. Even Nelly Dean is impressed. "No angel in heaven could be more beautiful than she appeared; and I partook of the infinite calm in which she lay. . . . I instinctively echoed the words she had uttered a few hours before. 'Incomparably beyond, and above us all! Whether still on earth or now in heaven, her spirit is at home with God!' " (pp. 174–75). In admitting that Cathy's spirit may still be on earth rather than in heaven, Nelly shows herself more unorthodox than she will at the end of the novel. She also indicates a difference between Cathy and Eustacia. Where Hardy's heroine would have nothing to do with the heath, Emily Brontë's identitifies herself and Heathcliff with the elements of the moor, and they manage to become part of that impersonal world once they are dead. Eustacia has achieved only a personal victory. The heath goes on as it had before she appeared on it. Yet, as Hardy's picture of the elemental heath shows, that active impersonal world constitutes as worthy an archetype as the passive personal one to which Eustacia and Lord Jim resign themselves. As Hardy and Conrad saw it, personal identity could be maintained only by opposition to the impersonal environment. For Emily Brontë, it was still possible to look for harmony with an active environment, though only by cultivating an impersonal identity, as first Cathy and then Heathcliff did.

Unfortunately, cultivating an impersonal identity sounds to twentieth-century ears suspiciously like a euphemism for giving in to what Freud has taught us to call the death wish. Being truthful, we must admit that all these novelists demonstrate an involvement with the problem, as did the Romantic poets before them.

Perhaps a partial justification of their preoccupation with death comes from its being an important part of life. Vicariously, through observation and imagination, it is part of each individual's experience. The question is the extent. I referred in Chapter Two to the morbid power of *The Monk*. Similarly, it would not be difficult to make out a case for a death wish in Emily Brontë, Dickens, Hardy, and Conrad. In each case a psycho-moral judgment against the author would undoubtedly result.[2] But such a procedure seems to me mistaken. By a similar process, all great artists can be convicted of acute neuroticism, or worse. While I cannot agree with those who pretend that creativity is incompatible with severe psychic disturbance, I do agree that creativity aims, among other things, at righting emotional imbalance. A reasonable hypothesis might be that the heights of creativity are called into play only by the deeps of psychic disturbance. The conclusion could then follow that what the artist faces and attempts to solve is simply his own compelling version of the inner problems we all have, though we may be only dimly aware of them. One justification of art, then, and of its dealing with death, would be its ability to face such important problems.

Another justification is more in line with the approach we have taken so far. What we experience in these novels is not after all a literal, or even a pretend-literal death. It is fictional death, and in most cases figurative death. We saw this process most clearly in applying Jung's version of the theory of regression to *Lord Jim*. To become the hero, Jim must be born again. To be born again, he must die. As we saw, Conrad was slightly skeptical of this process because of his own experience and his strong reality sense. Yet he was compelled to trace

2. The most obvious model for this particular game is *The Romantic Agony* (1933) by Mario Praz. For a more positive Freudian approach to the problem of dung and death, see Norman O. Brown, *Life Against Death* (1959).

out the attempts of Wait, Kurtz, and Lord Jim to relodge themselves
in life after a deathly experience—a burial, a sickness, a jump into
the grave. Recalling Conrad's self-descriptive and revealing phrase,
"creative darkness," we can see the truth that lies behind the emphasis
on rebirth. All these novelists seem obliged to follow Stein's advice
and "immerse" in the dream, the destructive element. As Conrad put
it in the Preface to *The Nigger of the Narcissus,* "the artist descends
within himself, and in that lonely region of stress and strife . . . he
finds the terms of his appeal," an appeal "to that part of our nature"
that is "kept out of sight. . . . to that in us which is a gift and not an
acquisition." Knowing their emotions are the true "destructive element,"
such writers still feel obliged to risk this descent into creative darkness, and are willing to die to the light of consciousness for the sake
of an artistic conception and in the hope of a rebirth.

It is not only these writers who depend on the darkness within, of
course. The question is one of degree. Some writers work mainly with
material taken from conscious memory and give it more or less the
temporal shape it had. Some have easy access to memories of incidents
which do not bear an emotional over-charge. Some through hard
labour can tap the Freudian unconscious of repressed emotion, a
valuable area for any artist. Jung called these repressions the personal
unconscious, which he contrasted with the collective unconscious,
where dwell his archetypes. In his essay on "Psychology and Literature," he was presumably working on that distinction when he contrasted the psychological "mode of artistic creation" with the visionary.[3]
"The psychological mode deals with materials drawn from the realm
of human consciousness—for instance, with the lessons of life, with
emotional shocks, the experience of passion and the crises of human
destiny in general—all of which go to make up the conscious life of
man, and his feeling life in particular" (p. 179). Although Jung says
this mode is concerned with "human consciousness," he presumably
intends the phrase "emotional shocks" to include material dredged up
into consciousness from the personal unconscious. Certainly he does
not wish to include such material in the visionary mode, which clearly
depends on archetypal experiences. That mode "is a strange something
that derives its existence from the hinterland of man's mind—that

---

3. This essay was included in *Modern Man in Search of a Soul* (London: Routledge & Kegan Paul, 1933).

suggests the abyss of time separating us from pre-human ages, or evokes a super-human world of contrasting light and darkness. It is a primordial experience which surpasses man's understanding, and to which he is therefore in danger of succumbing. The value and the force of the experience are given by its enormity. It arises from time-less depths; it is foreign and cold, many-sided, demonic and grotesque" (pp. 180–81). The relevance of Jung's evocation to the patterns de-veloped in this chapter should be clear enough.

Not only have we seen a constant use of light and dark images in the novels studied; that use has been in a visionary context, from the "superhuman world" of *The Monk* where Ambrosio succumbs to "a primordial experience," through the "demonic and grotesque" world of *Bleak House,* to the "foreign and cold" vision of "timeless depths" common to *Wuthering Heights, The Return of the Native,* and *Lord Jim.*

Jung argues for the "primordial" quality of such visions by analogy. "In the physical structure of the body we find traces of earlier stages of evolution, and we may expect the human psyche also to conform in its make-up to the law of phylogeny. It is a fact that in eclipses of consciousness—in dreams, narcotic states and cases of insanity—there come to the surface psychic products or contents that show all the traits of primitive levels of psychic development" (p. 190). Regard-less of how we feel about Jung's logic, his case is quite similar to that of Hardy and Conrad. We have seen, for instance, both novelists con-ceiving of a character who makes contact with the primitive by giving up consciousness, Diggory Venn as automaton and Singleton as oracle. Both authors insisted that the poetic imagination also makes contact with this primitive realm. The result is animism, Hardy's "barbaric idea which confuses persons and things," a figurative mode of per-ception.

In the artist as initiated magician this primitive vision is transmuted from a limiting superstition to an enlarging attempt to connect man and nature, inner and outer reality. In the aesthetics of Conrad, "a work of art is very seldom limited to one exclusive meaning and not necessarily tending to a definite conclusion. And this for the reason that the nearer it approaches art, the more it acquires a symbolic character. . . . [T]he symbolic conception of a work of art has this advantage, that it makes a triple appeal covering the whole field of life. All the great creations of literature have been symbolic, and in that way have gained in complexity, in power, in depth and in beauty" (*Life and*

Letters, II, 205). Of these four terms, I have taken "beauty" for granted and allowed "complexity" to speak for itself in analysing the various novels taken up. "Power" and "depth" are the two notions most emphasized by Jung as characterizing the archetypal world, which is by definition symbolic. Perhaps the key point about the irrational in fiction is its charging of seemingly everyday, descriptive detail with added psychic meaning, the symbolic conception that strives to connect the inner and outer world in a suggestive and harmonious whole.

To achieve this primitive vision leading to high art, such a writer not only descends within himself but characteristically forces one of his characters, usually the hero, to do the same. We saw in the last chapter one image connected with that inner plunge, the descent into the well or cauldron. This image is important not only for Conrad, but for Dickens and Hardy as well. And, because the descent into creative darkness is like a death, even these writers feel ambiguous toward it. Thus Conrad refers to Jim's well as a hole and a grave.

Dickens, a little like Conrad, connects the well with darkness and burial. These connections are striking in his description, in *Bleak House*, of the Smallweeds "digging, delving, and diving among the treasures" of the late Krook (p. 423). Out of a "well or grave of waste paper" (p. 424), they bring valuable documents. Like Krook and the Chancellor, however, the Smallweeds are after money, not truth. The treasure which they dig up and then hoard is, in Dickens' opinion, a poor substitute for life. He therefore has Jarndyce explicitly contrast for Esther her own worth against the family tree of the Woodcourts and any hidden hoard of the past. "I would not have my Esther's bright example lost . . . I would not have her admitted on sufferance into the line of Morgan ap Kerrig, no, and for the weight in gold of all the mountains in Wales!" (p. 649). The moral here is a fairy tale moral, one that we saw pointed to in the indifference of the youth, Iron Hans's protegé, to treasure and money.

As the epigraph to *Youth*, Conrad took from Grimm a quotation similar to the one Dickens had in mind. "But the dwarf answered: 'No; something human is dearer to me than all the wealth of the world.' " Those who sell their souls for physical gold are digging in a grave where only darkness and death have power. The true well, human nature, is best plumbed by impersonal agents like Bucket, who can dip into the darkness of the human mind with impunity, or by the artist as initiated magician.

Our final example of the well image will also bring us back to the

problem of creativity and unconscious thought. The well appears in
The Return of the Native not only as a source of pure water for
Eustacia, but also as a habitat quite different from the heath. It contains "strange humid leaves, which knew nothing of the seasons of the
year," and a bucket which is characterized first as "a dead friend come
back to earth," and then as "a falling body" (III, 3) when it slips back
down into the well. This hint of resurrection is all we need to connect
Hardy's well to Conrad's. But the image is best pursued in another
context, also connected with Eustacia. First in her dream and finally
in her life, Eustacia dives into a pool (which is called a caldron) where
she expects her dreams to come true. As we have already observed,
she does in fact achieve apotheosis in this plunge. It could be said that
her immersion in the well of truth brings her rebirth as the splendid or
perfect person she had desired to be.

But we must also remember Jung's characterization of the "time-
less depths" of the archetypal world as "foreign and cold." In one sense
Eustacia's act partakes of these qualities. But that is because they
partake of that world. It is a cold, inhuman world, foreign to our warm
passions and social obligations. As imaged by Hardy, it is a world of
succeeding seasons and contending elements, each with its essential
characteristics and its own beauty, but none conscious of man. If
Eustacia achieves harmony with that world it is because chance rules
that she is ready to abnegate her human desire at the season when
nature is generally celebrating the death of passion and the dissolution
of individual desire. Hardy understands this process in nature because he understands it in his own depths.

Like other novelists in the nineteenth century, those we have been
discussing were involved with the psychological mode, presenting the
struggles of characters to achieve personal identity. But, behind the
groundwork of recognizable reality which may connect their world to
our everyday one, informing its details, each of these novelists
cherished a vision which he tried to render in his work. Each was
driven by primordial impulses which shaped his fictional world. Beneath the ordered society of his time each saw an unordered chaos, a
world disintegrating, a new order waiting to be established. Each saw
such a spectacle, perhaps because it was true of Victorian society,
but more fundamentally because each had descended within himself
and confronted in that heart of darkness not only the death of life
but the unborn shape of future life. Their novels embody that life.

Index

Abyss, 32–33, 37, 139, 174
Adam Bede, 99
Alice in Wonderland, 15
Alien, 60–61, 66, 67, 102, 107, 168
Alienation, 118
Allegory, 15, 25, 32, 80, 100, 135, 155
alter ego, 75, 80–82, 83, 87–90, 99, 145, 152–53, 169
American Novel and Its Tradition, The, 24–25, 167
Ancient Mariner, The, 31, 38
Angel, 35, 55, 69, 93
Anima, 144, 148, 154
Animals and animal imagery, 68–69, 81, 84–85, 87, 90, 107–8, 153; cat, 87–88, 90, 91, 97; dog, 44, 55, 66–69; lion, 43 n3, 80; mole, 113; stag, 47–48, 63, 70; wolf, 81, 84. *See also* bear, bull
Animism, 105–7, 110, 174
Apuleius, 14, 43
Arabian Nights, The, 41
Archetypal: analysis, x, 35, 146, 149, 151–54, 156–61, 164–66, 169–71; experience, 34, 58, 121–25, 138–39, 160; identity, 169–72; world, x, 44–45, 144–45, 153–54, 160, 171, 173–76
Archetypes, vii, ix–x, 17, 27, 60, 128, 135, 144–45, 148, 161, 173
Aristotle, 16–17
Austen, Jane, 16, 18, 23, 169
Automaton, 55, 113–14, 117, 174

Barbaric ideas, 104, 111, 134, 162, 174
Bear, 43 n3, 55, 81–82, 84–85

Beast (character and motif), 43, 45–46, 51, 55–56, 59–60, 65, 67, 68, 82, 87, 89, 90
Beauty (character and motif), 43, 46, 51, 55, 59, 67, 78, 103
Biographia Literaria, 26
Blake, William, 57, 70
Blindness, 37, 113–14, 117, 165
Blood, 19, 31, 67, 109–10, 112, 120–21, 160–61
Bronte, Emily, ix, 13, 16, 21, 42, 43, 47, 50–51, 54–57, 58, 59–71, 73, 99, 168, 170–73; *Wuthering Heights,* 16, 27, 47, 50–51, 54–57, 58, 59–71, 73, 81 n3, 167–68, 170, 171, 174
Buber, Martin, viii n2, x n5, xi
Bull, 47–48, 63, 153
Bulwer-Lytton, Dickens' letters to, 82, 90, 94, 95, 127
Byron, Lord, 39, 57, 100
Byronic hero, 23, 39, 50, 100, 118

Calderon, 139
Campbell, Joseph, 34, 35, 116 n16, 149 n7
Carroll, Lewis, 15
Castle of Otranto, The, 19, 21–23
Catacombs, 33, 35, 36
Cauldron, 124, 149, 175, 176
Cavern, 124, 139, 156, 157
Cervantes, Miguel de, 138–39
Cervoni, Dominic, 137–38
Chase, Richard, 24–25, 26, 27, 42, 53, 167–69
Christ, 132, 157–58

Christianity, ix, 14, 32, 74, 76, 96, 111, 117–18, 131–32, 136, 170
Clodd, Edward, 104–5
Cold, image of, 26, 30–32, 33, 159, 174, 176
Coleridge, S. T., 26, 29, 31, 38–39, 42, 53–54, 100
Collins, Wilkie, Dickens' letters to, 95, 130
Conrad, Joseph, ix, 13, 21, 42, 47, 99, 127–40, 141–66, 168, 170–76; *Heart of Darkness*, 128, 139, 151, 157, 162–63, 164 n13; *Lord Jim*, 128–29, 138–40, 141–66, 167, 170–72, 174 (*see also Patna*, Patusan); *The Mirror of the Sea*, 135, 137, 139; *The Nigger of the Narcissus*, 128, 131–32, 133–37, 141, 157–58, 159, 173; *Notes on Life and Letters*, 154; *An Outcast of the Islands*, 151; *A Personal Record*, 127–40 passim, 159; *Within the Tides*, 128; *Youth*, 175
Conrad's Polish Background, 144

Daemon (daimon), 60, 62, 86, 145, 169. *See also Alter ego*
Dark powers, 142, 154
Darkness, ix, xi, 33–34, 67, 121, 143, 149, 173, 176; creative, 130, 173, 175; images of, 26, 33–35, 50, 56, 84–93 passim, 124–25, 151–59 passim, 174; of Heathcliff, 60–63; of Krook, 86–87, 97; of Egdon Heath, 101, 104, 110–11, 115, 119; of Eustacia, 101, 119, 125
Darwin, Charles, 15, 99, 170
Daydream, 13, 27, 29, 33 36, 54, 123, 142, 169
Defoe, Daniel, 20, 21, 23
Demonic, the, 22, 38, 39, 74, 93, 103, 169, 174
Depth, images of, 26, 47, 67, 82, 92, 135, 139, 157, 163–65, 170, 174–76. *See also* Abyss, Hole, Well
Depths, descent into the, ix, 33–36, 139, 149–50, 160, 175. *See also* Grave
Devil, 60, 62, 93, 111, 145. *See also* Satan
Dickens, Charles, ix, 13, 16, 21, 42, 47, 50, 73–97 99–100, 119, 127–31 passim, 140, 159, 168, 170, 172–73,

175; *Bleak House*, 27, 47, 73–97, 168, 170, 174, 175; *A Christmas Carol*, 74, 80–81, 100; *David Copperfield*, 75–76; *Dombey and Son*, 74; *Great Expectations*, 99; *Household Words*, 74, 75, 94, 168; *Martin Chuzzlewit*, 73; *A Tale of Two Cities*, 95
Don Quixote, 138–39, 157
Dragon, 84, 87, 88, 90, 160. *See also* Monster
Dream, xi, 13–17, 24, 26, 27, 29, 42, 104, 112, 115, 134, 142–44, 155, 165–66, 167–73. *See also* Daydream, Nightmare, Vision
Dream(s): Walpole's, 19; Lorenzo's, 32–34, 38; Hareton's, 55; Catherine's, 16, 66; Lockwood's, 67, 69–71; Eustacia's, 121–24, 176; Don Quixote's, 138–39; Jim's, 146–47
Dream world, 122, 143, 146, 166, 171. *See also* Archetypal world
Dreams and Nightmares (Hadfield), 16

Eclipse of God (Buber), viii n2, x n5, xi
Elemental imagery, 37, 56, 63, 71, 100, 104, 106, 109, 111, 119–21, 124, 134, 151, 171; earth, 109, 112, 119–20, 151 (*see also* Heath, Moor); fire, 106, 108–12, 117, 119, 121, 124, 156, 158 (*see also* Seasonal rites: bonfire); water, x, 37, 44, 45, 71, 117, 119–21, 124–25, 131, 143, 147, 149–51, 157, 163, 164, 176 (*see also* Sea); wind, 64, 71, 104, 106, 119
Eliot, George, 16, 18, 99, 100, 169
Elixir, 149–50
Enchantment, 31, 45, 48, 56, 66, 75, 83, 88, 139, 140
English Novel: Form and Function, The (Van Ghent), 60
Escapism, 14, 26, 42, 55
Evolution. *See* Natural selection

Fairy, 63–64, 68, 69, 77, 84
Fairy tale, x, 13, 14, 18, 24, 40, 41–51, 54–55, 59, 62, 63, 67, 68, 70, 74–80, 84–86, 135, 145, 149, 159–60, 167, 175. *See also* Folktales

Fairy tale characters, 75, 85–87, 159–
60; Blue Beard, 90; Cinderella, 51,
54–55, 76, 97; Dick Whittington, 78;
elves, goblins, 75, 88, 160; Prince
Charming, 54–55, 77; Snow White,
54–55. *See also* Beauty, Beast,
Dragon, King, Prince, Princess,
Queen
Fairy tale motifs, 14, 15, 17, 43, 47,
49, 51, 55, 70, 77, 80, 99–100, 127,
149–50, 159
Fairy tale patterns, 59, 63–68, 84, 97,
159–60
Fairy tales: *Beauty and the Beast*, 43,
44, 60, 65; *The Children in the
Wood*, 77–78; *Cinderella*, 50; *Cupid
and Psyche*, 14, 43; *The Fire-Bird*,
149; *The Frog Prince*, 160; *The
Gnome*, 160; *The Goose Girl at the
Well*, 160; *Hänsel and Gretel*, 64,
77, 78; *Jorinda and Joringel*, 78;
Mother Goose Tales, 41; *Mother
Holle*, 160; *Toads and Diamonds*,
160; *Valentine and Orson*, 81–82;
The Widow's Son, 149. *See also
The Glass Coffin, Iron Hans*
Familiar, magician's, 87–88, 91, 97,
109
Fanger, Donald, 73–74
Fantasy, xi, 13, 14, 26, 27, 38, 40, 42,
69, 167
Fate (*and* chance), 43, 49, 60, 76, 114,
123, 131
Fielding, Henry, 20, 21
Firor, Ruth, 110, 111, 115, 123
Flaubert, 96
Folklore, 128, 133, 153
Folktale, The (Thompson), 41, 44 n5
Folktales, 14, 15, 34, 41
Folkways, 105, 110, 114, 115, 123
Folkways in Thomas Hardy (Firor),
110, 115, 123
Frazer, James, 118
Freud, Sigmund, viii, 17, 27, 34, 49,
121, 122, 136, 172, 173

Galsworthy, John, Conrad's letters to,
130, 159
Garnett, Edward, Conrad's letters to,
130, 145, 151
Gestner, Theodore, 116
Glass Coffin, The, 47–49, 50, 51, 63,
70

Gold, 44–46, 63, 64, 84, 90, 160, 175.
See also Treasure
Goldberg, M. A., 103
Golden, 86, 102, 150, 159–60
Golden Ass, The, 14, 43
Gothic novel, the, 14, 18, 19–26, 41,
42, 49, 50, 54
Graham, R. B. Cunninghame, Conrad's
letters to, 132, 133, 134
Grave, 35, 69, 71 132, 136, 155–57,
173, 175. *See also* Catacombs, Cav-
ern, Hole
Grimm, Jacob and Wilhelm, 41, 43,
44, 50, 160, 175

Hadfield, J. A., 16
Hardy, Thomas, ix, 13, 15, 16, 21, 42,
47, 99–125, 128, 132–36, 168–76;
The Dynasts, 103, 106; *The Return
of the Native*, 15, 99–125, 133–36,
154, 167, 170, 171, 174, 176; *Tess
of the d'Ubervilles*, 105, 106, 170
Hawthorne, N., 24, 54, 167, 169
Heath, 100–25, 136, 167–68, 171, 176
Height, images of, 26, 47, 67, 82, 157,
170
Hero with a Thousand Faces, The, 35,
116 n15, 149 n7
Hole, 157, 159, 163, 175. *See   also*
Grave
Hurd, Bishop, 53

Identity, 23, 25–26, 43–45, 63, 67, 77,
169–71, 176 (*see also* Transformation); choice or exchange of, x, 65,
83, 92 (*see also* Initiation); archetypal, 169–72
Illusion, x, 13, 101, 104, 105, 114, 124,
129, 133, 158
Imagination, xii, 17–18, 20, 23, 39, 53–
54, 57–58, 99, 147, 168, 171, 172,
174; Conrad's, 128, 130–31, 135,
138, 139, 144, 164 (Marlow's) 161–
65; Dickens', 73–75, 95; Hardy's,
105, 118–19, 135; Lewis's, 26, 31, 39
Impersonality, viii, ix, 42, 56, 93, 106,
110, 111, 117, 156, 170, 175; of
environment, 100, 103, 116, 119,
133–34, 171–72
Incest, 35, 39, 48–49
Incubus, 31, 38
Initiates, 132, 137–39, 142, 174, 175

Initiation, 43–45, 49, 67, 131, 138, 146–47, 148–49. *See also* Identity, Transformation
Introduction to the English Novel, An (Kettle), 56–57, 60
Iron Hans, 44–47, 48–51 passim, 149, 159, 175
Irrational, 13, 16, 18, 21, 23, 24, 26, 29, 41, 57, 73, 127, 163, 167–69, 175

Jean-Aubry, G., 137
Johnson, Samuel, 21
Joseph Conrad: Life and Letters, 130–40 passim, 149, 159, 174–75
Joyce, James, 16, 96
Jung, Carl, vii–x, 17, 27, 34, 46, 49, 85–86 118, 121, 135, 136, 144–45, 148–52, 160, 172–76; *The Basic Writing's of C. G. Jung,* (ed. de Laszlo), vii, 135; *Modern Man in Search of a Soul,* 173; *Psyche and Symbol,* 18, 145, 148, 152; *Symbols of Transformation,* 27 n2, 34 n10, 144, 148–52 passim, 160

Keats, John, 57, 100
Kettle, Arnold, 56–57, 60
King, 44–46, 55–56, 101–2

Labyrinth, 121–23
Leavis, F. R., 18
Legend, 41, 137
Letters from Joseph Conrad 1895–1924, 130, 145, 151
Lewis, M. G., 22, 23–26, 27–40, 169, 171; *The Monk,* 22–26 passim, 27–40, 42, 49, 50, 54, 169, 171, 172, 174
Life of Matthew G. Lewis, A (Peck), 25
Life of Thomas Hardy, The 100, 105, 106, 113, 119, 135
Lifton, R. J., viii–ix
Light, images of, 26, 33–34, 50, 56, 63, 84, 86, 106, 108 124, 143, 155, 158–59, 163–64, 174
Love and death, 36, 171–72
Lyrical Ballads, The, 50, 54

Magic, 26, 29, 42, 43, 49, 68, 82, 84, 85, 92, 110–11, 124, 131

Magician, 48–49, 63, 82, 84–85, 87, 88, 90, 92–97, 127-40, 145, 174, 175
Marlow as narrator, 128–29, 154–59, 161–65
Materialism, ix, 14, 73, 132–33, 142
Melodrama, 17, 18, 22, 25
Mentor, 44, 136–38. *See also* Wise old man
Microcosm, 57, 96, 115
Mill, J. S., 105–6
Moll Flanders, 23, 56
Monster, 32–35, 67, 79–81, 87, 103, 163. *See also* Dragon
Moon, 101–2, 125, 135, 155–57, 161
Moor, 55, 63, 71, 73, 167–71 passim
Motif-Index of Folk Literature (Thompson), 42
Mysteries of Udolpho, The, 22–23, 24, 28, 169
Myth, 14, 15, 34, 35, 45, 135
Mythic patterns, 15, 25, 27, 35, 149, 160
Myths and Dreams (Clodd), 105

Natural selection, 15, 99, 106, 174
Nature, 36, 53, 57, 73, 99-100, 106, 108–10, 114-21, 127, 133, 135 168, 170, 174, 176
Nightmare, 29, 31, 33, 38, 115, 169
Nimbus, 101

Objectivity, vii–ix, 56–57. *See also* Realism, Impersonality
Origin of Species, The, 99

Paganism, 102, 108, 118, 136
Patna, 129, 142–44, 152, 154, 156–59, 161, 163, 164
Patterson, John, 117–18
Patusan, 140, 142, 144–56, 157, 159, 160–63, 167–68, 171
Peck, Lewis, 25
Perrault, 41, 50
Philosophy of the Unconscious, The (Von Hartmann), 136
Poe, E. A., 54
Popular Novel in England, The (Tompkins), 20
Primitive man, vii, 14, 15, 115, 127, 135–36
Primitive ways, 27, 105, 110–12, 115, 118, 136, 174–75
Prince, 43, 46, 62–63, 64, 65, 79, 82

Princess, 48, 51, 65, 66, 76, 77, 88, 159, 160
Promethean, 37, 108, 121
Providence, novelist as, 95–96, 128, 131
Psyche, 82, 99, 135
Psychic: energy, 71, 144, 175; problems, ix, xi, 14, 67, 172; processes, vii–xi, 18, 58, 82, 135, 174
Psychoanalysis, vii, 27, 42–43, 48–49, 63, 148, 151, 161
Psychological approach to literature, x, xii, 14, 16, 17–18, 172–73, 176; Conrad's, 127, 129–31, 139–40; Dickens', 50, 92–93, 94–97; Hardy's, 104–5.
Psychology, ix, xi, xii, 18, 136, 141, 173

Queen, 35, 55, 69, 77, 85, 93 101–2

Radcliffe, A., 22–23, 28, 169
Rasselas, 21
Realism in art, 17, 20–26, 53, 56–58, 70, 99–100, 103–6, 119, 162, 167–68
Reality, vii–viii, 42, 123–24, 128, 143, 155–58, 171–72, 176
Rebirth, ix, 15, 34, 115, 136, 148–52, 157, 172–73, 176
Regression, 34, 144, 148, 172
Repression, 90, 94, 173
Resurrection, 67, 117, 120, 131–32, 176. *See also* Rebirth
Richardson, S., 20–24 passim
Rise of the Novel, The (Watt), 21, 23–24
Ritual, 13, 15, 115–16, 128, 131–32, 136. *See also* Seasonal rites
Robinson Crusoe, 23, 56
Romance, genre of, 13–14, 16–17, 20–26, 28, 32, 39, 40, 42, 53–58, 59, 70, 75, 99, 138 141, 167–68, 171
Romantic poetry, 29, 38, 41, 53, 54
Romantic viewpoint, 15, 39, 71–74 passim, 101, 104, 123–24, 128, 133, 137, 140, 144–45, 165, 170, 171
Romanticism, 39, 75, 99–104 passim, 107, 114, 115, 118, 128, 132, 155, 161, 168, 170
Romantics, the, 14, 18, 21, 57, 70, 99–100, 169, 172

Sartre, viii
Satan, 29–31, 36–37, 110
Satanic, the, 23, 111, 141, 145, 161, 165, 167
Scott, Sir Walter, 39
Sea, 132, 133, 135, 142, 143, 146, 156, 158, 164 168
Seasonal rites, 15, 100, 108–9, 115–20 (*see also* Ritual); bonfire, 106, 108–9, 111, 114; gypsying, 102, 108–9, 117, 122, 125; maypole, 108–9, 117; mumming, 101, 108–9, 114, 115
Self limitation, xi, 35, 39, 50, 61, 63–66, 69, 76, 78–79, 80–81, 86, 90–91, 120, 125, 160, 163–64; of positive characters, 108–9, 112–14, 115–16, 134–35
Self, potential of, ix, 45–46, 55–56, 61–62, 69, 76–77, 103, 145, 146–47, 158, 160, 164 171. *See also* Transformation
Sensation, 21, 23–25, 139, 140, 169
Sensibility, 13, 20–21, 23–25, 169
Sex, 28–30, 32, 37–38, 50. *See* Incest, Love and death
Shadow, 26, 76, 80, 81, 84, 96 n25, 128, 137, 139, 144, 152–56, 159; as *alter ego,* 75, 144, 152–53
Shelley, P. B., 57, 100
Silas Marner, 100
Stone, Harry, 74
Strange Story, 82
Sun, 37, 85, 101–2, 109–10, 121, 135, 155–59, 161, 164
Supernatural, 19, 21–22, 24, 26, 29, 38, 132, 169
Symbolism, ix–x, 57, 59–61, 63, 108, 135, 167, 174, 175

Taboo, 35, 39, 42, 48–50, 117
Talisman, 30, 49, 63, 83, 145, 146, 153
Test, 43. *See also* Identity, Transformation
Thackery, W. M., 96
Thespis (Gastner), 116
Thompson, Stith, 15, 41, 42–53, 44 n5
Three Essays on Religion (Mill), 105
Through the Looking Glass, 70
Tomb. *See* Grave
Tompkins, J. M. S., 20
Transformation, ix, x, 15, 43–51, 54–56, 62, 65, 69, 70, 76, 77, 99, 122, 124, 150, 152

Treasure, 44, 45, 46, 47, 63 n2, 87, 147–8, 159 n11, 175. *See also* Gold

Ulysses, 102–3, 137–38
Unconscious, vii, ix, 108, 133–34, 136, 142–43, 148, 161, 164, 173, 176; collective, viii n2, ix, 135, 144, 173. *See also* Archetypes

Van Ghent, Dorothy, 56, 60, 62, 69 n6
Von Hartmann, 136
Victorian novel, the, ix, 26, 40, 43, 50, 54, 57, 73–74
Victorian society, ix, 14, 15, 43, 50, 57, 70, 73–74, 77, 89, 100, 132–33, 170, 176
Vision, 22, 173–76

Walpole, Horace, 19–20, 21–22, 39
Walpole, Hugh, Conrad's letters to, 149
Warmth, images of, 26, 30–31, 37, 61, 111, 119
Watt, Ian, 21, 23–26, 53, 56, 58, 169
Well, 44–47, 94, 120–21, 149, 157, 159–60, 163, 164, 175-76
Well of truth, x–xi, 94, 159, 163, 165, 167–76
Wise old man, 44–45, 49, 50–51, 85–86, 89, 93, 94, 136, 144, 145, 148, 152
Witch, 31, 64, 68, 69, 75, 78–79, 84, 87, 110–11, 113, 117, 124, 144, 149, 161 n12. *See also* Magician
Woman in White, The, 95
Womb, 34–35
Wordsworth, W., 50, 57, 100, 119

Indexed in English Novel
Explication, Supplement I